)5ᵘ

GEORGE TICKNOR
and the Boston Brahmins

DAVID B. TYACK

GEORGE TICKNOR
AND THE BOSTON BRAHMINS

1967

HARVARD UNIVERSITY PRESS
CAMBRIDGE · MASSACHUSETTS

For Dee

Acknowledgments

A full acknowledgment of indebtedness would require an autobiography. Recognizing that neither in my notes nor here can I adequately express my gratitude for assistance, I should still like to mention a few people and organizations. I am deeply grateful for fellowships from Harvard University, the Danforth Foundation, and the American Council of Learned Societies which supported my research and writing during graduate study and during a leave of absence from my teaching at Reed College. I am indebted to President Richard Sullivan for arranging this leave and to my colleagues Hugo Bedau, Mason Drukman, Dorothy Johansen, Roger Oake, David Ray, Werner Schlotthaus, and Charles Svitavsky for their advice and encouragement. To Bernard Bailyn, under whom I began this study, I owe special thanks for his penetrating questions, his wise counsel, and his stimulating example. A number of other scholars have given me valuable guidance on topics treated in this biography: Mrs. Cynthia Brown, Theodore Crane, Robert Dalzell, Oscar Handlin, Thomas Hart, Benjamin Labaree, Reginald Phelps, Frank Ryder, William Taylor, Walter Whitehill, and Donald Williams. Lawrence Cremin, Thomas Gaddis, Frank Jennings, and John Tomsich gave useful appraisals of the biography as a whole, as did my father, Samuel Tyack, and my father-in-law, Claude Lloyd. Obviously none of these people should be judged guilty by association with my errors.

I should like to thank the many librarians who assisted me in my search for manuscripts and extended many courtesies, in particular the staffs of the Baker Library at Dartmouth, the Archives and Houghton Collection of the Harvard College Library, the Massachusetts Historical Society, the Boston Public Library, and the Boston Athenaeum. To these libraries, and to the literary heirs of the authors whose writings I have used, I should like to express appreciation for permission to quote from manuscripts. I am especially indebted to Nathaniel Dexter, George Ticknor's descendant, for permission to quote from the Ticknor papers.

To my sons, Peter and Daniel, I owe countless pleasant distractions; to my wife, Dee, I give thanks first and last.

D.T.

Reed College
October 1966

Contents

Illustrations

Following page 130

GEORGE TICKNOR
and the Boston Brahmins

Introduction

In long lines, unread on library shelves, sit hundreds of lives and letters of nineteenth-century patrician worthies, men eminent in their day and forgotten in ours. Dutifully, sons, wives, and friends wrote these biographies in a tradition stemming from Puritan diaries, lives of the saints, funeral eulogies, and notices of departed colleagues (*pro forma* in Brahmin clubs). Many a patriarch wrote his letters and journals knowing that one day posterity would see his thoughts embalmed in print. In a community schooled in deferring pleasures biographers might praise their subjects when they were dead with an emotion not decorous to reveal when they were alive. In *The Late George Apley* John Marquand has caught both the humor and the pathos of the genre; in describing his *Education* Henry Adams has written in this tradition as if he were his own disillusioned son.

As historians penetrate the marmoreal propriety of these family records, they may find a wealth of social evidence on the American patrician class. Written not only to memorialize the dead but also to give moral instruction to the rising generation, the Victorian lives and letters were consciously didactic. Despite omissions and varnish, these biographers provide the historian with clues — intentional and unconscious — about the Brahmin life-style and conscience. Such a source is the *Life, Letters, and Journals of George Ticknor,* a work edited by his wife, his daughter, and his friend George Hillard. With suitable discount for wifely, filial, and friendly distortions, this book, like dozens of others, reveals a rich and complex stratum of American society during a period of rapid change. The *Life* fascinated Ticknor's Boston, a city dubbed "Ticknorville" by other patricians. In his mansion at Nine Park Street George Ticknor dominated the social life of proper Boston as fully as Daniel Webster its conservative politics and the Boston Associates its financial affairs. Today Ticknor shares the obscurity of many who loomed large in the social and intellectual community of his day —

when Boston and Cambridge engrossed a large share of the nation's intellectual life — while others, unknown or disdained in their time, now have secure fame.

Ticknor's niche in history today rests on his attempted educational reforms at Harvard, his liberal and commanding role in founding the Boston Public Library, and his erudite *History of Spanish Literature*. Some recall that he preceded Longfellow and Lowell as the first professor of modern languages at Harvard. Some associate him with the other New England historians of the golden age of gentleman-scholars. But his image has become blurred, his world obscured in a romantic haze generated by antiquarians.

This is an unfortunate fate for Ticknor, for in life he was anything but blurred, obscure, or romantic. He was a man of decided tastes, opinions, and personality, a social cynosure in his time. Raised as a Federalist, a Federalist he remained while he observed Andrew Jackson, the Civil War, and President Grant. He judged the political events of his lifetime by standards anachronistic or irrelevant to his compatriots, as if today a man born in 1885 were to judge American foreign policy by the code of Theodore Roosevelt and government economic policies by the canons of President McKinley. A frank elitist, he lived in an age of rampant egalitarianism. He was a militant mediator between the Old World and the New in a day when nationalism was as fashionable in literature as in politics.

Typically, the life of an intellectual offers the biographer few dramatic outward incidents. So it is with Ticknor. With the exception of his first trip to Europe, his career is barren of adventure, his love life unexceptionable in cold-roast Boston — and hence bereft of spice. But his inner life, the clash of his ideas with new heresies and conditions, generates dramatic and illuminating conflict.

It is this conflict of his inner life, together with his social setting, on which I have focused. The years of Ticknor's youth were a time of ferment in Boston, a period of apocalyptic visions and passion in politics, of transition and muted conflict in religion and letters, of new economic opportunities in a society whose moral and social character was still largely conservative. During these years, from his birth in 1791 to his departure for Europe in 1815, Ticknor acquired a set of mind and character which he retained tenaciously throughout his eighty years. His European journey confirmed his preconceptions about the Old

World and laid the foundations for his scholarly and social career. From 1819 to 1835 he taught modern languages at Harvard and introduced several generations of students to European thought and literature. Familiar with the best contemporary European and American schools and universities, he was convinced that Harvard was anachronistic in its structure and inefficient in its operation. Unsuccessfully he fought a battle with academic orthodoxy and anticipated changes which would follow when his nephew Charles William Eliot became president of Harvard after the Civil War.

In his *History of Spanish Literature,* as in his Harvard lectures on French and Spanish literature, Ticknor expressed both the hopes and the anxieties of the cultivated men of his circle. For Ticknor literary history was a mode of political allegory whose message was ominous. A literary nationalist in creed, he was provincial in taste. As arbiter of patrician society in Boston he interpreted the New and the Old Worlds to each other. Together with his fellow Brahmins he helped to build the ramparts of proper Boston and to create one of the few cohesive and exclusive patrician groups of his day. He questioned much of the "conventional wisdom" of the common man and helped to shape the "covert culture" of the elite. Politically at home neither in Europe nor America, he was that anomaly, a republican Tory. To Ticknor the republic remained an experiment, ever precarious, subject to the dangers proclaimed in his youth and beset by new threats which subverted his occasional optimism.

In this study of George Ticknor I have tried to look, with the reader, over Ticknor's shoulder at his world, to see the moral questions of his time as much as possible from his perspective. As a conservative who always spoke his mind, Ticknor neither solicited piety nor flinched from censure. What he sought from his contemporaries was comprehension, and this, I trust, is what he expected from posterity.

I

The Formative Years

To a man of mere animal life, you can urge no argument against
going to America but that it will be some time before he will get
the earth to produce. But a man of any intellectual enjoyment
will not easily go and immerse himself and his posterity for ages
in barbarism.   *Samuel Johnson*[1]

In the spring of 1814 George Ticknor, a young lawyer of
Boston, decided to transform his avocation into his vocation. A zealous
scholar, he began to chart and justify a career devoted to his chief
pleasure, literature. Clearly he foresaw the reefs of his course. Instinctively he agreed with the opinion of his townsmen that anyone "who is
not believed to follow some useful business, can scarcely acquire or
retain even a decent reputation." Reputation was all-important to Ticknor, and he realized that he could achieve his ambitions only by obeying
the dictates of his community. Still he believed that America had men
of affairs in abundance, but few men of letters. Would his land be a
second Carthage, prospering for a time but leaving no trace of its
existence? Or might Ticknor witness "the dawn of our Augustan age,
and . . . contribute to its glory?" [2] In the meantime he knew what his
mission would be.

Although Ticknor became a pioneer New England intellectual, he
shared throughout his eighty years the universe of habits and morals of
his father's generation. His parents inculcated convictions and traits of
character which never wavered. The Boston of his youth — its social
character, its political and religious contests, its literary coteries, its
moral and intellectual assumptions — shaped his decision to become
a scholar. This eighteenth-century education never ceased to direct his
role and his response to the transformation of America during his lifetime. Like Henry Adams, he was trained to live in a world which was
to dissolve before his eyes, yet to the end Ticknor's character retained
the cast given it during the formative years.

1. *The Schoolmaster*

The world of Elisha Ticknor, George's father, was one of sure dimensions and clear imperatives. Calvinist and Federalist, he had no trouble discerning the children of light and the children of darkness. He was tall and thin, with sharp features and a grave expression. Boston knew and respected him as Deacon Ticknor, mainstay of the Old South Church, public-spirited and politically orthodox, socially respectable though not fashionable. As a father he was affectionate — even indulgent, he feared — but he always had a Biblical sense of righteous superintendence. "The eye, who mocketh at his father," he quoted approvingly, "and despiseth to obey his mother, the ravens of the valley shall pick him out, and the young eagles shall eat him." [3]

"A young scholar," Elisha wrote in 1793, "by pursuing his studies, by avoiding bad company, and cultivating morality, may rise to eminence." Elisha's own example modestly proved the point. A descendant of four generations of American farmers, he was born in Lebanon, Connecticut, in 1757. After learning Latin at Nathan Tisdale's Academy he moved with his parents in 1774 to a frontier farm in Lebanon, New Hampshire, where he taught in the district school and farmed for five years. He and his father both fought in the Revolutionary War.

The local college, Dartmouth, scanty and provincial as it seemed to his son George, a Boston boy, enlarged Elisha's intellectual horizons. To his death he remained a grateful and loyal alumnus. President John Wheelock, the baron of this educational fief in the wilderness, exemplified to Elisha the union of Calvinist piety and practical intellect. Wheelock became Elisha's mentor, and at times of decision in his life Elisha turned to him for parental advice, his own father being a simple farmer. [4]

After a brief stint as instructor at a preparatory school in Hanover and in a private school in Pittsfield, Massachusetts, Elisha looked about for richer harvests. Writing to Wheelock in 1785, he inquired if there were still a "vacancy for a schoolmaster in Boston, useful and reputable," adding that he was "still inexpressibly fond of teaching the 'young idea how to shoot'; but that the contractedness of the world is so great, that the prospects of a comfortable living, in this way, appear, in no sense encouraging." He became a reading master of the Franklin public school in Boston and continued in this work until 1794.

During this time he composed a little book which combined parsing and correct opinion: "The people are foolish." "The mob is dispersed." "Despise pleasure. Remember death." "This is the Constitution which secures your rights." To Elisha the schools were powerful engines of church and state designed to inculcate orthodox values and liquidate error. The "young idea" should be taught to shoot straight theologically and politically.[5]

These were trying times for the friends of righteousness. On the day in 1792 when Louis XVI was beheaded, the friends of liberty paraded through Boston with a skinned ox on a sledge followed by two carts of bread and two hogsheads of punch. At the ensuing feast in front of the city hall, the Jacobin mob rioted, throwing hunks of roast ox and bread at the bystanders and roaring for equality and fraternity. The fifty-foot pole they raised, the ox head grotesquely perched on top, grimly symbolized the menace of the foolish people.

Although Bostonians had long valued the schoolmaster as the foe of Satan and disorder, they felt a teacher should find his reward in heaven and know his proper place on earth. Ticknor's pay as reading master was a pittance, and the town added insult to injury by paying teachers by town orders, or money warrants, which instructors had to sell at a discount. When one of Ticknor's colleagues, Caleb Bingham, advertised in the newspaper for "a town order for sale at a liberal discount," the town fathers ordered the impudent fellow to apologize. Rather than apologize he stood up in town meeting and declared: "I have a family and need the money. I have done my part faithfully, and have no apology to make to those who have failed to do theirs." They paid him in cash. But so great was the range of training and ability that the standing of teachers was ambiguous at best, and shocking at the worst. A Boston writing master named John Tileston, for example, became a symbol of antediluvian absurdity: Tileston opposed the cloth pen wiper because *his* writing master had always wiped his pen on his little finger and then cleaned his finger by wiping it on the long hair beneath his wig.[6]

Little wonder, then, that energetic and respectable men like Elisha Ticknor and Caleb Bingham left a calling they honored. Elisha had long been tempted by other careers. Once he wrote to John Wheelock that "if Providence should open a door . . . I could embark with pleasure, surmounting the boisterous surges of a selfish world." In 1795 Providence opened the door into the grocery business, a vocation Ticknor never liked but in which he prospered. He branched out into insurance and banking and helped to found the Provident Institution for Savings and the Massachusetts Mutual Fire Insurance Company.

Never buoyant on "the boisterous surges of a selfish world," he retired in 1812 to devote himself to public school reforms, which had engrossed him since 1805. He campaigned for primary schools in Boston — prior to 1815 the town grammar schools excluded children who could not read — and served on the Primary School Committee in 1818.[7]

In 1790, at the age of thirty-eight, Elisha Ticknor married Elizabeth Billings Curtis, the daughter of a Norfolk farmer and the widow of a surgeon. She was attractive and gentle, more cultivated than most ladies in a day when the education of women was stunted. When her first husband died, she opened a fashionable school for girls in her home. She continued to teach for a time after her marriage to Elisha. George, the only child of Elizabeth and Elisha, was born on August 1, 1791. The four children of Elizabeth's first marriage were all considerably older than George. This was a time when a code of austerity dissuaded parents from demonstrating their affection for their children and when fathers often adopted a distant and autocratic role. The mutual love and respect between George and his parents was unusual; they understood and appreciated his interests and aspirations.[8]

As an infant George was sickly, sheltered and petted by his mother and half brothers and sisters. As he grew older his father insisted on more Spartan ways. George sometimes had to shovel out the snow that drifted in his open bedroom window during the night. Often he would rise early and uncover the ashes on the kitchen fire to sit by the blaze and read. Once he came down, sleepy-eyed and half dressed, to find the servants still up; they raucously packed him back to bed.

In 1802 George and his parents made the long and arduous trip through the forests of Massachusetts and New Hampshire to visit Dartmouth College and his grandfather in Lebanon. In a coachee drawn by a pair of horses they spent a week traveling one hundred and twenty miles on corrugated and dusty roads and fording swift white rivers. At his grandfather's farm he worked in the hayfield and kitchen garden in a checked frock which his mother had made. The months spent working on the rocky farm and playing in the barns gave the Boston boy a taste of his father's hardy youth; but he had no lasting interest in country life.[9]

As the only child of two schoolteachers, George never lacked instruction. By the age of four he could write a good hand; before the age of ten he had passed the admission examination for Dartmouth in Cicero's orations and the Greek Testament. His father taught him Latin and Greek so well that when George went to a private school taught by Ezekiel Webster, Daniel's brother, he already knew all that Webster tried to teach him, and he amused himself by reading Pope's translation of Homer. He studied French and Spanish with Francis Sales, a courtly French refugee who dressed and powdered his hair meticulously but who had a poor provincial accent. Precocious — perhaps a bit priggish — George was deadly earnest about his studies. To James Freeman, minister of King's Chapel, he wrote at the age of fourteen to thank him for a copy of Cervantes: "Don Quixote is a book, which, if thoroughly read will extend the reader's knowledge of the Spanish language very much; and it shall be my endeavor to read it in this way." Dartmouth in 1805 was bound to disappoint such a budding scholar.[10]

2. *The School of the Prophets*

When George was eleven years old, he painted a delightful landscape of the "auspicious plains of Dartmouth" with a prospect of the main buildings of the college and a glimpse of the slopes behind, forested with pine, maple, and hemlock. Here was Old Main, with its dome glistening in the sunshine, and chaste white brick walls in characteristic academic Georgian. Surrounding it were the other buildings — more plain, even barracks-like in George's sketch, except for the president's imposing house, with a gambrel roof, tall granite front steps, and an ornate doorway. Often the Ticknors stayed here. Young George was struck by the incongruity of the furnishings in the Hanover wilds — delicate linen sheets on the beds and lace-trimmed pillows, but no carpets on the floor — and hated to sit down to dinner at Mrs. Wheelock's table, for "the cookery was detestable." In the foreground of his painting, on the plain that stretched from hills to the east of the college to bluffs overlooking the sparkling Connecticut River, stood a mixed array of village caricatures: a pot-bellied cleric trailed by a timid dog; dandies in bright colored smallclothes courting young ladies; an absent-minded scholar stumbling across the rough plain while reading a book; and a boy in tall boots returning with his fishing rod from a foray to the river.

It was a whimsical view of the sort of peaceful, orthodox town that was the delight of Yale President Timothy Dwight, who used to spend his vacations wandering over New England. Hanover was a village where almost everyone had a decent dwelling and enough to eat, where men were independent but accepted the God-given fact of social and economic hierarchy, where a union of ministers and magistrates and merchants held sway, where the rule of the Bible and the rule of law tempered men's contests with each other and with rude nature.[11] Beneath his watercolor of the campus and the village folk Ticknor inscribed a poem:

> Where late the Savage roam'd in search of prey,
> Fair science spreads her all enlivening ray.
> The ancient forest fall'n; its inmates fled;
> See seats and sons of learning in their stead;
> 'Tis scenes like these, that freedom's pow'r disclose,
> She makes the desert blossom like the rose.

Technically a member of the freshman class since his admission at the age of nine, Ticknor entered Dartmouth on advanced standing as a junior at the age of fourteen. Such cases of early admission to college were common at the time: witness Henry Wadsworth Longfellow who entered Bowdoin at fourteen; and George Bancroft and Edward Everett, who both were Harvard freshmen at thirteen. As Ticknor soon learned at Dartmouth, the colleges of the period often as not were merely glorified secondary schools.

In Hanover George lived with his half sister Eliza Curtis Woodward and her husband William, later the defendant in the Dartmouth College case, a far-reaching contest over the sanctity of the school's charter. A conscientious moralist like Elisha knew the dangers of dormitory life in the colleges of the day. George recalled that he "ran into no wildness or excesses" at Dartmouth. Perhaps his father also thought that Calvinist Dartmouth would be a safer place than Harvard, where Henry Ware, a Unitarian, had just been elected Professor of Divinity.[12]

Elisha's chief reason for sending George to Dartmouth was undoubtedly his loyalty to his mentor, John Wheelock. Dartmouth was John Wheelock, and John Wheelock was Dartmouth. Looking on the college as a personal possession, he was dictatorial in manner to students and faculty, imperious even to the trustees. Daniel Webster recalled that Wheelock had once justified one-man rule to his trustees by reminding them that " 'It was Jason . . . who stole the Golden Fleece, it was Hercules who slew the Lernean tiger, and the Erymanthian boar.' " With thick brown hair, parted in front and clubbed behind, a bulbous nose, and a grave falsetto voice, he impressed George as "one of the most formal men" he ever met. Once an acquaintance of Wheelock's decided to see whether he could give the last bow on saying goodbye to the President, as a contest of politeness, but Wheelock, determined to win, followed his guest to the gate and bowed him out of sight. When students came to visit him, he would say, when he wanted them to leave, "Will you sit longer, sir, or will you go now?" It would have taken the Lernean tiger himself to resist such an invitation to depart. George never "felt the smallest degree of familiarity with him," nor did he share his father's high regard for Wheelock as a moral and intellectual model. As cleric and instructor, Wheelock left much to be desired. Never formally educated for the ministry, he sometimes found himself at a loss for prayers. Once, after visiting the science laboratory, he prayed in his high-pitched voice "We thank Thee O Lord for the oxygen gas; we thank Thee O Lord for the hydrogen gas; we thank Thee O Lord for the nitrogen gas and for all the gasses." [13]

Learning at Dartmouth was a mechanical and deadly serious matter; the sing-song recitation system was the established mode of teaching. John Smith, professor of languages, was a kindly and timid man, bald and weighing over two hundred pounds, exact within the narrow limits of his knowledge, but not so good a teacher as Ticknor's father. George had already studied most of the Latin and Greek which constituted two thirds of the rigidly prescribed curriculum during the first three years of college. He also learned a little mathematics and science. In his senior year he met New Light Calvinism, together with a discreet mixture of "political law" and science; his lifelong distaste for metaphysics may have been fortified by an overdose of Jonathan Edwards at the age of sixteen. "I was idle in college," Ticknor summarized, "and learned little."

Even to the fourteen-year-old George Hanover seemed provincial and its learning lilliputian. Dartmouth's curriculum was narrow and rigid, its library and equipment meager, its teachers drillmasters. It could hardly have been otherwise in a school so remote, so poor, and so purely conservative. In 1802 the library — much of it theological — numbered three thousand volumes, many of them duplicates. The "Museum," the apple of Wheelock's eye, contained curiosities, the chief of which was a stuffed zebra which mysteriously roosted from time to time on the chapel roof.[14]

Most of the students were rustic and scantily prepared. Crotchety John Quincy Adams despised them. On a visit to Hanover he met one graduate who had "to perfection the appearance and manners which have distinguished all the young gentlemen from that seminary with whom I have had any acquaintance, — the same uncouthness in his appearance, the same awkwardness in his manners, and . . . the same vacancy in his countenance." Realizing that it was not common to find a man who was both a scholar and a gentleman, Adams was impressed with the uniform inability of Dartmouth students to be either. His jaundiced view, however, hardly fits the facts. Dartmouth produced eminent graduates far out of proportion to its size and prospects, the most notable of whom were Daniel Webster and Rufus Choate, both Whig senators from Massachusetts and later friends of Ticknor. Some of Ticknor's classmates became his lifelong friends; but it was clear that the college was not a finishing school of scholarship and gentility like Harvard, with its corps of young aristocrats who were able to smooth the rough edges of their talented rustic classmates. They were, however, a spirited group, and restive under the regime of the martinet president. "When I visited my *alma mater*," George wrote to a friend shortly after his graduation, "I found her at variance with her children, who had risen up in rebellion against her — The School of the Prophets tottered to its centre; but by the grace of God and by the assistance of John Wheelock it still stands — it still triumphs." [15]

In view of George's irreverence towards the Prophet, it is ironic that his father wrote to Wheelock for advice about his son's future. "If I can learn . . . from you," said Elisha, "that he has been, while under your direction, judicious, studious, manly in his deportment, and persevering in whatever he undertakes; and at the same time sensible of the necessity of a religious moral principle . . . I shall be strongly inclined to give him advantages, considerably beyond those of common professional men." The time had come to begin thinking of George's future. Elisha and John Wheelock thought that his character and conduct thus far boded well for a career "useful to himself and the public." George was approaching a turning point in his life.[16]

3. *A Compact, United, and Kindly Community*

The next few years were among the happiest in George Ticknor's life. Later he looked back on the Boston society of his youth as a lost, golden age:

Business, which had never been so engrossing as it has since become, during five years of commercial embarrassments, relaxed something of that hold on the thoughts of men, which is always so tenacious . . . we . . . felt involved in each other's welfare and fate as it is impossible we should now, when our numbers are trebled, and our affairs complicated and extended till their circumference is too wide to be embraced by any one mind, and till the interests of each individual are grown too separate and intense to be bound in by any general sympathy with the whole. Notwithstanding our old political quarrels, therefore, and notwithstanding our coming theological dissensions, which already cast their shadows before, we were then a more compact, united, and kindly community than we have ever been since, or ever can be again.[17]

In this period from Mr. Jefferson's Embargo in 1807 to Mr. Madison's war ending in 1815, Boston was thrown on its own resources; and all these resources were open to George Ticknor, who returned in 1807 to continue his education.

If Boston seemed provincial to those who knew the greater world, it was still an exciting place to the boy of sixteen who had spent the last two years in Hanover. The houses that lined the narrow, crooked streets were surrounded with trees and flowers and vegetable gardens. From the three hills on the Boston peninsula one could see the town nestled by the wharves stretching out into the harbor and see the square-riggers tacking past the islands in the bay. The sea breeze brought the smell of oakum and cod. Sailors told of adventures in Canton and Java, Astoria and Martinique. Timothy Dwight found Boston, with its population of thirty-four thousand, large enough "to ensure all the benefits of refined society, and yet so small, as to leave the character of every man open to the observation of every other . . . His virtues and his vices, his wisdom and his folly, excite here much the same attention, and are examined in much the same manner, as in a country village." It was rare to find a child, he said, "who could not tell me both the street and the house for which I inquired." Bostonians were adventurous in a circumspect way, and spoke and moved quickly as if they had no time to spare.[18]

George Ticknor had graduated at sixteen, but both he and his father knew that Dartmouth had only begun his education. Soon he must choose his vocation — and what was there for him but law, medicine, the ministry or business? But meanwhile Elisha decided that George should study the classics with an acknowledged master of Latin and Greek, Dr. John Sylvester John Gardiner. Gardiner, minister of Trinity Church, was a former student of Dr. Samuel Parr, the best and vainest classical scholar in England. In Gilbert Stuart's painting Gardiner is a white-haired, portly, and jovial gentleman of the old school. A man who fancied himself the Dr. Johnson of Boston, he loved to talk about Pope and Addison late into the night over good cigars and madeira. He received Ticknor "in his library, in his slippers and dressing gown," and together they read Horace, Livy, and Tacitus, Aeschylus, Euripides, and Thucydides. Although Gardiner could be sarcastic and abrupt to the inattentive, to the enthusiastic Ticknor he was cordial and open mannered. In contrast to the somber instructors at Dartmouth he showed George that scholarship and pleasant conversation could mingle: "much knowledge was communicated by an easy, conversational commentary, the best part of which could not readily have been found in books, while the whole of it gave a life and interest to the lessons that could have been given by nothing else." [19]

Soon Gardiner invited Ticknor to small literary suppers at which some of the leading intellectuals of the town gathered. "These little *symposia* were always agreeable," Ticknor remarked, "perfectly simple and easy, full of fun and wit, and always rich in literary culture. It was my first introduction to such society." There he met the Reverend Joseph Buckminster, an early Unitarian scholar who had a profound influence on Ticknor's career; Buckminster's sister Lucy, a charming and literate girl; Ticknor's life-long friend, the antiquarian James Savage; and William Smith Shaw, the founder of the Boston Athenaeum. It was an easy step from Gardiner's symposia to Buckminster's Sunday night suppers where Ticknor discussed literature, politics, and theology with men of affairs like Samuel Dexter, one of Boston's foremost lawyers, and Chief Justice Isaac Parker, a red-faced, bald, and convivial judge who knew everyone and everything of import in Boston. At his own house Ticknor gave hasty-pudding frolics on Saturday evenings where he and his friends read and wrote Latin. They recorded their meetings in Latin poetry and prose so abusive of each other that Ticknor decided to burn the minutes.[20]

Frequently George was a guest in the home of the leading merchants and professional men of Boston, who accepted him as a social equal though his father took little part in fashionable life. Elisha Ticknor's position was respectable but not eminent. His bearing was stately, his manners decorous, his standing as teacher and grocer reputable, his politics sound, his morality impeccable. But as the son of a backwoods farmer and as grave alumnus of Calvinist Dartmouth, he did not belong to the "genial, pleasure-loving group" of local grandees headed by Harrison Gray Otis, a man who "considered himself the most polished corner of the social temple in Boston." City born and bred, well-off though not wealthy, an appreciative listener and budding man of letters, liberal in religious sentiments, attractive in person and manners, friend of the intellectuals of the town, George Ticknor found it easy to emulate the life-style of the elite and encountered no serious social barriers.[21]

Some of the social badges which had marked the colonial elite still persisted. Social station was no small matter to a community which had evolved from a theocracy to a Federalist society. Talk in the counting houses and political assemblies smacked of the quarter-deck. People accorded a habitual deference to the clergy, wealthy merchants, magistrates, lawyers, and doctors. In the Brattle Street Church on the Sabbath one could still see the gentry wearing their cocked hats, scarlet coats, lace ruffles, and silver-buckled shoes. Bostonians tried to live up to their reputation as the flower of New England fashion by importing exotic fruits and wines for their banquets and by giving balls accompanied by Turkish bands. Harrison Gray Otis had the gusto and flair of the earlier colonial aristocracy. A free-spending, colorful, eloquent Federalist, he flaunted the gout with four meals a day beginning with *pâté de foie gras* for breakfast and put ten gallons of punch out daily for his guests. Two paintings by John Singer Sargent, "The Tea Party" and "The Dinner Party," give an intimate glimpse of the colorful oval drawing rooms, the spacious scale and rich ornament of the Federalist mansions of the day. Self-consciously, Otis' sister complained in her diary that she was introduced to some *printers* at a dance. Another lady spoke of a ball of two hundred people which was "not mixed, but consisted of all the respectable people in town." [22]

Despite pretensions, porcelain walls and peacocks, and the attempt to imitate the social lineaments of provincial times, Boston society was not rigidly stratified. Political orthodoxy was more important than genealogy: "I should as soon have expected to see a cow in a drawing room as a Jacobin," one lady remarked. Boston had much of the flavor of a market town. A contemporary of Ticknor's recalled that "almost any morning might be seen Col. Thos. H. Perkins, Harrison Gray Otis, William (Billy) Gray, Ben Bussey, Peter C. Brooks, Israel Thorndike and other wealthy towns folk, trudging homeward for their eight o'clock breakfast with their market baskets containing their one o'clock dinner." [23]

Boston society during Ticknor's youth was transparent and intimate. "We were then comparatively a small people," Ticknor said, "seemed all to know one another, as we met in the streets." Certain families which had achieved a respectable position before the Revolution — the Danas, Wendells, Winthrops, Otises, Phillips, and Prescotts among them — did fancy themselves a step ahead of the post-revolutionary parvenus. But most of the men rising to leadership of Federalist Boston were self-made merchants and lawyers who had seized new opportunities created by the Revolution and the turmoil in Europe.[24]

Samuel Eliot, Ticknor's future father-in-law, was a case in point. Born the son of a poor bookseller, he was apprenticed to a prosperous merchant. Before the Revolution he opened a modest variety shop on Dock Square in which he waited on each lady "as if she were a duchess." One customer predicted that if Mr. Eliot treated all customers in this manner, he should soon ride in his own coach. So he did in time. Encouraged by his success, he married the daughter of a rich merchant, Joseph Barrell, who lived — like the aristocrats in Watteau's paintings — in a mansion with a sweeping grand stairway, rich paneling and formal gardens. By 1798 Eliot became president of the Massachusetts Bank, "the highest pinnacle of honor to which a merchant could attain." In an era when apprentice grocers could become merchant princes, when mechanics and ship captains could rise to eminence, there was unquestionable economic mobility in Boston. With a Midas touch these men could transform ice and granite into gold. The badges of status had a ready price, but it was not all a matter of cash: already romantic lore was spreading about the dour Yankee merchants, a feeling that they were more adventurous, more scrupulous, more cultivated, more princely than their counterparts elsewhere.

Surely the newly rich merchants had no doubts about their own power or wisdom. Samuel Eliot used to stand while the minister preached his sermon, nodding if he agreed and turning his back to visiting preachers whose opinions he condemned. Since common sense was the measure of all things — and since they had demonstrated their eminent good sense by making fortunes — they did not hesitate to lead in matters intellectual and religious as well as mercantile. Eliot endowed a chair of Greek literature at Harvard. Two of his daughters married Harvard professors, Ticknor and the Unitarian pope, Andrews Norton. Some of the business elite had crises of conscience over the conflict between God and Mammon, or the uneasy marriage of commerce and culture; but most of the time they were too busy and too self-confident to worry about such things. They seemed as solid and unruffled as marble busts.[25]

Occasionally a gadfly appeared to disturb the peace of the patriarchs. Francis Jeffrey, editor of the *Edinburgh Review,* was one of these — a stout, restless little man who moved like a puppet jerked on a wire. At a dinner party, when Jeffrey was discoursing on Jeremy Taylor, Harrison Gray Otis made the cataclysmic blunder of asking who Taylor was. Sarcastically, Jeffrey echoed, "You don't know who *Taylor* is?" The story quickly ran across the little town, much to Otis' mortification. A local bookseller profited from the provincial embarrassment by issuing an edition of Taylor's works.

Ticknor and the young intellectuals were delighted with Jeffrey who gave all his listeners the same degree of deference, but "the old men and the politicians found their opinions and dignity too little regarded by the impetuous stranger." Yet Ticknor admitted Jeffrey's lack of decorum: "I was not disposed to claim from *him* that gentleness and delicacy of manners which are acquired only by early discipline, and which are most obvious in those who have received, perhaps, their very character and direction from early collision with their superiors in station or talents." [26] Despite his condescending tone, Ticknor enjoyed Jeffrey's irreverence. He was beginning to suspect that the provincial mind of Boston deserved to be ruffled now and then. Still, it was his home, and he was a loyal son.

After three years of studying with Dr. Gardiner, the time had come to choose a career. Studying the classics and establishing a reputation as a scholar and socially eligible young man was not enough. But what path to take? In 1810 he drifted half-heartedly into the law — perhaps because some of his literary friends were doing so, and because he hoped to continue his favorite studies at the same time — and he began to read law with William Sullivan, a skilled advocate and high priest of Federalist orthodoxy.

4. *The Fear of Apocalypse*

In the early American republic no elder son could expect to inherit a title; no younger son could count on an assured position in the church or the military; no wealthy and titled patrons stood ready to support and honor the man of genius. The avenues to eminence were limited, and politics and public administration were one of the few highroads for the ambitious. As Ticknor's friend Edward Everett observed, political "office here is family, rank, hereditary fortune, in short, Everything, out of the range of private life." [27]

Surely the statesmen in the generation following the Constitution possessed extraordinary talents and could boast of bold achievements. Yet Ticknor and most of his friends had no desire whatever for a political career; more than that, they thought politics disreputable. Earlier, many able young lawyers with intellectual interests — men like John Adams, Thomas Jefferson, John Quincy Adams, Fisher Ames, Alexander Hamilton, and James Madison — had turned as a matter of course to affairs of state. But as Ticknor came to maturity he dismissed a political career. He and his mentor Sullivan witnessed the decline of the Federalist party.[28]

The fear of political apocalypse dominated Ticknor's thoughts about society. Rarely has American political partisanship been more virulent, or anxiety about the fate of the nation more acute than in the Boston of Ticknor's youth. One of George's earliest and most vivid memories was the death of Washington. News of the event had spread across the town in waves marked by the closing of shops in street after street. "My father came home and could not speak, he was so overcome; my mother was alarmed to see him in such a state, until he recovered enough to tell her the sad news. For some time every one, even the children, wore crape on the arm; no boy could go into the street without it."

A terror of Jacobin violence was in the air George breathed. A fellow schoolboy declaimed in 1798 that "False patriots are the street orators and coffee-house politicians of every large town; they are the *Ciceros* of the mob . . . the vapors of putrifying democracy." A current of reaction against the excesses of the French Revolution swept across the town. "Our days are made heavy with the pressure of anxiety," the lugubrious Federalist Fisher Ames said, "and our nights restless with visions of horror. We listen to the clank of chains, and overhear the whispers of assassins. We mark the barbarous dissonance of mingled rage and triumph in the yell of an infuriated mob; we see the dismal glare of their offerings, and scent the loathsome steam of human victims offered in sacrifice." [29] The French Revolution became a new metaphor of sulfureous hellfire. Like a child in an earlier day terrified of being a sinner in the hands of an angry God, a boy growing up in a time of such political turmoil was predisposed to anxiety.

The elders of the community, alarmed by the example of France, regarded the American republic as a fitful and precarious experiment. Hypochondriacs, they daily took the national pulse. Fisher Ames feared that in the normal course of events a demagogue would transform the republic — a mixed government in which the wise and good could check the majority — into a hateful democracy. In turn, the people would tire of democratic misrule and would soon welcome a dictator like Napoleon. It was the duty of the Federalist leader to warn and chastise the people. Like a schoolmaster, he should rap the knuckles of erring students; like a minister, he should berate the populace for their sins. The common man was by nature envious and easily misled, but not smart enough to be dangerous by himself. Only demagogues could turn the people into a dangerous mob. If respectable men, who should know better, persisted in following the Jacobin Jeffersonians, the proper remedy was social ostracism. As for upstart foreigners and newspaper scribblers, the Alien and Sedition Acts would take care of them.

Federalists reserved their most potent venom for visionary, "metaphysical" theorists. "The biggest fools we have are our sensible fools,"

Fisher Ames wrote, "whose theories are more pestilent than popular prejudices. They are more stubborn, more tinctured with fanaticism, and with the rage of making proselytes." He ridiculed the "dreams of all the philosophers who think the people angels, rulers devils . . . that a man is a perfectible animal, and all governments are obstacles to his apotheosis." [30] The Boston Federalists had little faith in the future, and the more pessimistic among them seemed almost to have a death wish.

The Boston Federalists placed their chief trust not in the fickle legislature, but in the executive and judicial branches. These were the anchors to windward. Their regard for George Washington amounted to idolatry. After the calamity of Jefferson's election in 1800, they entrusted their fate to Chief Justice John Marshall and the power of a conservative judiciary. Ticknor's friend Jeremiah Mason later commented that if "Marshall had not been Chief Justice of the United States, the Union would have fallen to pieces before the general government had got well underway." [31]

Many Federalists never accepted the necessity of political parties and took little interest in creating an effective party organization. Commonly they assumed that certain people were suited by birth, talents, and virtue — buttressed by wealth — to rule in the interests of the nation. Rejecting the idea that individual or class interests necessarily conflicted and should be resolved through parties, they inclined toward an organic conception of the body politic in which virtuous leaders would promote the welfare of the whole society. Washington himself had warned Americans to "drive far away the daemon of party spirit . . ." William Tudor, Jr., a spirited intellectual of Ticknor's circle, proposed in 1810 that every city erect a statue to George Washington and hold yearly rites when all citizens should gather to honor him and experience "the delicious feelings of filial gratitude." Although he hoped that such a ceremony would shame the partisan politicians, he feared that once the statue of Washington was out of sight they would again "stifle the generous, social affections awakened in their breasts towards a common country, and perform the unhallowed rites, the foul, malignant sacrifices of faction." Another member of the Federalist literati wrote disdainfully that "Our caucus, instead of being the caucuses of old, where the Gods met together to decide on the affairs of the world, is now the aldermen's hall, whose walls are stained with the smoke of roast beef and 'smell woundedly' of the breath of fat and greasy citizens." The sensitive man, he added, couldn't enjoy his wine without the assault of an "ode for the occasion, from the nose of a twanging psalm singer." [32]

This was more than a precious complaint that politics should resemble a Federalist drawing room. No one really expected political assemblies to be the meeting of the gods "to decide on the affairs of the world." The objections of Ticknor and his friends went beyond mere snobbery or utopianism: their refusal to consider political careers stemmed from their adherence to the alternative ideal of the man of letters and from the discouragement facing young Federalists seeking office during the second decade of the nineteenth century.

Joseph Stevens Buckminster, the eloquent and learned young minister of the Brattle Street Church, gave a speech in 1809 to the Harvard chapter of Phi Beta Kappa on the "Dangers and Duties of Men of Letters." It marked an epoch in the lives of Ticknor and several other young intellectuals, who applauded it "with a turbulent rapture." "The young man, who is to live by his talents and to make the most of the name of a scholar" must not prostitute intellect in the service of political faction, Buckminster warned. This would win only an early but soon blighted reputation. If he courts public favor, "his time, his studies, and his powers, all in their bloom, are all lost to learning . . . His leisure is wasted on the profligate productions of demagogues, and his curiosity bent on the minutiae of local politics. The consequence is that his mind is so much dissipated, or his passions disturbed, that the quiet speculations of the scholar can no longer detain him . . . It is, perhaps, one of the incurable evils of our constitution of society that this ambition of immediate notoriety and rapid success is too early excited, and thus the promises of literary excellence are so frequently superseded." Buckminster's melodious voice, his earnest manner, his message, Ticknor wrote, "sank deep into many hearts; and more than one young spirit, we have reason to think, was, on that day and in that hour, saved from the enthrallment and degradation of party politics and party passions, and consecrated to letters." [33]

Even if a young Federalist like Ticknor had wanted to become enthralled and degraded, success in politics would have been difficult indeed after the fiasco of the Hartford Convention. Even before Mr. Madison's war, the politics of Boston had been a rocky battleground. "Party spirit then ran very high," Ticknor recalled. "Since the time of the Revolution, it has never been so bitter or so violent as it was in the four or five years immediately preceding the War of 1812. Many men among us, during that disastrous period [of the Embargo], felt that they were struggling for their subsistence, — for the home-comforts of those dearest to them, — for the order and well-being of society."

During the war itself feelings ran so high that lifelong friends refused to speak to each other. The Hartford Convention split Boston down the middle. Some New Englanders feared that extremists would propose that New England withdraw from the Union. While it was in session, Ticknor happened to visit John Adams to request some letters of introduction. Adams launched abruptly into a discussion of the horrendous affair. A dark green coat, buttoned tightly over his rotundity, cramped his vehement style. "As he grew more and more excited in his discourse, he impatiently endeavored to thrust his hand into the breast of his coat. The buttons did not yield readily; at last he *forced* his hand in, saying, as he did so, in a very loud voice and most excited manner, 'Thank God, thank God! George Cabot's close buttoned ambition has broke out at last: he wants to be President of New England, sir!'" Ticknor beat a hasty retreat from the splenetic prophet, for he was intimate with Cabot, William Sullivan, Harrison Gray Otis, and other prime movers of the Convention.[34]

Hartford struck the death knell for Federalism. Whatever the motives of the leaders who gathered in Hartford, the Convention seemed to their enemies — and to some of their friends — traitorous at worst and ridiculous at best. It gave new arguments to those Republicans who wanted to proscribe Federalists from all public positions. It effectively prevented the rebirth of Federalism as a force in national politics. Sullivan wrote the epitaph of his party: "So fell federalism. Not from its own want of talent, integrity, or patriotism; not for its perversion of power; but as the Spartan band fell at Thermopylae, beneath a mound of calumnies and slanders." [35]

Not all Bostonians were ready to attend the funeral of Federalism. Some hoped that in the "era of good feelings" President Monroe would favor the regenerate with offices (William Tudor even made the fantastic suggestion that Monroe should abandon the Republicans in New England and turn patronage over to the Federalists). The optimists soon learned that few Federalists would fatten on Monroe's "soft corn." Others sought to amalgamate the parties in such a way that men of Federalist principles could slip in unnoticed. This was the obscurantist tactic of Daniel Webster and the Whigs. But this would never do for the Federalist of the old school, as one stalwart confessed to another: "The old Federal doctrines, as first delivered by the true apostles of that faith will never again be extensively professed. But with new glosses, I think, they are coming gradually into use. The truth is, you ancient apostles expounded your doctrines in a manner ill-suited to the corrupt taste of your hearers . . . You divided the saints from the sinners." [36] The new glosses would make a new act in the drama of conservative politics, one which Ticknor would help to write but in which he had no desire to perform.

The political lessons Ticknor learned in his youth made him forever a member of the party of the past. He would observe anxiously but would rarely act. Convinced that the only party to which he could wholeheartedly subscribe was extinct, he would seek instead to build other institutions by which the sovereign majority could be shaped and curbed. Sometimes hopefully, sometimes sadly, he would look for another Washington. Although his later experience would broaden his perception of political theory and practice and although there was a revolution in political leadership during his lifetime, to the end he would remain "one of the seven sleepers who have dreamt from the days of the Hartford Convention." [37]

5. *Liberal Christianity*

At the same time that Ticknor and his friends were fighting a rearguard action to preserve Federalism, they were also participating in a silent revolution in religion. The attention of the community was riveted on political conflict, but a subtle and pervasive change was taking place in theology, one which would transform the dominant Boston religion from an attenuated Calvinism to Unitarianism. Most of the radicals who wrought this revolution were mild and respectable men who had no intention of disturbing the peace; most of their fathers were orthodox Calvinists, and the sons had no desire to be unfilial.

Ticknor played a modest part in this upheaval. Raised and educated as a Calvinist, he early came under the influence of a group of literate and persuasive "rational Christians" and gradually discarded what he considered the outmoded metaphysics of Calvinism. Yet he never rejected his father's clear distinction between the morally regenerate and the reprobate. The lasting religious lessons of his father were the requirement of strict attention to duty and the need to cultivate a forceful will. Ticknor's conception of morality is suggested by the first example of the "Imperative Mode" in his father's *English Exercises*: "To *command* your passions." Josiah Quincy has described the climate of the Boston of Ticknor's youth as theologically foggy but morally bracing: "Many of the peculiarities of Puritanism had been softened, and so much of the old severity as remained supported the moral standards . . . A few men were accepted as the leaders of the community, and lived under a wholesome conviction of responsibility for its good behavior." [38]

Elisha was a deacon of the Old South Church, whose pastor, Joseph Eckley, was one of the most orthodox in town. Dr. Eckley was a stern minister of the old school whose demeanor terrified the young members of his congregation; he fought the amenities of life as the snares of Satan. Once his parishioners replaced his old pulpit with a new one of elegant mahogany. The next Sunday he rebuked them in a long prayer, saying that "he hoped the Lord would soften the hearts of the congregation, and not keep them as HARD as the ma-ho-ga-ny which they had introduced into His house." He was so angry that his wig nearly fell off. Contrasted with the crotchets of such a man, the genteel tone and liberal views of men like Joseph Buckminster attracted Ticknor.

Several ministers, especially the most literary whom Ticknor came to know well through the Anthology Society, undermined orthodox doctrine, though by disregarding it more than by attacking it. William Emerson, father of Ralph Waldo Emerson and one of the founders of the Anthology Society, delivered liberal sermons in a graceful and cool manner. The genial John Kirkland, president of the Anthology Society and later president of Harvard, preached in a flowing and literate style from odd scraps of paper which he assembled while the congregation sang the hymns; he was even known to slip a joke into his sermons now and then. But the preacher who had the most lasting effect on Ticknor was Joseph Stevens Buckminster, a man whom Ticknor emulated in religion as in scholarship. He was a young man of extraordinary learning; a master of Greek, Latin, and French so alert to new scholarship that he learned German to read Eichhorn; a distinguished preacher and writer and a talented musician. His church attracted many of the leaders of Boston. It was a personal blow to Ticknor as well as a loss to the community when the epileptic Buckminster died in 1812. To Ticknor and two of his friends fell the apostolic task of editing Buckminster's papers.[39]

Buckminster "placed himself on the impregnable Protestant ground of the Bible, authenticated by miracles as the only binding creed, and the only rule of faith and practice, and in the right and therefore the duty of private judgment in everything relating to its interpretation." The liberals claimed that *they* were the true Bible men, and that they were simply discarding the excrescences of superstition which their common sense could not accept. Common sense — that was philosophically sound and the measure of all things, the proper basis for the "private judgment" of religious truth.

How did men know that the Bible was divinely inspired? The evidence for this, in Ticknor's opinion, was the record of miracles in the New Testament. Andrews Norton, Ticknor's future brother-in-law, would spend his life proving that the miracles really did occur, and hence that revelation was authentic. The historicity of miracles was a subject with which a sensible man, a lawyer or a historian, could come to terms. Later when William Prescott, Ticknor's closest friend, wished to judge the Christian religion for himself, he turned to his father, an eminent judge, for guidance. Together they canvassed the Bible and the eighteenth-century skeptics and apologists — Hume, Gibbon, Middleton, Watson, Brown, Butler, and Paley — and concluded that the Gospels were indeed authentic. And, as Ticknor remarked of Prescott's decision, "He might have added, that it was the safer, because the person who had helped him in making it was not only a man of uncommon fairness of mind, but one who was very cautious, and, on all matters of evidence, had a tendency to scepticism rather than credulity." Rational Christianity, then, was to be a lawyer-proof religion.[40]

For a time the liberal Christians had hoped to avoid controversy, to preserve the peace of the mother Congregational Church. The outspoken Unitarian Andrews Norton blamed his colleagues for not being "sufficiently explicit in their opinions." The tart Episcopalian J. S. J. Gardiner sneered that "the candour of a Unitarian resembles the humanity of a revolutionary Frenchman. It is entirely confined to words." The theological battles between orthodox and liberal became more virulent after the election of Henry Ware to the Hollis Chair of Divinity in 1805. Men began to taunt one another by asking, "Are you of the

Boston religion or of the Christian religion?" or by retorting, "Are you a Christian or a Calvinist?" [41]

Ticknor was not much interested or involved in these bitter theological exchanges. For him, as for many other respectable Bostonians, the central issue — the validity of Calvinist theology, Oliver Wendell Holmes' "One Hoss Shay" — was already settled, and he saw little value in "metaphysical" contests. He was interested in what he called "practical metaphysics," the art of making people happy and not "crazy or quarrelsome." Most of his friends were liberals, and he knew that neither he nor they were miserable sinners. Having seen "to what absurdities the Calvinists were carried, by their perverse intellectual philosophy," he rejected a dark view of human nature in theology while embracing it in politics. Later he and some of his friends would have doubts about the outcome of the religious revolution in which they took part, but as a young man he was pleased with their handiwork.[42]

6. *The Anthology Society*

In 1810 Ticknor was invited to become a member of the Anthology Society. This was a convivial and cultivated group of professional men who edited *The Monthly Anthology and Boston Review*. This association with the leading intellectuals of Boston and Cambridge profoundly shaped Ticknor's conception of literature and the social role of men of letters. The Society seemed at times a Unitarian club: John Kirkland, Joseph Buckminster, and William Emerson, for example, were charter members. Dr. Gardiner, also an editor, gave a witty Johnsonian ring to talk in the club. Over good suppers of mongrel goose and claret, they discussed contributions to the journal in a rough and ready fashion. Ticknor enjoyed this seminar in contemporary literature where Latin puns and a magisterial manner were considered good form. The ladies of Boston would not "invite company on Anthology evenings, because the meeting of the club robbed them of the most agreeable gentlemen." In America there was too little *esprit de corps* among literati, the Anthologists believed, and standards of scholarship and taste were too crude. They pictured themselves as "gentle knights who wish to guard the seats of taste and morals at home from the incursions of the 'paynim host' . . . as insensible to the neglect or contumely of the great vulgar and the small as they are to the pelting of the pitiless storm without when taste and good humor sit round the fire within." Behind a condescending manner and pedantic tone lay a dream: that they would help to usher in a new Augustan age, that they would create an Athens in Boeotia. Dr. Johnson had thrown down the gauntlet: only a boor, he said, would go to America to "immerse himself and his posterity for ages in barbarism." But Bishop Berkeley had painted a contrasting vision of a westward course of cultural empire moving from Europe to the New World.[43]

The founders of the Anthology Society saw clearly the role of the scholar in fulfilling Berkeley's prophecy. William Emerson sketched this ideal — quite different from his son Ralph Waldo's view of "The American Scholar" a generation later — in a preface to the December, 1804, issue of *The Monthly Anthology*. There he expressed the Society's hopes for the foundling magazine. In astonishing detail this preface foreshadowed the actual career of George Ticknor. Emerson personified the young journal: "We are daily introducing him to the acquaintance of the wise and good, and laying plans to give him an excellent education." He shall learn ancient and modern languages, study at two or three universities, and enjoy membership in American and European learned societies. He shall travel for instruction to Europe, where he shall "inspect the colleges, hospitals, and armies of Europe, take now and then a peek into the cabinets of princes, and get a general acquaintance with the great affairs of the political world." He shall enter politics only "to be a judicious biographer of the great." Although he shall be learned, "he shall not be destitute of the manners of a gentleman, nor a stranger to genteel amusements." At home in the theater, at balls, in museums, and in "whatever polite diversions the town may furnish," he shall not be a learned recluse but "his dress and conversation shall borrow the mode and graces of the most polished circles in society."

The grand object of giving to our charge these expensive advantages, is to make him extensively and permanently useful. Having neither patrimony nor wealthy connections, he will be obliged to gain reputation by continual exertion of talent, and we feel confident that he will choose rather to lead a beneficent than luxurious life . . . If he should be unable to mend the constitution of our country, or save it from ruin, he may yet mend the morals of a private citizen, and can at least engage in the more

> Delightful task! to rear the tender thought,
> To teach the young idea how to shoot,

To pour the fresh instruction o'er the mind,
And fix the generous purpose in the glowing breast.[44]

This preface, like Buckminster's "Dangers and Duties of Men of Letters," delineates the ideal gentleman of letters as conceived by the intellectuals of Boston. The scholar was not a narrow specialist, but a man of the world interested in all civilized activity and inquiry. Naturally his first love would be literature, for letters and learning were indistinguishable, and literature more easily domesticated in America than the other arts. Buckminster believed that we "can never in this country possess many of the luxuries of the fine arts which the older countries enjoy; but we may learn to love the more refined and loftier elegances of literature and taste." A cosmopolitan gentleman, the scholar would be at home socially in all refined society on both sides of the Atlantic. He would temper the noxious passion of his countrymen for money and encourage them to serve a "Pantheon of better gods."

By his example the gentleman of letters would oppose the lust for money which threatened to turn America into a rich but culturally barren land. Fisher Ames had warned against this preoccupation with money-making: "the single passion that engrosses us, the only avenue to consideration and importance in our society, is the accumulation of property; our inclinations cling to gold, and are bedded in it, as deeply as that precious ore in the mine. Covered as our genius is in this mineral crust, is it strange that it does not sparkle?" Abhorring political or religious enthusiasm, the intellectual would call "away the student from questions which gender strife," and would decry fanaticism. The man of letters would mediate between the riper civilization of Europe and the culturally parched New World, and would make his pilgrimage to the Old World much as the English *vir bonus* had visited Greece and Rome. He was to play in the republic of letters the role of the Federalist leaders in the political republic.[45]

Ticknor and the Anthologists believed that there was a close connection between literature and morality. This influence moved both ways: corrupt literature undermined the foundations of society, and a sick society infected literature. "A man who has seen anything of life," Alexander Everett wrote Ticknor, "tends not to be startled by examples of great profligacy and corruption of all kinds — but I love to believe that literature and philosophy afford the best security that one can have of general integrity." Literature must be didactic and moral; "my mind delights to dwell on the severe morality of Johnson," exclaimed Buckminster's best friend, Arthur Walter. "I admire Johnson for his continual propriety. Other writers sometimes relax from rectitude, but he is always consistent." In literature, at least, one could fight the "pernicious notion of equality," and maintain a republic, not a democracy, of letters. This battle would be no easier, or less fateful, than the contests of Federalists and Jacobins. "We know that in this land, where the spirit of democracy is everywhere diffused, we are exposed . . . to a poisonous atmosphere," lamented Andrews Norton, "which blasts everything beautiful in nature and corrodes everything elegant in art." Norton deprecated the lust for popularity

> Which courts the rabble's smile, the rabble's nod,
> And makes, like Egypt, every beast its God.[46]

With every vulgar scribbler trying to get into print, attempting to turn the republic of letters into a democracy, the reviewer in the *Monthly Anthology* had no easy task. As one anonymous critic said, "It is our duty to destroy useless, unnecessary, and pernicious productions, as the ancient Grecians exposed their most puny and imbecile offspring to perish. Therefore the office of the reviewer is in the republick of letters as beneficial and necessary, though as odious and unpleasant, as that of the executioner in the civil state." It was not enough to prosecute and condemn vicious writers; it was essential to exterminate trivial ones as well. After all, Buckminster said, they were breaking the rules of the literary republic. In former times, "the method of conducting literary journals was to be ascertained by experiment, and an author was to be flattered into a quiet acknowledgement of . . . [the critic's] privileges; now every candidate for fame has it in his power to consult innumerable precedents, statutes, and declarations of criticism, by which the verdict of the publick and the sentence of the reviewer may be previously and probably conjectured." [47]

Judicial criticism could go no further. Ticknor took smug delight in pointing out "Ridiculous Literary Blunders" and in wearing the judge's gown. Yet he and some of the younger members of the Anthology Society were beginning to wonder whether the work of literature could really be adjudicated like a case at law. Ticknor conceded that critics "certainly ought to give place to those who without or even in defiance of art and rules, perform wonders in literature." [48] Sympathetic to some of the early romantic writers, Ticknor and his friends could not share the Olympian assurance of Gardiner that the standards of Dr. Johnson were beyond question.

The issue came to a boil in the Anthology Society in a debate between Gardiner and Buckminster on the merits of Gray's poetry. For Gardiner the question of Gray's worth had been settled once and for all by "the superior authority of the mighty Johnson. 'These odes (says the doctor) are marked by glittering accumulations of ungraceful ornaments. They strike rather than please. The images are magnified by affectation; the language is labored into harshness. The mind of the writer seems to work with unnatural violence, *Double, double, toil and trouble.*'" Though Buckminster had talked of "precedents" and "statutes" of criticism, he disagreed with Johnson and his arch vicar Gardiner; for him the issue came down to the "single question, is there such a description of poetry as the lyrick?" Arguing "that there is a higher species of poetry than the mere language of reason," Buckminster claimed that Gray's indistinct language raised "a glow, which . . . seems to consist in a certain felicity of terms, fraught with pictures, which it is impossible to transfer to the canvas." He appealed to the vivid emotions aroused by this couplet:

> O'er her warm cheek and rising bosom move
> The bloom of young desire, and purple light of love.

Irregularity, varied cadences, and unexpected and forceful epithets were Gray's virtues as a lyric poet. "For my own part I take as much delight in contemplating the rich hues that succeed one another without order in a deep cloud in the west, which has no prescribed shape," Buckminster wrote, "as in viewing the seven colours of the rainbow disposed in a form exactly semi-circular." Arrant nonsense, replied Gardiner. How could such a talented writer — a clergyman at that — waste his time "in the defense of absurdity"? Obscurity is just another name for corruption: "Indeed I lay it down as a general maxim, that WHATEVER IMAGERY A GOOD PAINTER CANNOT EXECUTE ON THE CANVASS, MUST NECESSARILY BE INCORRECT." As for that epithet about the *"purple light of love,"* Gray, in his desire "to write like no one but himself," was simply inappropriate and unintelligible.

This pre-romantic crossfire was beginning to disrupt the Anthology Society. As the battle continued, Gardiner wrote a further reply to Buckminster in which he included a satirical personal comment on the young minister. After he had finished reading his article to the Society, he glanced at the stony faces about the table and threw his manuscript into the fire. From that time on, no one in the Society ever referred to Gray again. Yet it could not be denied that faction had appeared in the republic of letters. The icy assurance of the establishment was cracking.[49]

Ticknor and the other younger Anthologists began to wonder what sort of Augustan age they should help to usher in. Might it be that some of the writers whom they were trying to expose to the wintry wind were not "puny and imbecile offspring," but rather the precursors of a new American literature? By what standards should one judge his country-men? Gardiner had said that "all sensible Americans will rely on the great writers of . . . [England] as authorities, till we can produce equal excellence. We know of no American language, that is not Indian, and feel no inclination to resort to the Choctaws, the Chickasaws, the Cherokees, and the Tuskaroras for literary instruction. Whilst we speak and write in the English language, we are satisfied to be guided . . . by approved English authorities, by which we shall guard against modern foppery and provincial impurities." Samuel Thacher, another Antholo-gist, disagreed: Poetry need not ally itself with riches and refinement, Americans should not "import the style and imagery of England, much as our merchants do its wares." "The birth place of the original poet has often been where, as in our country, nature appears in all her rude-ness, where the mountains rise in their unsubdued and gigantick eleva-tions, the cataracts fall without mechanical precipitation, and the rivers roll without artificial meanders." [50] Provincial impurities or rude gran-deur, refinement or nature, classical and universal standards or unique nationality — the terms of a great literary debate of the nineteenth century were emerging. Ticknor and the men of letters in his Boston circle would be as ambivalent in this debate as in the distressing conflict between Gardiner and Buckminster.

After almost a decade — a long life as literary journals went in America — the *Monthly Anthology* died in 1811. As secretary of the Society in its declining years, Ticknor recorded in the minutes that the members hoped to have a last issue good enough for the community to lament the passing of the magazine, but in the last months they disgustedly threw the contributors' poems under the table. "It is really a grievous thing that these blockheads will not suffer us to die in peace," Ticknor complained. "In our better estate we could endure it; but to be kicked by every ass in our weakness and decrepitude is heaping insult upon injury."

In truth, the Anthology had outlived its usefulness, and would soon be replaced by the *North American Review,* a far more distinguished and sophisticated periodical. But the Anthologists had gained a priceless sense of intellectual community and a preview of critical struggles to come. Like the transcendentalists to follow, but in a far different manner, they scorned the lust for money, the materialism, of their countrymen; they deplored the shallowness of much of the partisan politics of the day; they anxiously inquired about the cultural estate of the nation and asked what role scholars could play in bringing forth a vigorous intellectual life; they raised many important questions about the character of American literature and art; somewhat alienated from the society around them, they expressed a concern for the vocation of the intellectual. Ticknor's experience as a member of the Anthology Society had sharpened his distaste for the law and given direction to his vague quest for a scholarly career. Now he must pursue a more decisive course.[51]

7. *Abandoning the Law*

From 1810 to 1813 Ticknor read law with William Sullivan and was admitted to the bar in 1813. One year of practice convinced him that he would be unhappy as a lawyer. Like several other young men of literary tastes he had drifted into the law for lack of an acceptable alternative. "I read law with some diligence, but not with interest enough to attach me to the profession. I continued to read Greek and Latin, and preferred my old studies to any other." His work with Sullivan had followed the familiar path of the legal apprenticeship — Plowden's Reports, Coke and Blackstone — and provided little of the intellectual challenge which later students would find in Joseph Story's enthusiastic teaching at the Harvard Law School. Law and letters did not mix for Ticknor. One suspects that he was describing his own experience when he wrote in the *Monthly Anthology* that "nothing is more fatal to legal success than pursuing the study in hot and cold fits — by starts and after frequent interruptions." Ticknor's decision to desert the law hardly surprised those who knew him; his father realized that George's true love was letters.[52]

Compared with literature the law was musty, and to make matters worse it wasn't even profitable. Ticknor's mentor Sullivan recognized that "none of the departments of intellectual labor, presents a more discouraging view, to one who can choose his own cast in society" than the law. In New England he said, "the lawyer is ever ready to escape from his slavery when the proper opportunity offers." Sullivan reported that of 127 lawyers admitted to the bar between 1784 and 1813 none had retired early with a competent fortune, nineteen had died of whom "a majority left no property," and many had abandoned the law for other vocations. Samuel Eliot had advised his son not to enter the law, for "in the present day, when every young man almost is becoming a lawyer, in addition to the innumerable host that crowd the courts, I see not the prospect of obtaining, by honourable procedure, a comfortable subsistence." [53]

The law bored several of Ticknor's friends. Judge Story, himself a poet, suggested one reason: "the technical doctrines of a jurisprudence . . . must have a tendency to chill that enthusiasm, which lends encouragement to every enterprise, and to obscure those finer forms of thought, which give to literature its lovelier, I may say, its inexpressible graces." Admitted to the bar at the same time as Ticknor, Edward T. Channing soon gave up the law to teach rhetoric at Harvard, where his students included most of the famous writers of New England's golden day — Emerson, Thoreau, Holmes, Dana, Motley, and Parkman among them. Ned Channing, Ticknor's witty companion of the hasty-pudding suppers, earned a reputation as the most famous teacher of composition in the nineteenth century:

> Channing, with his bland, superior look,
> Cold as a moonbeam on a frozen brook,
> While the pale student, shivering in his shoes,
> Sees from his theme the turgid rhetoric ooze.

Another lawyer, Henry Wadsworth Longfellow, became Ticknor's successor at Harvard and the best-known American poet of his time, Ticknor's life-long friend and Harvard colleague, Joseph Cogswell, who later founded the New York Public Library, became disgusted with

his legal practice in Maine when he heard that "our first lawyers, and
even our judges avow that no man can succeed here by uprightness of
character and honorable dealing." Alexander Everett also studied law
under Sullivan's auspices and opened an office next door to Ticknor's
on Court Square, but he too grew dissatisfied with the work and embarked on a distinguished career as a diplomat and writer. William
Hickling Prescott, Ticknor's best friend, briefly practiced law before
becoming one of the great historians of the nineteenth century.[54]

Ticknor believed that he was not yet equipped to become a professional man of letters. He was already approaching the limits of American
literary training. His real education had been more informal than
formal, shaped by his membership in literary clubs and by reading in
his excellent library. He agreed with Buckminster that one of the dangers
of American scholars was that their studies were too often "loose and
undirected," their inquiries "superficial and unconnected." "I began,
long ago, a course of studies," Ticknor commented to a friend, "which
I well knew I could not finish on this side of the Atlantic; and if I do
not mean to relinquish my favorite pursuits, and acknowledge that I
have trifled away some of the best years of my life, I must spend some
years in Italy, France, and Germany, and in Greece, if I can." [55]

When he decided to study abroad, Ticknor did not know what career
to pursue on his return. He knew that New England would never lack
skilled lawyers, but that it did lack excellent scholars and teachers. He
had come to know several Harvard professors and tutors and his fellow
Anthologist John Kirkland, who became Harvard's president in 1810.
Probably he had reason to hope that he might win a professorship there.
This appealed to him: "I am not sure I should not prefer to have a friend
of mine an able professor rather than an able lawyer," Ticknor commented. The Anthologists never tired of calling for better colleges.
William Tudor, Jr., urged that "a university should not only be a place
of instruction for youth; it should be a home to the cultivators of learning. In her shades they should find a shelter, in whose calm retreats
they may devote their lives to the active pursuits of science and literature,
unharassed by the cares of the world." [56] (An attractive ideal, this,
though it might have struck the college teachers of the time as hopelessly
utopian.) Were Ticknor a professor, he could at least justify his literary
career to the world.

Proper Bostonians at this time never went to Europe merely for the finishing touches of the Grand Tour. They went for a variety of reasons — which they were always at pains to point out — for health, for private or public business, or for education unobtainable elsewhere. For Ticknor it was to be a study tour, "a sacrifice of enjoyment to improvement. I value it only in proportion to the great means and inducements it will afford to me to study — not men, but books." Many of Ticknor's friends had made the pilgrimage to the Old World already, among them Buckminster and several members of the Anthology Society. They had charted the way so clearly to Liverpool, to London, to Paris, to Rome, even to Göttingen, that Ticknor felt that he had been there too. Edward Everett — the astounding young man who had been chosen minister of the Brattle Street Church at the age of nineteen and had become Professor of Greek at Harvard the next year — decided in 1814 to complete his education in Europe.[57]

Everett and Ticknor heard about prodigies of scholarship at the German universities from some of their friends. During his junior year at Harvard Everett had paid weekly visits to Buckminster to discuss theology and literature. In Buckminster's rich library he first formed "a vague and youthful ambition of pushing these studies to their fountain head at a German University." From Samuel Thacher Ticknor learned about the extraordinary library at Göttingen that made the Harvard library seem like a mere "closetful of books." Ticknor's interest in the German universities, originally aroused by Madame de Staël's *De l'Allemagne,* was further whetted by Charles Viller's enthusiastic portrait of Göttingen in his *Coup-d'Oeil sur les Universités.* Viller talked of the freedom of teaching and learning and the diligence and brilliance of the professors that made the German universities "schools for all civilized nations." "I understand! I understand!" a French professor had exclaimed; the "Germans begin where we leave off!" In Viller's excited description Göttingen was indeed the fountainhead, high above the sleepy English universities or the French schools corrupted by the Revolution and Napoleon. Later Ticknor wrote of Viller's pamphlet that it was "the book which in 1814 determined me to go to Germany." [58]

Thus during the summer and fall of 1814 Ticknor turned with characteristic energy to learning German and preparing himself for his odyssey. Although there were scholars in New England who could have smoothed his path in learning the language and understanding the culture, Ticknor seems to have been unaware of the fact. He studied

German largely on his own; the tutor he could find had an Alsatian accent, and Ticknor ransacked his friends' libraries to obtain a grammar and dictionary. With the connivance of William S. Shaw, founder of the Athenaeum, he managed to get a copy of Goethe's *The Sorrows of Young Werther* from John Quincy Adams' library (without permission — Henry Adams claimed that Ticknor never returned the volume). Although the choice of *Werther* was a strange one for an upright Bostonian, Ticknor rendered it into English as an exercise in learning the language, and produced a remarkably good translation. It was a *tour de force* which demonstrated Ticknor's extraordinary skill as a linguist.[59]

As part of his preparation for his European education Ticknor decided to make a tour of the United States. To be an effective mediator between the New and Old Worlds he must first sample the best which his own country could offer. In this way he could guard against the expatriate's disaffection. A further practical reason for visiting the great men of America was to obtain letters of introduction to the worthies of Europe.

8. *Pilgrimage in the New World*

Ticknor's trip to Virginia in the winter of 1814–15 turned out to be a successful dress rehearsal for his European voyage. Ticknor was then twenty-three years old, quick in walk and gesture, slight in stature, with a complexion so ruddy, hair so black and thick, and eyes so dark, that people thought he looked Spanish. He was an eager and perceptive listener and a good talker, his memory full of "fact, anecdote, and quotation."

He had a life-long knack for good timing; he always seemed to be about when interesting things were happening. Ticknor's first destination on his pilgrimage was Hartford where the Convention was then in session. He traveled there with a hearty and decisive merchant prince, Samuel G. Perkins, who talked as the coach bounced along about his experiences during the Revolution in Santo Domingo. Ticknor and Perkins stayed with the members of the Massachusetts delegation — among them George Cabot, the president of the Convention, Harrison Gray Otis, and Judge William Prescott, father of the historian. The talk ranged far and wide. "I, of course, learnt nothing of the proceedings of the Convention, which sat with closed doors; but it was impossible to pass two days with such men," Ticknor commented, "and hear their free conversation on public affairs, without feeling an entire confidence in their integrity and faithfulness to duty." [60]

In New Haven Ticknor heard Professor Benjamin Silliman give an animated lecture on chemistry to a group of 180 students who listened attentively and took notes. This was the way to teach, Ticknor believed, not routinely grinding through a recitation. Silliman had gone to Europe to prepare for his Professorship at Yale. He too had been a lawyer before beginning his academic career. Outside the town was Eli Whitney's musket factory, where Whitney developed the principle of interchangeable parts. In old age Ticknor remembered "still with great interest the conversation we had with Mr. Whitney," the man whose invention of the cotton gin "gave the Slave States their resources for rebellion."

New York City seemed large and cosmopolitan to Ticknor. He visited a double-hulled frigate that Robert Fulton had designed to defend the harbor; the vessel had topsides five feet thick, forty cannon, and a steam engine placed between the two hulls. He had dinner with William B. Astor, who had recently returned from Germany, and from whom he could have gleaned much information about Göttingen; but for some reason the subject of Germany never arose in their conversation.[61]

The greatest attraction in Philadelphia was the elegant dinner parties where Ticknor saw for the first time a service of silver plate for twenty people and liveried servants with epaulettes. At one of these parties he met John Randolph who looked like a boy of fifteen when he was seated, but who towered over Ticknor when he stood to shake hands. He resembled a pyramid: thick long legs and broad feet, tiny head and shoulders, and long hair like an Indian's. In his "shrill and effeminate" voice he talked with Ticknor about his loneliness in a melancholy vein "which made me think better of his heart than I had before."

Randolph, however, rarely let down his guard. At the dinner table the suave Portuguese minister to the United States, the Abbe Correa de Serra, who had just been to Virginia to visit Jefferson, commented that he was surprised that so few gentlemen-planters lived in luxury. Quick to resent any slight on his native state, Randolph retorted "Perhaps, Mr. Correa, your acquaintance was not with that class of persons." "Perhaps not; the next time I will go down upon the Roanoke," replied Correa, "and I will visit Mr. Randolph and his friends." The bitter Randolph persisted: "In *my* part of the country, gentlemen commonly wait to be *invited* before they make visits." With flushed face, and looking slowly at the guests about the dinner table, Correa softly asked "Said I not well of the *gentlemen* of Virginia?" [62]

January of 1815 was a sad time to visit Washington. Following the road the British had taken when they marched to burn the government buildings, Ticknor's coach traversed a desolate plain leading to the rise where the ruined Capitol stood without "even a hill to soften the distant horizon behind it, or a fence or a smoke to give it the cheerful appearance of a human habitation." When Ticknor had dinner with Madison in the White House, the President was anxiously awaiting news of Jackson's battle with the British in New Orleans, unaware that the peace treaty with England had already been signed at Ghent on December 24, and that Jackson had scored his astonishing victory on January 8. It was little wonder that Madison seemed preoccupied, but he talked freely with the young Federalist about religion — intimating "his own regard for the Unitarian doctrines" — and education, only once or twice giving his comments a political coloring.

The Congressmen whom Ticknor met were not so reticent. The bankrupt condition of federal finances brought bitter carping from the Federalist members. When one Democrat in exasperation asked a Federalist if his party would take the nation if the administration turned it over to them, the Federalist replied "No, sir; not unless you will give it to *us* as we gave it to *you*." Ticknor thought that the Democratic administration was about to adopt "violent and desperate" measures. The news of Jackson's triumph and the peace treaty would soon blow away the clouds of gloom. But the change in political weather would hardly help the Federalists.

From Washington to Monticello the journey was arduous. Ticknor had to help break the ice in streams so that the horses could pull the coach across the fords; he had to trudge miles in the snow; and he went for twenty-four hours without food. "You, my dear father, often talk to me of your sufferings as a Revolutionary soldier," Ticknor wrote, "and you, my dear mother, look down a little on the pet your indulgence has made. — but now I can answer you both." He also had a taste of the miserable poverty of the southern poor white and Negro. In one hovel which passed as a tavern, he found that humans and animals lived on the "borry" (borrowing), and after the pigs were dismissed from the room, Ticknor and five others slept on the floor while the wind whistled in through cracks in the doors and windows. At the next house he found "sickness and suffering even more moving than we had seen yesterday." [63]

Later another New Englander, Henry Adams, made his pilgrimage in Virginia over impossible roads. "To the New England mind," Adams wrote, "roads, schools, clothes, and a clear face were connected as part of the law of order or divine system. Bad roads meant bad morals. The moral of this Virginia road was clear, and the boy fully learned it. Slavery was wicked . . . and yet, at the end of the road and product of the crime stood Mount Vernon and George Washington." A further paradox awaited George Ticknor, for his destination was Monticello and his host the arch foe of Federalism, Thomas Jefferson. The winding and steep climb up the forested slopes of Carter's Mountain, on which Jefferson's house perched, Ticknor thought "as pensive and slow as Satan's ascent to Paradise." [64]

As Ticknor entered Monticello through the glass folding doors he saw the hall with the "strange furniture of its walls," indices of Jefferson's catholic interests: a mastodon's head, animal horns, a painting of the "Repentance of Saint Peter," and Indian maps and paintings. Nothing was so surprising as Jefferson himself. Finding a tall man, instead of the small figure conjured by his imagination, "with dignity in his appearance and ease and graciousness in his manners," Ticknor was delighted with the old philosopher who loved "old books and young society." He could talk well on almost any subject and was the soul of hospitality. Ticknor was impressed with his "sobriety and cool reason." Two incidents demonstrated his remarkable composure. When Jefferson's grandson came from Charlottesville to report Jackson's victory at New Orleans — which Jefferson had thought impossible — Jefferson had retired and "refused to open the door, saying he could wait till the morning." And when Jefferson's dam was washed away — a large project which would cost $30,000 to replace — Jefferson announced it as if it were no great matter.

True at times Jefferson seemed less philosophical, as when he took great satisfaction in showing Ticknor his collection of books on the scandalous behavior of kings and queens. Still, Ticknor could now dismiss the political vagaries of the Jacobin as "curious *indicia* of an extraordinary person," part and parcel of his "notional philosophy," which confirmed him in his habit of wearing "very sharp-toed shoes, corduroy small-clothes, and red plush waistcoat, which have been laughed at till he might perhaps wisely have dismissed them." The bond of Jefferson and Ticknor as bibliophiles, and as men ambitious for high scholarship in the new republic, was too firmly welded for politics to split. Jefferson was delighted with Ticknor, and wrote to John Adams that "if Mass. can raise a few more such, it is probable she would have been better counseled as to social rights and social duties." In the light of this remark it seems safe to assume that the two scholars did not discuss the Hartford Convention or the virtues of Federalism.[65]

On his return to Boston Ticknor stopped again in Washington, where he visited the Supreme Court. There he heard eminent lawyers pleading a case before Chief Justice John Marshall, an awkward, tall man with a thick shock of hair. In conversation Marshall was mild and conciliating, in appearance somewhat careless, Ticknor thought; but his eyes disclosed his acute mind. Ticknor had dinner with Martha Washington's granddaughter, Mrs. Thomas Peter, who served a bottle of wine from Washington's cellar and regaled the company with stories about her grandfather's family life and a vivid account of the British attack on the Capitol. She was a patriotic Tory, a woman after Ticknor's heart, who named her daughters Columbia Washington, America Pinckney, and Britannia Wellington.

This tour, Ticknor's "first real sight and knowledge of the world," whetted his appetite for seeing the wider world of Europe and provided him with letters of introduction to some of the notable men in the Old World. Yet Ticknor knew that he would sacrifice the security and pleasures of home when he embarked on his next pilgrimage. His must be the straight path of duty, of strenuous study, not the nostalgic and provincial by-ways of Washington Irving who traveled across Europe "with the sauntering gaze with which humble lovers of the picturesque stroll from the window of one printshop to another." [66]

Indeed, Ticknor was not unrealistic or hypocritical when he spoke to a friend of the sacrifices he would undergo. With the War of 1812 barely ended, travel was uncertain and more difficult than it would soon be when there were guidebooks and well-beaten tourist paths. Even before his experience abroad, Ticknor knew of the prodigious labor necessary before he could measure up to decent European standards of scholarship.

As Ticknor embarked, Jefferson, an older but still hopeful pilgrim, predicted to Elisha Ticknor that George "will return fraught with treasures of science which he could not have found in a country so engrossed by industrious pursuits as ours, but he will be a sample to our youth of what they ought to be, and a model for imitation in pursuits so honorable, so improving, and so friendly to good morals." [67]

II

A Yankee Abroad

"You [Americans] are the advance guard of the human race —
you are the future of the world." *Madame de Staël* [1]

Ticknor's experience in Europe tested and proved the durability of his Yankee education. Never did he lose a clear image of himself and his mission in the labyrinth of the Old World. "Travel rather in the manner of a clergyman," his father had told him. "The great object of your journey I am sure you will keep in mind, and never turn to the right hand nor to the left, viz. to improve in solid science, the arts, and literature, and in the knowledge of men." Elisha had every reason to believe that his son was a triumph of the Bostonian ideal of education: he was clear thinking, decorous, loyal and filial, with a distaste for enthusiasm and the show of emotion but with deep underlying affections, dignified and socially gracious, and magnificently self-assured. Well aware of the snares and opportunities of Europe, George had no intention of being a lotus-eater.

With characteristic diligence he had prepared himself beforehand by reading everything he could find on Europe and by talking with travelers. His model man of letters, Joseph S. Buckminster, had preceded him in 1806 and had charted the reefs and channels. Ticknor knew what to expect. Did not a Bostonian know in his heart, as Emerson was later to confess, that "England is the best of actual nations"? Did not a Federalist know what he would find in Paris? And any good classicist remembered Cicero's remark that "none but a Barbarian can be a *stranger in Rome.*" [2] There might be some surprises, but the fewer the better.

Ironically, it was the Europeans who were confused. Ticknor met people who thought that Americans were cannibals and criminals or, alternatively, the advance guard of the human race. How could they fit these "new Americans," Ticknor and his fellow literary pioneers — Edward Everett, George Bancroft, and Joseph Cogswell — into their preconceptions. "You must not think me extravagant," wrote Cogswell to a friend at Harvard, "but I venture to say that the notions which the European literati have entertained of America will be essentially changed by G. and E.'s [Ticknor's and Everett's] residence on the Continent." [3] How could Europeans explain these scholarly and self-possessed young men who perversely refused to match Old World images of Americans, who were unwilling to adapt flexibly, as Benjamin Franklin had, to the incongruous expectations of Europeans.

Throughout his pilgrimage Ticknor remained the stern republican, the moral gentleman, and the earnest scholar. Like Cogswell, who insisted on wearing plain black republican dress in the courts of the Continent, Ticknor was determined to retain his political convictions and to interpret the "ominous ripeness" of Europe allegorically to his countrymen. He was resolved to wear the armor of innocence to deflect the temptations of the corrupt Old World. He had made up his mind to carry home the spoils of culture but to resist envy and nostalgia. To a large degree he saw what he expected to see and comprehended what he was taught to comprehend. The blinders of the moralist, the literalness of the diligent scholar, and the dogmas of the conservative republican caused his impressions to be "received and conveyed," as Henry Adams observed, "as absolutely within certain limits as the habitat of a family of plants." [4]

1. *Our Old Home*

On April 16, 1815, Ticknor boarded the Liverpool packet with some of his closest friends: Edward Everett, who was also destined for Göttingen; Nathaniel Haven, a Portsmouth gentleman of literary tastes; and Mr. and Mrs. Samuel Perkins. Edward Everett's brother, Alexander, teased Ticknor about his affection for the charming Mrs. Perkins, whom Talleyrand had known when he visited Boston and who was, he said, one of the most beautiful girls he had ever met. Alexander wanted his brother and George to wait until he could accompany them across the Atlantic, "but Mrs. Perkins, has come . . . like a blazing star and dragged off" Edward and Ticknor in her train.[5]

As the ship neared Liverpool, the pilot brought the alarming news that Napoleon had returned to Paris to wage war again with the righteous. "Even in this age of tremendous revolutions," Ticknor wrote his father, "we have had none so appalling as this." Every honest man in Christendom had rejoiced when Bonaparte fell, believing that "he had a surer hope of going down to his grave in peace, and leaving an inheritance to his children. But now the whole complexion of the world is changed again . . . God only can foresee the consequences, and He, too, can control them. Terrible as the convulsion may be, it may be necessary for the purification of the corrupt governments of Europe, and for the final repose of the world."

These were exciting days to be in England. Bred as he was "in the strictest school of Federalism," Ticknor was astounded to learn that there actually were respectable men who rejoiced in the resurrection of Napoleon. Dr. Samuel Parr, the ancient friend of Johnson and Dr. Gardiner's former master, told Ticknor in his dogmatic lisp, "thir, I should not think I had done my duty, if I went to bed any night without praying for the success of Napoleon Bonaparte." Sir James Mackintosh wrote a vehement article for the *Edinburgh Review* arguing that a new war with Napoleon could only hurt England; just as the article was about to be distributed, Wellington's victory at Waterloo "came like a thunderclap," and the essay was suppressed.[6]

Liverpool reminded Ticknor of Boston, as it had Buckminster. Ticknor noted in his journal that the population of Liverpool had diminished by five thousand during the Revolutionary War, so close were the commercial ties between the city and America. If anything, the Liverpool merchants were more bustling than those in Boston; but they were not content to be merely "mercenary and commercial," Buckminster had commented, because they realized that "something more than great riches is necessary to make a place worthy of being visited." William Roscoe, founder of the Liverpool Athenaeum and biographer of Lorenzo de Medici, was one of the merchant-scholars Ticknor admired. He was a cultivated, self-made man who had earned a fortune in trade and lived on the same estate where his father had been a gardener.

Liverpool proved that there need be no antinomy between culture and commerce. Ticknor saw no essential difference between Yankees and Europeans in their love of money. The English should throw no stones at the Americans for worshipping Mammon, Ticknor commented, for "the love of the useful and profitable is the first feeling bred in Englishmen from childhood and prevails during life over every other, more than in any other nation besides." Indeed, businessmen were everywhere the same. Once, while he listened with amusement to German merchants in a tavern boasting of attendance at a German fair, he observed "how exactly these people from Hamburg . . . are like the Merchants in Amsterdam, London and Boston." [7]

Although Ticknor later concluded that with respect "to the love of money and the pursuit of it, I find little difference in different countries," he was deeply moved by the remnants of antiquity in England, by the reminders of a past absent in the New World. Irving had spoken of ruins, paradoxically, as the unique promise of Europe. As Ticknor journeyed to London through the lush spring green of the Welsh hills, he wrote excitedly in his journal about the valley of Llangollen.

The recollection of all I had seen during the day pressed confusedly on my memory — the moon shone brightly on the village church, which was in full view of my bed — and the harper was still playing some of his airs in the room beneath me, and when I finally sunk to rest, the last tho'ts that floated indistinctly in my mind and seemed almost to rise into reality before my senses, were of the days, when the castle on the mountain stood in its pride and strength — when the Abbey was filled with the incense and anthems of the holy men of old, who worshipped there — and the valley echoed thro' all its windings to the harps and songs of bards who were the delight of genera-tions, that have been for ages forgotten.

Birmingham shattered his revery. There he saw noisome columns of black smoke and pitiful tubercular children whose hair had turned green in the copper factories.

At Hatton Ticknor stopped to visit Dr. Parr, the best Latinist in England. A vigorous old man who wore a coat and waistcoat like Dr. Johnson's and who had the same "dirty bob-wig," he rolled about in the chair as he talked about American politics in a declamatory tone "as dictatorial as an emperor's." Unconcerned about his ignorance of Ameri-can affairs, he told Ticknor that he had hated to see the Americans called rebels and that he "was always glad that you beat us." Ticknor was delighted with his grotesque solemnity, his evocation of an earlier era.[8]

London was the high point of Ticknor's trip through England. In "the world's metropolis" ancient met modern — Westminster Abbey and counting houses, the living men of letters of England and the living traditions of literature. Ticknor walked through the Stock Exchange into the old stone London Exchange, to Lloyd's Coffee House, and to

Guildhall. He visited Benjamin West's gallery of paintings and the theater. But above all it was in the literary drawing rooms and in the author's suppers that he tasted the flavor of English intellectual life.

One of the first celebrities Ticknor met was the famous chemist Sir Humphry Davy. This handsome and animated scientist talked rapidly and excitedly about his last trip to Italy and his friend Madame de Staël, to whom he gave Ticknor a letter of introduction. Ticknor was surprised to hear him say that if he had to choose between fishing or philosophy he would be most uncomfortable. He met the satirist William Gifford, had "a genuine booksellers' supper such as Lintot used to give to Pope, Gay [and] Swift," with John Murray and a group of authors, and frequently saw Lord and Lady Byron. Nowhere did social and intellectual triumph mean more to Ticknor than in England, and he was well pleased with his first acquaintance with literary society in the Old World. From this time on he would achieve a social reputation that would have astounded anyone with less self-assurance.[9]

2. *The Personification of Earnestness*

"If Ticknor had taken it into his head to go to Olympus," commented the literary critic Edwin Whipple, "the first person he would have sought, with a letter of introduction in his pocket, would have been Jupiter." As Ticknor continued with his European pilgrimage, he went from victory unto victory. His ability to ferret out intellectual celebrities surprised everyone but Ticknor. What was it about this young man, people asked, that made him such a good lion hunter?

Ticknor was determined to make the most of his time abroad for he did not know whether he would ever return. He had come not only to read books and to study in universities but also to understand "that sort of undefined and indefinite feeling, respecting books and authors, which exists in Europe as a kind of unwritten tradition." Obviously the best way to understand this tradition was to meet the foremost authors and scholars themselves. Never doubting the importance of his mission, and having no qualms about his own competence to perform it, Ticknor sought out many of the most prominent writers and scholars of the period: Wordsworth, Scott, Robert Southey, Madame de Staël, Chateaubriand, Alexander von Humboldt, Friedrich and Augustus von Schlegel, Ludwig Tieck, Byron, Goethe, and many others. With some he became fast friends. Characteristically, when he was in Rome, he obtained an audience with the Pope.[10]

Ticknor recognized that some of the members of this international republic of letters were not fashionable people — indeed, in Germany few scholars were admitted to the upper reaches of society. Conversely, he realized that those fashionable intellectuals whom he did meet did not typify the aristocracy. Of Lord Holland and his circle he commented, "Fashionable people, they certainly were in one sense of the word, for all of them were of the first class wherever they might be; but they did not belong to that class which makes fashionable intercourse its chief object and occupation in life. This, however, is no inconsiderable proportion of those who constitute the first division of society in London, and that is one reason why the life they lead is so laborious and why it is so inaccessible to strangers." [11]

"What was his 'Open Sesame' . . . ?" rhetorically asked an Englishman about Ticknor. He was young — only twenty-three when he came to Europe in 1815 and twenty-seven when he left in 1819 — and had no particular claim to attention, no official diplomatic or recognized scholarly or literary position. He was merely the son of a Boston grocer with a zeal for literature. To be sure, he carried letters of introduction from eminent Americans like John Adams and Thomas Jefferson. To be sure, he was an attractive person; he had dark expressive eyes and an alert face, impeccable manners and familiarity with social forms, obvious uprightness of character, facility in learning languages, and a marvelous memory which served him well in conversation. To be sure, he seemed discreet, not the scribbling kind of fly-by-night visitor who writes travel books. Still, as one Englishman observed, "there was nothing striking about him in look, air, or manner. He had no wit, humour, or vivacity . . . he was voted rather heavy in hand in circles which are caught more by quickness of perception, fertility of fancy and flow of language, than by the extent of knowledge or solidity of thought." The key to his success was his attitude, said this Englishman.

> 'Wherefore? you ask. I can but guide your guess.
> Man has no majesty like earnestness.'

Ticknor was "the personification of earnestness" in an age when respectable people were agreed on the importance of being earnest. Aptly, one acquaintance suggested that Ticknor abroad fulfilled the role "which belongs in fiction to Scott's colorless heroines. The passive personage of a novel to whom everything happens corresponds to the judicious hearer to whom everything is said." [12]

Undoubtedly Ticknor's status as an American affected the nature of his reception. Had he been simply the son of a moderately successful Liverpool grocer, the tale would probably have been different. To find this young American taking the worthies of the Old World so seriously was flattering: did not his approbation resemble the grave judgment of posterity? The vast ocean separating Europe and America gave him perspective. His self-assurance gave his opinions an Olympian ring. As usual, Ticknor's timing was perfect; he arrived in Europe right after the Napoleonic wars, when the frayed fabric of relations with the New World was just being rewoven. Europeans were eager to learn about this new nation across the sea which had fought a successful revolution and had weathered a war which had prostrated half of Europe.

To some it came as a surprise to find such a civilized young man emerging from the wilds of America. Ticknor was annoyed at the comment of a cockney who was surprised that he "spoke so good English." In Germany Ticknor found a mulatto featured in a circus side show "as a Cannibal caught near Philadelphia," and he wryly commented that he and Everett had been admitted to a literary club in Göttingen "as a kind of raree-show, I suppose, and we are considered, I doubt not, with much the same curiosity that a tame monkey or a dancing bear would be." Reviving an affront that had angered Americans for decades, the ill-tempered Lady Holland declared that she had heard that convicts had colonized New England. Ticknor, an obvious refutation of such an outrageous charge, knew how to deal with such insults. He reminded Lady Holland that her own ancestors had been prominent in founding that Bay Colony. The waspish hostess was delighted with such a spirited reply, and came to like Ticknor, but Ticknor never conquered his dislike of her. [13]

More often than not Europeans responded favorably to Ticknor as an American. His citizenship in a classless republic baffled any attempt to estimate his social position except by his evident dignity, his decorous manners, and his scholarship. Here was a Yankee who came not to drum up trade but disinterestedly to pursue knowledge, a man who carried in his pocket letters of praise from the most eminent men of the American republic. Madame de Staël announced to him "you are the advance guard of the human race, you are the future of the world." Even the Pope told Ticknor and Cogswell that "the time would soon come" when Americans "should be able to dictate to the Old World." [14]

Ticknor was not alone in seeking celebrities. Edward Everett, George Bancroft, and Joseph Cogswell skillfully stalked big intellectual game. At times there was a friendly competition among the young hunters. Ironically, two of the authors most friendly to the Yankees abroad were men most suspect to the elders at home; Byron and Goethe. Somewhat to their surprise, and with a kind of uneasy exhilaration, Ticknor and his friends found Goethe and Byron not morally repulsive, vain, and affected, as they had expected, but respectable in appearance and conversation, and sympathetic and well-informed concerning America.

Ticknor had pictured Byron as a deformed little man with a pinched and anxious face. Instead he found him well-proportioned, except for his crippled foot, with a round, smiling face, and a relaxed and affable manner. Toward his wife Byron was affectionate and respectful; his menage seemed to Ticknor a picture of domestic bliss. He asked all about America — inquiring, one supposes with a desire to pull Ticknor's leg, "whether we looked on Barlow, as our Homer" — and said that he wanted to visit the United States. He wanted to see the Indians and the wilderness and stand "in the spray of Niagara." He spoke repentantly of his early escapades and modestly about his poetry. "In everything . . . he is unlike the characters of his own Childe, and Giaour and Corsair, and yet those who know him best . . . say that these stories are but the descriptions of his early excesses." Byron told Ticknor that "he never envied any men more than Lewis and Clark," and he gave him a "splendid pistol" to give to the perverse Ali Pasha when Ticknor should travel in Greece. No wonder Ticknor confessed "that I have come from him with nothing but an indistinct, tho' lively impression of the goodness and vivacity of his disposition." [15]

Ticknor was also eager to meet the author of *Werther*. In Weimar he and Everett met Goethe, a man "not only respectable but imposing," who spoke "in a quiet, simple manner, which would have surprised me much, if I had known nothing of him but from his books." Everett was not so impressed as Ticknor. He wrote to his brother, Alexander, that "As I gave Ma a high-flown account of the interview, I will state to you the facts as they were . . . He was very stiff and cold, not to say gauche and awkward. His hair was gray, some of his front teeth gone, and his eyes watery with age." Cogswell, though, shared Ticknor's regard for Goethe and became quite intimate with him. He persuaded Goethe to give a set of his works to the Harvard Library. Cogswell had expected Goethe to be "vain and affected," but discovered "the politeness of a real gentleman." He thought that Goethe made "juster and more rational observations" on the United States than any other European he met. Bancroft, too, fell under the sway of the old man.[16]

When confronted with these earnest and innocent young men, both Byron and Goethe seemed to become candidates for the Unitarian ministry. In turn, their writings and personalities appealed to a latent romantic streak in the Yankees. Ticknor reread *Werther* when he felt melancholy. In Wetzlar he stopped to see the scenes depicted in the story. Imagining the scenes between Werther and Charlotte, Ticknor recalled that the chilly wind "gave me a sensation of sadness such as I have seldom felt. I was quite alone." Later he mounted the rocks where Werther passed the night after leaving Charlotte, "and in the village itself, I needed no guide to show me the red church — the lime trees — the burying ground, and the village houses which he has described with such fidelity. On returning to the city I stopped again on the rocks — read the description of his despair and stayed until the departing sun had almost descended behind the hills." Bancroft, younger and more romantic than the others, reveled in hikes in the sublime Alps and odysseys with Byron. Cogswell, no youngster, wrote at the age of thirty-two about his exultation, like Manfred's, in "leaping from cliff to cliff amid German clouds. Then I lived." Somewhat apologetically Ticknor revealed similar emotions during his climb in the moonlight near Mont Blanc, with the music of waterfalls above and the sound of herdsmen singing the Ronce des Vaches: "if in a scene like this, my thoughts and feelings took the hue of romance more than a traveler's commonly do, I am still not disposed to look back on them with ridicule."

Longfellow, too, responded to the same mood later when he wrote *Hyperion*. He read *Werther*: "the language and imagery are beautiful. In England and America the book is sneered at, I think it is not understood." *Werther* was a story of a youth "of fine intellect, and a heart overflowing with a love for the good and beautiful — full of the religion

of Nature — of violent passions — unrestrained by Christian principle."
He decided, however, that "such books are not favorites with me. The
impression they leave in the soul is one of unrest and pain." [17]

The ambivalence of the New Englanders towards Byron and Goethe
could hardly have been more aptly expressed than in Longfellow's comment. Ticknor's father had doubts about George's association with Byron.
You ought to be grateful for Byron's kindness, however corrupt his
character, Elisha said, but do not see him again, for it "will be of no
credit to you in this country." Elisha was right. Daniel Webster expressed
the proper Boston attitude toward Byron when he wrote Ticknor later,
after he had read Thomas Moore's *Byron,* that "Byron's case shows
that fact sometimes runs by all fancy, as a steamboat passes a scow at
anchor . . . He was an incarnation of *demonism.* He is the only man
in English history, for a hundred years, who has *boasted* of infidelity and
of every practical vice." Clearly a good Bostonian couldn't give way to
these romantic impulses. Satan — or ridicule — stalked the unwary.
George Bancroft failed to heed the common sense of home when
Andrews Norton wrote to him to avoid bizarre manners and dress.
When he arrived in Boston with a brightly colored waistcoat, yellow
gloves, and a beard, and kissed Andrews Norton on both cheeks, everyone knew that Europe had spoiled him. Not so Ticknor; he would have
no trouble re-chilling his blood to an appropriate New England tem-
perature.[18]

3. *The Fountainhead*

Ticknor had been delighted with London society, the stories of the
age of Johnson, the feuds of writers, and the exploits of Nelson and
Wellington. Still after a month he had felt he must continue his pilgrimage. After traveling through Holland with the Perkins and Nathaniel
Haven, Everett and Ticknor parted with them at Utrecht and went to
Göttingen. When Ticknor arived in the crowded medieval town in early
August 1815, he found lodgings on Weenderstrasse, a cobblestone street
lined with three- and four-story shops and apartments. The public walks
flanked by elms and buttonwood trees gave a prospect of hills in the
distance which reminded him of the mall in Boston with the sun sinking
behind the hills of Roxbury and Brookline.

In other respects his life was different from anything he had known before. After spending three months learning German with Professor Benecke, who taught English literature, he settled down to a grueling schedule of lectures and private study. Almost without interruption from five in the morning to ten at night he studied Greek, German, natural history, Biblical exegesis, fine arts, and literary history. "Learning is here as much a profession and occupation," he wrote, "as merchandise . . . while in America learning is generally an accomplishment and a show — a gala dress but not homely wear." At Göttingen he found the best marketplace of scholarship in the world: "what in all other languages is called a *lesson* is called in German 'an hour,' " he noted. The "hours" he bought from his instructors were productive beyond his most optimistic expectations. His Greek tutor, Dr. Schultze, who was almost his own age, astonished Ticknor by the range and accuracy of his learning. "Every day I feel anew," Ticknor lamented, "under the weight of his admirable acquirements, what a mortifying distance there is between a European and an American scholar! We do not yet know what a Greek scholar is; we do not even know the process by which a man is to be made one." [19]

Before coming to Göttingen Ticknor had written of the "pools of stagnant learning in Germany" and had wondered whether he would want to stay the five or six months he had allotted for study there. After seeing Göttingen first-hand his doubts evaporated; in fact, he became oppressed by the time already lost. He studied there almost two years. Viller and the others had not exaggerated. The erudition and industry of the German scholars, the library, laboratories, seminars and lectures of the university, all exceeded their reputation. Founded in 1735 by Baron Gerlach von Münchhausen and advanced by Heyne, Göttingen was in 1815, Ticknor thought, the foremost university in Germany. It had suffered less than the others from the "intellectual mildew" of the French Revolution and the depredations of the French occupation. Napoleon himself had "considered Göttingen as an University belonging neither to Hanover nor Germany but to Europe and the world." Other universities were plundered and attacked, but Göttingen was spared. As a result its faculty and facilities were intact. Although some schools had lost their students to armies, Göttingen kept a large enrollment of over 840 regular students.

Göttingen's library of two hundred thousand volumes, "the most important library for practical use in Germany, perhaps the world," was Ticknor's delight. Now in the long rows of stacks he could find books which he had formerly ordered at great expense from Europe, works he had known only by name, and volumes totally new to him. It was a bibliophile's paradise. Why the university *"consists* in the Library," Ticknor declared, while at Harvard "the Library is one of the last things thought and talked about . . . we are mortified because we have no learned men, and yet make it *physically* impossible for our scholars to become such." Göttingen's museums, scientific apparatus, and special collections supplemented this magnificent library.[20]

The forty-one professors and nearly forty private lecturers and instructors gave seventy or eighty courses of lectures each semester while engaged in research on every conceivable topic. Ticknor was especially impressed with Planck in church history, Blumenbach in natural history, Eichhorn in Biblical exegesis, Bouterwek in aesthetics and literary history, and Dissen in classics. With Dissen and others Ticknor pursued individual tutorials, which he, like Henry Adams, considered the most valuable part of a German education. Lectures only supplemented and directed this private study. In the lectures the professors gave comprehensive and philosophical views of the topics. There was no better way, Ticknor thought, to communicate the *"general* view of the *whole* subject" and clear "notions of the *relative importance* of the several parts." The philosophical seminar was a third effective means of instruction, a small class in which the students explicated difficult passages in Latin and Greek and criticized each others' dissertations. The method of approach was most important, Ticknor wrote Jefferson: "I am exceedingly anxious to have this spirit of pursuing all literary studies philosophically — of making scholarship as little of drudgery and mechanism as possible, transplanted to the U. States, in whose free and liberal soil I think it would, at once, find congenial nourishment."

To their friends Ticknor and Everett wrote enthusiastically about scholarship at Göttingen — so lyrically, in fact, that Elisha warned George not to be too extravagant lest people expect too much of them when they returned. George Bancroft came to Germany after graduating from Harvard in 1817 on their recommendation and with some financial assistance from President Kirkland of Harvard. Joseph Cogswell, who had drifted disconsolately from one job to another after deserting the law, learned about Göttingen while he was in Marseilles, and hastened to join his friends in November of 1816. The four men were not the first Americans to study at Göttingen, but they cleared a path to the German universities for later Americans to follow.[21]

Ticknor and his four friends recognized that the pattern of German education was not comparable to the structure of American schools. They saw that the universities could accomplish such scholarly feats only because they were constructed on the firm foundation of the gymnasia. During their vacations at Göttingen they investigated some of these schools that prepared students for the universities. At gymnasia like the Schul Pforta, the Thomas Schule, and the Meissen Schule, Ticknor found instruction more effective, libraries and other facilities more comprehensive, and graduates more learned than at the best American colleges. Usually entering these schools at twelve or thirteen, the students underwent for six or seven years the most rigorous and unremitting kind of preparation for graduate work. They began the day at four-thirty in summer and five-thirty in winter, and worked ten or twelve hours a day with alternate recitations and private study. Often chosen because of unusual intelligence and force of character, the students were a natural aristocracy.

At the Schul Pforta, for example, 132 out of 160 boys held full scholarships. Under such circumstances it was not surprising to find intense intellectual competition, with some boys arising at three in the morning to out-do classmates in an essay contest or to win a prize from the king for a Greek composition. Ticknor did not believe that this zeal undermined the boys' health or spirits, even though they normally had only two hours a day for play. They worked willingly and obeyed cheerfully. After such a regimen, when the students graduated at eighteen, nineteen, or twenty, they were able to read and write Latin with ease, were at home with the best Greek authors, and had a fine grounding in history, mathematics, physics, chemistry, music, French, English, and their own literature. Thus they were liberally educated and ready for advanced instruction in the universities.

Here was an institution which America might well emulate. Ticknor saw features of the gymnasium which he would "gladly see transferred" to other schools, among them a spirit of emulation, close and imaginative questioning by instructors rather than the parrot-like recitation common in the United States, short summer vacations and above all thoroughness of instruction. Learning was serious business to these students both in the gymnasia and in the universities, for these institutions were the main pathway to advancement in the professions and the government.[22]

In Germany more than any other country Ticknor visited he found that intellectuals formed a genuine republic of letters. "We have always been accustomed to hear and to talk of the republic of letters," Ticknor commented to his father, "as a state of things in which talent and learning make the only distinction; and the good-natured Goldsmith even went so far as to make a book about it, and describe it as accurately as a dealer in statistics and topography. But . . . the thing itself remained as unreal as Sidney's 'Arcadia.' " The system of patronage in England, the court in France, and the big and little tyrants of Italy, Spain, and Portugal, Ticknor believed, had "prevented everything like a liberal union of men of letters, and an unbiased freedom in the modes of thinking in all these countries." In Germany, however, the case was different. With little patronage, with no metropolis like Paris, with few tyrants, except under Napoleon, the German men of letters "have always been dependent for their bread and reputation on their own unassisted and unembarrassed talents and exertions." Separated from royal courts, and from active political and business life, German intellectuals came to form "an entirely separate class throughout all the German States, and have long ceased to be amenable to any influence but that of their own body. In this way a genuine republic of letters arose in the north of Germany." This society admitted "no man to its honours, who has not written a good book." These intellectuals — mostly university professors — were loyal to their guild, not to a particular country: "talk with a man of letters, and you will instantly perceive that when he speaks of his country he is really thinking of all that portion of Germany, and the neighboring teritories, through which Protestant learning and a philosophical mode of thinking are diffused." [23]

The German intellectuals readily welcomed Ticknor and his American friends into this republic of letters. When Bancroft arrived at Göttingen, he wrote to President Kirkland that the German professors respected Ticknor and Everett for their competence and zeal. The normally undemonstrative German scholars also displayed a great affection for the Americans. "The ladies seem to like Mr. Ticknor better," he said, but everyone praised Everett's ability too. The Greek scholar Dissen, whom Göttingen regarded as superior to Heyne, refused to accept pay from Ticknor for discussing literary history with him "saying that what he could do for me in this way he should not consider as instruction, but as an amusement." Ticknor visited him at his house twice a week in the evenings and rarely returned home before eleven.

Ticknor and Everett spent Saturday and Sunday evenings at their professors' homes, and became well acquainted with Eichhorn, Blumenbach, and the historian Heeren. When Blumenbach's wife and daughter went to the baths at Ems, the old naturalist dined with Ticknor and Everett. He took a boyish delight in teasing Ticknor about the barbaric ways of Americans, quoting travelers' accounts of Indian customs and inserting remarks indicating that the practices were common in Boston. Once Ticknor caught him off guard by noting that the book he was supposedly quoting from was published thirty years before the colonists came to New England; but Ticknor confessed that "if I have the best of the argument, he always has, and always will have, the best of the joke." Blumenbach thoroughly liked his young man from the wilds: "In the space of nearly 42 years during which I am Professor of our University," he wrote Ticknor's mother, "I made the nearer and lasting acquaintance of a great number of excellent young men, but there are very few which occupy so high a rank in my heart and who will live always so fresh in my memory as my dear friend G. Ticknor."

Ticknor and Everett became members of the only literary club in Göttingen, a group composed of professors and a few students chosen by the professors. "Like all literary clubs that ever survived the frosts of the first winter," George wrote his father, "its chief occupation is to eat suppers . . . We come from such an immense distance, that it is supposed we can hardly be civilized; and it is, I am told, a matter of astonishment to many that we are white, though I think in this point they might think me [Ticknor had a swarthy complexion] rather a fulfillment than a contradiction of their ignorant expectations. However, whatever may be the motives from which we were taken in, there we are, and we have as good a right to be there as the best of them." [24]

During the spring of 1816 Ticknor and Everett looked forward to a visit from Mr. and Mrs. Perkins. Everett had supervised their son who was attending a gymnasium. He resented Mr. Perkins' attempts to pay him for this favor, but realized that a merchant would have trouble thinking in other terms. He explained to his brother that he was really doing it for "the love I bear his mother." The incongruity of the merchant and his beautiful wife amid the unfashionable diligence of the university

amused the two men: "more of the domesticks (sense abstract) of Boston
are in a fair way of being talked over, in this learned city, than might
otherwise for many years have taken place." They wondered in what
language Mr. Perkins and stout old Eichhorn would converse — Eichhorn speaking no English and Perkins no German — and settled on
French. What should the two men discuss? "Mr. P. has not wandered
far into antiquity, nor Eichhorn ever sent a ship to the Northwest Coast;
but Mr. P. shipped much tobacco to Holland, and E. for forty years has
not ceased to smoke it, and as Ticknor and I shall set by, to pull the
bell, we shall take care that it sounds the right note."

When Mr. and Mrs. Perkins left Göttingen, homesickness and depression overwhelmed Ticknor. "I know that I now write in a moment
of unusual and even unnatural depression," Ticknor confided in his journal, "and I feel that the sensation of the loss I have suffered makes me
ungrateful for the happiness I have just enjoyed, but still I do not think
that I could ever desire to meet Mrs. Perkins again to be again separated
from her, Indeed — indeed — I never felt so entirely alone in the world
— so forsaken — as in the two days which have just passed, and I can
hardly imagine a form of happiness which I could wish to purchase at
so dear a price." Werther kept him melancholy company in his lonely
room on Weenderstrasse.[25]

The Yankees respected the intellectual accomplishments of the German scholars, but a note of nostalgia for home, of desire for the society
which Mrs. Perkins represented, of distaste for the poor manners and
corrupt opinions of German scholars, of condescension, even, runs
through the letters and journals of Ticknor and his friends during their
stay in Germany. Was the German republic of letters an adequate model
for American men of letters? Curious about the society which had produced this republic, Ticknor noted in his journal the social and political
differences between Germany and the United States. He conceded that
the German scholars had "a prodigious advantage over us . . . as far
as mere learning is concerned." But he pointed out that their freedom
was anomalous in a society whose "despotick . . . Governments by
their very form — and especially by their system of police . . . must
still press heavily upon this dense population and tend to keep every man
in the place where birth or accident has cast him." In America all citizens enjoyed opportunities not accessible to the average German because
of "the freedom of our government and the sparseness of our popula-

tion." In crowded Germany a man "cannot rise but at the expense of another." German peasants formed a class unknown in the United States. Gross and ignorant, they were losing their religious faith, their patriotism, and their links with an ancient social order. The merchants were less enterprising and liberal than American businessmen. In contrast to the adventurousness of American overseas merchants, they were parochial and niggardly in their internal trade. Ticknor believed that the nobility no longer served any useful function, having been shorn of power by the French occupation and corrupted by the manners and morals of the French court. He feared revolution, since the old traditional ties of reverence for the Church and for social station had given way to sentimentality, formality, and skepticism.

From the cradle to the grave the only time when Germans were free from relentless constraint was while they were in the universities. It was thus not surprising that both students and professors tended to abuse their freedom, Ticknor believed. The German intellectuals were not an integral part of their society — a displeasing fact to Ticknor, who wished to be a *gentleman* of letters and who would not have accepted the definition of a professor as "a man who thinks *otherwise.*" The German men of letters suffered from their social isolation and abused their anomalous freedom.[26] Eminent in scholarship, they were in other respects distasteful to the Yankees.

To Ticknor and his fellow New Englanders, reared in communities of precise moral standards and social propriety, the German professors and students often seemed boorish and immoral. After calling Christian Wolf perhaps the greatest philologist who ever lived, Ticknor added that "the more I admire his character as a scholar the more I dislike it as a man. In his youth he was addicted to the most vulgar debauchery — at Halle he was in the scandalous coterie of Bahrdt . . . and now in his old age stories are told of him which almost shake faith in human virtue." Ticknor was shocked to find that almost all the intellectuals he met swore abominably, even professors of divinity and the ladies "in whom such an intimation is horrible"; and Blumenbach, who lived for a while in England and was "more tinctured with English manners than anybody I have met" — even Blumenbach cursed. German scholars commonly violated the Sabbath by holding parties and compounded their sin by being "very dull." Few knew the art of conversation. Friedrich von Schlegel, the "short, thick little gentleman with the ruddy, vulgar health of a full-fed father of the Church" was one of only two intellectuals whose talk reminded Ticknor "of the genuine, hearty flow of English conversation." Scholars were often arrogant and rude; Cogswell noticed that he rarely found a professor who was "attentive and affectionate to his wife." One German intellectual, reacting to the priggishness and condescension of the Yankees, said, "They annoy me most when they seek to dignify their dry capacity for understanding by a dismayed Puritanism and turn themselves . . . against the so-called immorality with an arrogance which completely irritates me, as the most free, most pious, most righteous and most moral people on God's earth." [27]

As merchants of learning, eagerly competing for academic posts and struggling to live, German men of letters well knew the value of time and meted it out to students as carefully as a goldsmith his gold on the scales. Their routinely industrious life seemed quite as limited in its own way as the drudgery of the peasant stock from which some of them came. "In one word," scoffed Bancroft, "they learn Hebrew, because it is better to teach Hebrew than till the earth." Ticknor's friend and fellow Brahmin George Hillard later commented about the literary historian Friedrich Bouterwek that he "was one of those laborious and conscientious German scholars who begin to write books before they are out of their teens, who labor in their literary vocation with the patient industry of a mechanic toiling at his daily trade, and die at last with a proof-sheet in their hands." Diligence was a good thing, surely; but this was carrying a good thing too far. "Today closes my second semester in Göttingen," Ticknor wrote in the fall of 1816, "and I am grateful to Heaven that another period of imprisonment has passed, for five so miserable months as the last have never before darkened my days." Later generations of Harvard men would associate this jingle with the august name of Göttingen:

> Where 'er with haggard eyes I view
> This dungeon that I'm rotting in,
> I think of those companions true
> Who studied with me at the U-
>   niversity of Göttingen
>   niversity of Göttingen.[28]

The German students, even more than the professors, alienated the Yankees by their barbaric manners and vulgar tastes. Bancroft contended that in a society where the "distinctions of rank are kept up," few German scholars could rise socially above their origins; but in America "the son of an honest countryman is perhaps the most likely to think freely and sublimely." The German students "dress, *all of them,* as no civilized man ought to dress," Bancroft wrote to Andrews Norton. Their shirts were black with dirt; their leather pants were stained with tobacco juice and beer; they spat on the floor and had foul table manners; and they were grossly immoral and impious.

Ticknor and his colleagues were ambivalent also about the value of German academic freedom. Ticknor found at Göttingen "an extreme freedom, and as I should call it, latitudinarianism, in thinking, speaking, writing, and teaching on all subjects, even law, religion, and politics, with the single exception of the actual measures of the government." (This exception was hardly a minor one.) The Yankees thought that some of the effects of German academic freedom were odious: skepticism in religion and irresponsibility in morals and politics.[29]

Ticknor complained as bitterly as the more theologically minded Everett and Bancroft about the flippant attitude of Eichhorn, who explained miracles as the delusions of witnesses or as natural events. He called the death and resurrection of Christ mere suspended animation. "His faith in Christ is, as far as I can understand it," Ticknor complained, "precisely like his faith in Socrates," except that Eichhorn believed that Xenophon and Plato were more trustworthy witnesses than Galilean fishermen. As a Unitarian Ticknor felt that he should "have no objection to a serious and thorough examination of the grounds of Christianity," but he lamented Eichhorn's skeptical treatment of "all that I have been taught to consider solemn and important." Everett, too, was embarrassed that he should feel so squeamish about examining his faith, but he wrote Bancroft that "I have very little superstition, and I hope still less illiberality, but I did not think the attendance of lectures in this strain likely to be favorable on my mind and heart." Who could tell where all this skepticism would lead? Ticknor was convinced that Professor Wegscheider's false theological views produced the prostitution prevalent at Halle. Perhaps it was a good thing that public opinion exercised such a firm check on professors in America.[30]

The German republic of letters made the Yankees uneasy. "A man as a scholar must be completely *upset,* to use a blacksmith's phrase," wrote Cogswell; "he must have learnt to give up his love of society and of social pleasures, his interest in the common occurrences of life, in the political and religious contentions of the country, and in everything not directly connected with his single aim. Is there any one willing to make such a sacrifice?" The Yankees conceded that the devotion of the German scholars had worked wonders, but they didn't want to be *"upset"* any more than Longfellow wished to undergo the *"unrest and pain"* which Goethe aroused.

Ticknor firmly believed that a nation's educational system should be an organic part of its culture. Because of the significant differences he saw between the United States and Germany, he would never propose wholesale imitation of German education. He would be selective and eclectic in approach. Was not Harvard — Federalist, Unitarian, proper — better adapted to the political, religious, and social character of New England than a carbon copy of Göttingen?

The response of Ticknor and his friends to the German universities was more critical than that of many Americans who went to Germany after the Civil War. Devout and self-consciously gentlemanly, the former had a stout if provincial frame of moral and social reference in terms of which the Germans were conspicuously deficient. They were as excellent classicists as America could produce at that time, fluent linguists, and self-confident and brilliant young men. Ticknor spoke for all four when he said of his and Everett's admission to the elite literary club that "we have as good a right to be there as the best of them." [31]

In November of 1816 Ticknor received news from Cambridge which altered not only his European journey but his scholarly career as well. A letter from President Kirkland offered him two overlapping and concurrent professorships, one in belles lettres and the other the newly endowed Smith Professorship of Modern Languages. News of Ticknor's success at Göttingen had reached Kirkland and the Harvard Corporation, and they wished to reap the advantage of his education. Ultimately all four of the Americans at Göttingen would teach at Harvard. The professorships appealed to Ticknor since they would settle the difficult question about his role in society on his return. But since he had only sketchily studied French and Spanish literature at Götttingen, and then only as an avocation, Kirkland's offer would require a change of plans.

Characteristically, Ticknor consulted his father about the professorships and left the decision in his hands. He pointed out that the salary of one thousand dollars with a maximum of five hundred dollars in additional fees was too little to support a family and that thus he could accept only if Elisha were "able and willing to make up income to the amount necessary" to support a wife and children. He hastened to add that "I assure you my hopes are not fixed on any particular person, yet I know very well that in any country, and most of all in America, marriage is a sine qua non to happiness." If he accepted, he would need to spend another six months in Europe at his father's expense to study Spanish literature, about which he knew next to nothing. With his letter to his father Ticknor enclosed two letters to Kirkland, one affirmative and one negative. "For myself," he wrote, "I say freely, that the occupation would be pleasant to me, and I doubt not, in this office, I could, better than in any other, fulfil my duties to God and my neighbor; but still, if you be not satisfied, I do not desire it." Elisha knew his son well and consented, suggesting that he had long hoped that George would teach at Harvard: "I read carefully your letter to me . . . and made up my mind . . . that a seat at the University is much more congenial to your taste, genius, and habits . . . than to be employed on the boisterous ocean of law and politics." Elisha had not enjoyed his own attempt in the grocery business to surmount "the boisterous surges of a selfish world," and took great pride in his son's apostolic task. "Whatever time you spend," he wrote, "let it be for useful purposes, — let them be like seed sown in a rich soil, from which we may expect some thirty, some sixty, and some an hundred fold." [32]

4. *A Vast Bright Babylon*

Ticknor's next goal on his European journey was Paris, a "vast bright Babylon" for him as for Henry James's Lambert Strether. A faithful son of New England, Ticknor had already acquired a healthy scorn for the city, but he believed that his professorship required him to study there. Here again, Joseph Buckminster had gone ahead to point the way: "A man leaving N. England with that degree of moral sensibility, which our education generally produces, will continually be shocked upon his arrival in Paris. If he stays long, conscience will lose some of his power and his moral perception will be blunted . . . in no part of the world are all the contrivances of sensuality so concentrated as in Paris."

It was then probably with a sense of relief that Ticknor recorded in his journal on April 3, 1817, that "I entered the city, with little excitement of spirits and alighted at my lodgings near the Boulevards as composedly as I should have done in a German village." Ticknor observed that "Americans, coming from the rigid purity of a religious people, against which no one can offend without receiving an exemplary punishment from publick opinion, and finding themselves here freed from all such restraints, plunge into gross and vulgar excesses which surprise even the hardened libertinism of Europe." He was determined that this wouldn't happen to him.

Bancroft, a more malleable — Boston would say a more easily corrupted — young man, felt differently. After he had spent three months in Paris — a time "all too short" for him — he wrote President Kirkland that the visit "served to cure me of many ungrounded prejudices and false views of French character, which I had brought with me from America. How easy it is to call a nation fickle or corrupt: of fierce, determined vice England will show a stranger more in a night than France in a month." Bancroft was delighted to find that the Parisian literati were impressed with his friend Ticknor. Since they were more worldly and sophisticated than the German scholars, their judgment was more perceptive.[33]

The warmth of Ticknor's welcome underlined the irony of his experience in Paris. Armed with letters of introduction from Jefferson and others, Ticknor instantly entered a dazzling literary society composed of Madame de Staël, François de Chateaubriand, August W. von Schlegel, Alexander von Humboldt, Madame Récamier, Benjamin Constant, and Robert Southey. Ticknor captivated them all; Madame de Staël, slowly dying, insisted on seeing him against doctor's orders. But Ticknor refused to be seduced by Paris and wrote five months later that he had never "left a city of any importance with so little regret."

Ticknor tried to preserve in Paris the habits of study he had acquired at Göttingen. From six in the morning until five in the afternoon he studied French language and literature and Italian. In each country he visited he employed an "oratorical reader . . . whose voice is round, and full, and melodious" to tutor him in the language. He succeeded so well in learning foreign languages in this manner that he became fluent in German, French, Italian, and Spanish; he was also able to speak and write Latin with ease. His visits to literary salons perfected his diction but his intellect never became so well adjusted to France as his tongue.

In the evenings Ticknor often attended the theater, then in full swing. He dismissed French tragedy as mere "theatre of proprieties and conventions," but he was enchanted with French comedy. He believed that the excellence of the comic theater in France was almost inevitable. The ordinary "forms of society and the tone of their conversation" were dramatic, and the foppish actors and coquettish actresses were "playing the same parts all day in common life that they represent to the public in the evening." Besides, the French "national character furnishes more material for" comedy than any other. "I do not regret that we have none of this comedy in English," Ticknor wrote a friend from Paris, "for I deprecate the character and principles out of which it grows, and should lose no inconsiderable proportion of my hope for England and America, if they had reached or were approaching that ominous state of civilization and refinement in which it is produced." In a contest incongruous for a man who was to become a professor of French literature, Ticknor vied with two Frenchwomen to prove that Shakespeare and Milton alone were superior to all French writers combined. As the women piled the table high with the works of Racine, Voltaire, and Corneille, Ticknor countered all "passages of the *first* order of poetry" with a little volume of *Paradise Lost* which he pulled from his pocket. This left in reserve all of Shakespeare.[34]

Like French comedy, French education was deigned to amuse, Ticknor thought, but not to instruct. After hearing the famous historian Charles Lacretelle give a lecture, Ticknor wrote in his journal that he had liked his fluency and his dignity — which contrasted sharply with other professors who sacrificed everything for wit and epigrammatic effect — but he concluded that even Lacretelle was too artificial, "still, to a certain degree, a Frenchman talking brilliantly." Ticknor later commented, "I have long awakened from the dream in which I supposed I could find instruction in the branches I pursue, in the German way, from French lectures." He went to hear A. F. Villemain of the Academy of Paris Faculty of Letters lecture to three hundred and fifty students on Rousseau's *Emile* and decided that his remarks were "a kind of amusement which ought to come rather under the great and indefinite class of what is called in France *Spectacle,* than what in any country should be considered a part of public instruction."

The Parisian salon was just such a *spectacle* of epigram and wit. Although Ticknor called the ladies of Paris "ostentatiously gracious," he was charmed by Madame de Staël's declamatory death-bed manner and her daughter's calculated naiveté. Madame de Staël had sported several lovers in the past — though in her youth Gouverneur Morris thought she had "very much the appearance of a chambermaid." Now she was a decorous prophet whose face lit up when she spoke in aphorisms of America. "Especially when she said of America," Ticknor recalled, " 'vous êtes l'avant garde du genre humain — vous êtes l'avenir du monde,' there came a slight tinge of feeling into her face, which spoke plainly enough of the pride of genius." Ticknor enjoyed Benjamin Constant's conversation and the soirees at his house where "the wit — the criticism — even the good nature and kindness had a cast of nationality about them and took that form which in France is called amiability; but which every where else would be called flattery." [35] All Paris matched Ticknor's Yankee preconceptions.

It was no accident that the man in Paris who made the most lasting impression on Ticknor was a German, Alexander von Humboldt. One morning after Ticknor had visited Constant's salon he wrote in his journal about the amusement of the night before, but he added that "the interest and excitement you feel in French society is necessarily transient and this morning . . . my strongest recollections are of Humboldt's genius and modesty — and his magical descriptions of the tropical scenery of the Orinoco, and the holy solitudes of Nature, and the Missionaries." This extraordinary scholar, whose vigor of mind and body astonished Ticknor, made night and day into "one mass of time which he uses for sleeping, for meals, for labor, without making any arbitrary division of it." Equally at home on the slopes of Chimborazo, in the study, or in the salon, Humboldt rendered the scholars and literati of Paris puny and artificial by comparison. One day Humboldt met Ticknor and a fellow Bostonian in the street and offered them both tickets to a scholarly meeting. After Humboldt left, Ticknor's companion turned to him and asked, "Now, is there a Frenchman in all Paris who would have done that?" Ticknor was also impressed by another German, August von Schlegel, though after a troubled life, in which Schelling seduced his wife and Schlegel followed Madame de Staël on her travels to Germany, Sweden, Italy, and England, he looked like "a careworn, wearied courtier, with the manners of a Frenchman of the gayest circles, and the habits of a German scholar, — a confusion which is anything but natural and graceful."

More disconcerting to Ticknor than the gay insincerity of Parisian society was the political extremism of the ideological roués who had experienced the *ancien régime,* the Revolution, and the military despotism of Bonaparte. They seemed drunk with the heady wine of excessive hope or unrelieved despair. Madame de Staël and her circle welcomed the South American revolutions as a new dawn for humanity, but Chateaubriand's view of the future seemed as dark as his black hair and eyes. While everyone laughed at witty remarks in the salon of the Duchesse de Broglie, Chateaubriand sat glumly at the funeral of Western civilization. When the talk turned to the fate of Europe, he said to Ticknor in somber and exalted tones, "which made me almost think better of the language itself than I am accustomed to," that "for fifty years I foresee nothing but military despotisms — and in an hundred, — in an *hundred!* The cloud is too dark for human vision; too dark, it may almost be said, to be penetrated by prophecy . . . *perhaps* we live, not only in the decrepitude of Europe, but in the decrepitude of the world." [36]

Ticknor could accept neither their unrelieved gloom nor their utopian hopes. What could a Federalist expect in Paris? Ticknor's visit only confirmed him in his belief that France was the home of glittering but empty high society and a bloodthirsty proletariat. One day, when he was examining the dank vaults beneath St. Geneviève, Ticknor asked where was the tomb of Marat. His old guide replied excitedly, "I was one of those, Sir, who on the 28. July 1793 tore his [Marat's] body from its monument in that cell and cast it on the Ditch of Montmartre." Everywhere one saw "such effects of the French Revolution on individual character," Ticknor wrote, "and it is thus that such convulsions root out of human nature what is best worth preserving in it, by converting even the enthusiasm of principle into guilt and cruelty." It was clear that the French were doomed. Madame de Staël's daughter chided him for his pessimism about her country: "you are wrong to despise the efforts a nation makes to be free. All God's creatures are formed for a noble destiny, and you have no right to regard us as inferior beings." What could be more discouraging for a French liberal than to talk with Ticknor! [37]

The people of Boston had sung a *Te Deum* for Napoleon's defeat and had given a public illumination upon the restoration of the Bourbons. Ticknor, for his part, wrote in 1817 that "an impartial man would respect the present government and the Bourbon family." Yet early one June morning four policemen appeared at Ticknor's lodgings with a royal order to conduct a "severe search" for "all papers, libels or libellous writings, and books dangerous to the government." With customary aplomb, Ticknor opened desk and drawers, protested in a decorous way, and sat back while they examined his journals and correspondence for almost five hours. One of the men asked Ticknor why he kept his curtains drawn, implying that Ticknor wished to keep nefarious activities from the public gaze. The inspectors were suspicious about a Greek manuscript until they spotted the Bourbon coat of arms which identified it as borrowed from the royal library. Finally, after rifling through all of Ticknor's papers, they left, one of the men charitably assuring Ticknor that he was "not a dangerous person!" Ticknor wrote scornfully in his journal that night that to "one less sure of himself, this [search and accusation] would be an unpleasant though not an alarming circumstance — but to me it is simply ridiculous."

Ridiculous it certainly was. This was the first and last time that anyone would accuse George Ticknor of being a radical. Ticknor complained to Albert Gallatin, then American minister to France. Almost a month later Gallatin appeared at Ticknor's rooms early in the morning, embarrassed and hesitant. He handed Ticknor a paper, saying "That is the letter, sir, I wrote to the Duke de Richelieu on your case." The letter told the story of the inspection in a manner "more high-toned . . . than I supposed a man as cool and calculating as Mr. Gallatin would have made." Then he showed Ticknor the Duke's reply which claimed that no such search had been authorized and that the police would gladly arrest the impostors. Ticknor was certain that the inspectors had been policemen and that their royal orders had been genuine; thus it became his word against the Duke's. Ticknor hunted down one of the policemen, who admitted to Gallatin that he had searched Ticknor's papers, unaware that his orders had been disavowed by the Duke. There the case rested, except that Ticknor learned from Alexander von Humboldt that the person who had probably brought charges against him was an Englishman who made his living as a spy for the French government. Ticknor had argued with the ill-tempered informer, who apparently chose this novel means of retaliation.[38]

All in all, the search was a bizarre affair that confirmed Ticknor's prejudices against France. Paris appeared a Circe turning men into swine. Industrious Germans lounged away their time in cafés. Punctilious Englishmen violated social forms. Pure Americans forgot "at Paris the

manners of their homes and the principles and virtues of their youth."
The Palais Royal, with its bookstores, theater, and corporation of prostitution, was designed, Ticknor said, to satisfy all "within the compass of
human desires, whether innocent or guilty," and was "a kind of epitome
and concentration of Paris, of the French character and of the French
nation — a place where all without is dazzling, gay and gracious — and
all within crime and corruption." [39]

5. *Italiam! Italiam!*

Ticknor left Paris with little regret. He would never, he supposed, see
it again. On his way to Geneva he visited General Lafayette at his venerable castle at La Grange. The sixty-year-old general looked as vigorous
as a man of forty-five, and won Ticknor's respect and affection by his
"enthusiasm of character, his unalterable honesty, and his open simplicity." Later Ticknor would write an adulatory short biography of this one
French leader for whom he felt unmixed admiration.

The Calvinist city, Geneva, was "much more to my taste," Ticknor
wrote his father, "than the gayer and more witty circles of Paris, of
which I had a complete surfeit." Not only was it an abrupt change of
moral climate, but it fascinated Ticknor to find that almost all the men
of letters he met were also important government officials. The three
most important professors of the University were members of the Council of State; the chief magistrate of the state was a distinguished scientist.
"This is really not an unfair specimen of the state of letters in Geneva,"
Ticknor observed, "where they certainly form the first caste in society,
and where no man can hope to distinguish himself in private intercourse,
or even in the state, without being to a certain degree a literary or a
scientific man." Here was a model for Boston.[40]

From Geneva Ticknor followed the route of the Simplon to the summit
of the St. Bernard Pass, a magnificent road clinging to precipitous cliffs
through mountainous scenery reminiscent of Dante's Inferno. At the
peak of the road lay a stone marking the Italian boundary. As Ticknor
stepped on classic soil, he "could not choose but cry out with the son
of Aeneas — Italiam! Italiam! — for I seemed at once to have reached
another of the great limits and objects of my pilgrimage." And when he
saw for the first time in Europe some Indian corn growing in an Alpine

valley, he felt that he had returned to familiar ground at last. Across the rich plains of Lombardy he journeyed during the frolic season of the vintage. He passed through Milan, Verona, Venice and Bologna on his way to Rome, using as guidebooks his worn copies of Pliny, Livy, Horace, and Virgil.[41]

"On alighting at the Hotel de Paris, and finding myself, with a feeling, I can never forget or describe, *in Rome,* I set out," Ticknor wrote in his journal, "immediately, without guide or plan, determined to yield myself up to . . . accident, and see how much I should be able to recognize and discover from my recollections of history." As he passed the Column of Antoninus he pictured where Cicero and Cassiodorus might have stood; he visited the Bridge of St. Angelo, with the moon reflected below in the Tiber; in the "magical and indefinite light of the moon" the dome of St. Peter seemed suspended from the heavens and its pillars were "bewitchingly beautiful . . . broken and checkered with bold masses of light"; the darkened mass of the Coliseum, with shafts of moonlight piercing the ruins, and the broken columns of the Forum, in the still of a Roman night evoked "the fabulous age of Evander, Hercules, and Aeneas." Did the Coliseum in moonlight produce a romantic emotion that New Englanders like Ticknor and Hawthorne could safely feel? Or was it true, as Henry Adams claimed, that "Rome before 1870 was seductive beyond resistance" even though an "American parent, curiously enough while bitterly hostile to Paris, seemed rather disposed to accept Rome as legitimate education"? Ticknor, at least, believed that he could let his imagination run free in Rome. In his delight at finding his surroundings familiar he was reminded of Cicero's remark "that none but a Barbarian can be a *stranger* in Rome." To experience Rome was to justify the classical education of a gentleman; "if I were condemned to live in Europe," he wrote his father, "I am sure this is the place I should choose for my exile." "Rome is worth all the other cities in the world." [42]

Yet Rome could arouse anxious thoughts, for it was, like Venice, a fallen republic. Not the first American or the last to contemplate with Gibbon the decline and fall of this great nation, Ticknor was reminded of the prophecy Scipio uttered at the peak of Roman grandeur that the republic would fall. Even Nature had conspired to lay Rome low. The beautiful Campagna, the surrounding countryside, was releasing "poisonous exhalations" from its soil, the "Mal'aria," which was making parts of Rome and its environs uninhabitable, he believed. As he traveled through the Campagna he noticed that the sky was so transparently blue, the sun so clear and bright, the wind so soft, the vegetation so green and thick "that it seems as if nature were wooing men to cultivation . . . But when you recollect that this serene sky and brilliant sun . . . serve only to develop the noxious qualities of the soil . . . that this air is as fatal as it is balmy — when your eye wanders over . . . this strange solitude and meets only an occasional ruin . . . a gibbet still bearing the blackened remains of some poor wretch, whom this very desolation has tempted to some guilt . . . it is *then* you feel all the horror of the situation." If this be the course of empire, when even Nature turns against man and empties his cities, what must be the lesson for an American? [43] Ticknor would never adopt the view that nature, by itself, is redemptive.

One sure lesson Rome did teach: its glory survived its ruin. Unlike Carthage, a mercantile city which left no trace of itself in letters and arts, Rome still lived through the remains of its culture. Ticknor found that people of all nationalities came to Rome as he did to cultivate the past. These national coteries were rarely composed of "the empty and idle travellers who lounge through Europe to lose time . . . since Rome is not a common city, where vulgarity and dissipation can be contented as they are in Vienna or Paris, but one whose attractions it requires at least a moderate share of knowledge to understand." Since he believed the Romans themselves "worn out and degraded," he preferred the society of Germans and Englishmen, who maintained their national mores as they had failed to do in Paris. Only the French showed their shallowness by being unimproved by Rome: "Simond himself, though I think him in general a cool, impartial man, stands up a mere Frenchman as soon as you get him on the subject of antiquities, of which he seems to have as just notions as divines have of the world before the flood."

This was an important fault, for mistakes in taste were only slightly less serious to Ticknor than lapses in manners. Yet proper taste was not easy for a literal-minded American to acquire amid the perplexities of European art. Most music bored Ticknor. For judging painting and architecture he sought expert advice and formulae of criticism. He had few artistic instincts and at best was a sort of aesthetic stockbroker, a middleman and patron. At first his responses were somewhat primitive, though unquestionably precise. While in the gallery at Dresden he had copied down the exact measurements and values of many of the pictures he saw. He was especially impressed with a Correggio which was "only 15¾ inches by 13½, but which in the sale of the Modenese Gallery was estimated at 13,000 ducats." In time, however, he developed more sensitive criteria of artistic merit. At Rome he studied ancient statuary and ruins with a learned archaeologist. It was an excellent place for Ticknor to exercise his "unpracticed eye" and for any American artist to acquire a "classical tone." It was safer to make plaster casts of ancient statuary than to venture onto the uncertain terrain of modern art.[44]

At Göttingen Ticknor had translated Johann Winckelmann's "Thoughts upon the Imitation of the Works of the Greeks in Painting and Statuary," a work which rationalized some of his own prejudices. He quoted Winkelmann's dictum that the "only way in which we can become great . . . is by imitating the ancients . . . the Laocoön is . . . a perfect model of art." In ancient art the modern could discover "not only all that is beautiful in nature, but something beyond — that is — certain ideal beauties." This was Ticknor's key to judging art: it must idealize. He scoffed at the Dutch realists: "Their imitation of nature is too servile, and their subjects too common and vulgar. They present us no ideal beauty. They represent every thing with Chinese accuracy exactly as it is instead of relating it with Grecian fancy and talent to what it might be." Ticknor dismissed a Bacchus by Michelangelo by saying that it looked "too much like a merely drunken man." [45]

Ticknor believed that the fine arts were everywhere in decline in his age — a conventional aesthetic view at the time — but he saw no reason why Americans could not imitate the ancients as successfully as Europeans did. He later helped to raise money to patronize two American artists whom he especially admired, the painter Washington Allston and the sculptor Horatio Greenough. Allston, he believed, had learned the techniques of coloring and the axiom of idealization from the painters of the Renaissance, who in turn owed a debt to the ancients. And Greenough, he thought, profited from his acquaintance with Roman and Greek statuary. Ticknor would later help Greenough to study in Italy and to win a commission from Congress for a statue of George Washington.

Ticknor thought that Washington, of all people, was an apt subject for idealization, and was pleased with the model of the statue which

Greenough showed him in his studio in Florence: "It is plainly intended to represent Washington as an ideal; — to express as distinctly as possible his moral dignity and elevation — as one who relied on a power that came from above rather than upon the physical power of the sword. Whether this will be fully understood by the people of the United States, or whether a statue so little covered will not be complained of as a nudity, are different questions." Ticknor's fears were justified: when the statue was unveiled, the people of Washington took one look at the Olympian figure of Washington, with one hand raised, with bare torso and a cloth draped over the lower half of his body, and pronounced it a scandal.[46]

The doctrine of idealization was, perhaps, easier for Americans to accept in literature than in sculpture. Ticknor transplanted into literary history some of the criteria which guided his judgment in the arts. A nostalgia for older, more natural times, a praise of idealization, even the same diction — "noble," "elevated," and "pure" — colored his writing about literature as well as his reaction to art.

6. *The Riddle of Spain*

After Rome the next great stage of Ticknor's pilgrimage was Spain. There Ticknor planned to prepare himself to lecture on Spanish literature. The visit would have a far greater influence on his later life than he could have anticipated: it posed the riddle of Spain. Spain attracted and repelled him. In July of 1818 he wrote to a friend that "Spain and the Spanish people amuse me more than anything I have met in Europe. There is more originality and poetry in the popular manners and feelings, more force without barbarism, and civilization without corruption, than I have found elsewhere." Yet in December of the same year he wrote to his father that Spain is "a country dead in everything a nation ought to be . . . where all is stagnant and lifeless." Spain contradicted the present abruptly yet enticingly. "Would you believe it?" Ticknor asked a friend, "what seems mere fiction and romance in other countries is matter of observation here, and, in all that relates to manners, Cervantes and Le Sage are historians. For, when you have crossed the Pyrenees, you have not only passed from one country and climate to another, but you have gone back a couple of centuries in your chronology, and find the people still in that kind of poetical existence which we have not only long since lost, but which we have long ceased to credit on the reports of our ancestors." [47]

On May 10, 1818, Ticknor left Barcelona with three Spanish companions and spent thirteen days traveling the four hundred miles to Madrid. Never before, not even in Virginia, had a trip been so arduous. The roads through the desolate country were so miserable that their cart could make no more than twenty-two miles a day, though they struggled from four in the morning to seven at night. In the hovels where they spent the night, there was little food, and their rooms, usually over the stable, were "as full of fleas as if . . . under an Egyptian curse." They slept on stone floors which were "not so even or so comfortable as our sidewalks." Yet Ticknor said that it was the gayest journey of his life. His fellow travelers were courteous, hearty, and dignified, and while they jounced along in the cart Ticknor read *Don Quixote* aloud to them. "All of them used to beg me to read it to them every time we got into the cart," Ticknor wrote, and they roared with laughter and wept as he told of Sancho Panza and Quixote. It was a revelation "to witness the effect this extraordinary book produces on the people from whose very blood and character it is drawn." [48]

The poetic life of the common people in Madrid delighted Ticknor. As he walked in the evening he often saw them dancing the *bolero,* the *fandango,* and the *manchegas* in the streets or by the canal to the music of pipes and castanets. He listened to lovers playing the guitar and singing passionate *seguidillas.* He reveled in the bright colors and motion of the Prado, the beautiful public walk in Madrid ornamented with fountains and trees and statues. The splendidly dressed officers of the guard, the solemn monks in black cassocks, the dashing carriages of the king and the infantas, made "the most striking moving panorama the world can afford." After sunset the bell announcing evening prayers stopped the whole procession, and a hushed spell came over the darkened Prado while the multitude prayed.

Ticknor met all the intellectuals of consequence and became familiar with the members of the diplomatic delegations, who were far more interesting to him than most of the Spanish nobility. His closest friends in Spain were the French ambassador, the Duke de Laval, a brilliant and warm-hearted man of fifty, and Caesare de Balbo, the son of the Sardinian ambasador, an ardent young man of Ticknor's age who poured over Dante and Machiavelli with the dream of uniting Italy. Almost every day the three men rode together, and argued furiously with the confidence of the best of friends, Laval "as prompt, excitable, and enthusiastic as a young man of twenty," and Balbo "the model of all that is bold, vehement, and obstinate." [49]

Joseph Antonio Conde came to read Spanish poetry for two or three hours daily with Ticknor. Conde was one of the best scholars in Spain, formely librarian to the king and the head of public instruction. A simple and retiring man, awkward and open in manners, he occupied himself with the era of the Spanish Arabs, a safer period than the present time of turmoil when many of the Spanish intellectuals had been exiled or subjected to the Inquisition. Conde was the one man in Spain best suited to give Ticknor not only a knowledge of the Spanish classics but also the sort of bibliographical sophistication he sought. It was a decadent time for Spanish scholarship. Universities were in deplorable condition, intellectuals were harassed, libraries were in disarray. Ticknor found the Escorial and the other libraries disorderly, but a gold mine for systematic scholars who would bother to dig in their rich veins. Ticknor looked into a room of one large library where the "useless" books were stored; the first book he picked up was Laplace's *Méchanique Celeste*. Spanish literature offered to the diligent scholar the career of a lifetime; Ticknor was to make it his own.

Ticknor wanted to see all sides of Spanish life. One of the most distasteful to him was the bullfight. He was fascinated with the ancient traditions and ritual of this spectacle, which he traced back to the oldest Spanish chronicles, but he was sickened by the sight of slaughter and had to be carried unconscious out of the stadium by a guard. Astonished to find how passionately the Spaniards loved the bullfights, he learned that they would sell everything they owned to pay admission — one man even married the evening before a fight so that his new wife would give him a ticket. One reason for their zeal, Ticknor believed, was that the crowd felt their own power when massed in the stadium and enjoyed a sensation of freedom normally denied them. It resembled the ancient Roman bacchanalia. At the bullfights, men uttered what under other circumstances would have been revolutionary, or at least dangerous, comments: they would say that a particularly brave bull was "fit to be the president of the Cortes," and that another mild-mannered bull "was as cowardly as a king." [50]

Elsewhere Ticknor had rather enjoyed the ceremony of courts and the company of kings and nobles, but in Spain he despised the Court and the Church. Ferdinand VII he dismissed as "a vulgar blackguard. The obscenity — the low, brutal obscenity of his conversation and the rudeness of his manners are matters of perfect notoriety." Once Ticknor attended the theater when the court was there with all its pomp and circumstance. Whenever in the play "there occurred any indecent allusion, which was not infrequently, the whole pit, and indeed the rest of the house, turned directly to look at the King, so sure was every individual that these were the passages most to his taste. Nor were they disappointed, for every time he was in a broad laugh, although the Queen and the Infantas had the decency to look grave." [51]

The government was a unique "confusion of abuses." In theory the king's decrees were absolute, but in practice they were constantly flouted. Ticknor heard of one man in Barcelona who had protested an action of the government and had requested a hearing of his case. The king decreed a hearing but the tribunal refused; "he made a new decree, and so on to a third and fourth, each more peremptory than the preceding, and each one followed by similar gross disobedience, until at last the tribunal, wearied out with being thus teased, quashed the process they were ordered to examine, and told the injured individual to go about his business." The surest way to bring about a revolution would have been for the king to enforce his decrees, for government officials and the people found their freedom in the interstices of inefficiency and corruption which riddled the society. So pervasive was corruption that the Minister of Finance simply legalized bribery by calling it taxation and thus diverted the funds from venal officials to the treasury. A uniform set of fees — seven hundred and fifty dollars for bringing a case before the highest tribunal, five hundred ducats for the illegal practice of being a *corregidor* over two villages instead of one — systematized the worst corruption Ticknor found in Europe. "The very first principles of the social compact, all the political morality that keeps society together, seem to be put at auction by it, and in any other country a revolution would follow; but here this *may* be avoided by a tolerated disobedience."

Capping this grotesque social arch was the Inquisition. Ticknor thought it mostly a "bugbear" in Madrid — though occasionally persons did disappear rather mysteriously — but found it powerful in the south.

There he saw a decree "condemning anew the heresy of Martin Luther, and, as it was imagined to be making some progress there, calling on servants to denounce their masters, children their parents, wives their husbands, etc." Perhaps Ticknor recalled his conversation in Rome with the Pope, who had praised American religious toleration and said that "he thanked God continually for having at last driven all thoughts of persecution from the world, since persuasion was the only possible means of promoting piety, though violence might promote hypocrisy." [52]

Ticknor termed the middle class "oppressed and ignorant," the nobility "deplorable" and their way of life "monotonous, gross, and disgraceful"; yet the common people Ticknor thought "the finest *materiel* I have met in Europe to make a great and generous people." How could it be, asked Ticknor, that the people "are not so bad, as might reasonably be anticipated from all the means that seem to be studiously taken to corrupt them"? One answer, Ticknor believed, was that corruption and oppression infested chiefly the higher classes, and that the lower classes were as calm as the depths of the ocean untouched by the storm on the surface. The peasants led a pastoral life close to nature and folk tradition. They were the most orderly, loyal, and obedient people in all Europe; hardly a policeman was in sight, even in Madrid. And the poor had an instinctive dignity: "I have seen the lowest class of the people, such as gardeners, bricklayers, etc., who had never seen the king, perhaps, in their lives, suddenly spoken to by him; but I never saw one of them hesitate or blush, or seem confounded in any way by a sense of the royal superiority." [53]

After almost four months in Madrid, Ticknor packed his saddlebags and left on horseback for a long and hard journey through southern Spain. On a beautiful clear night he galloped over the dry bed of the Manzanares, thinking of the excitement of the Prado, the warm friends he had made — the most intimate he was to find in Europe — and the romantic scenes ahead. With a skin of wine and a haversack of bread attached to his saddle, he followed the mail courier to Aranjuez and mounted the pass through the dark mountains of the Sierra Morena to the point where Cervantes had freed the galley slaves. As he descended the steep slope, he welcomed the balmy air and olive trees in the valley of La Carolina. He visited the enormous yet delicate Mosque at Cordova and was welcomed by the open-hearted Andalusians.

The most exhilarating part of the trip was the Alhambra in Granada.

Here, where Sultans had walked under the great oaks and elms, he saw many Arab fountains, heard the singing of the birds circling overhead, and entered the magnificent halls of the palaces and the light and luxurious bathing rooms of the palaces. For Ticknor the Alhambra became "a name which will make my blood thrill if I live to the frosts of a century, not that the pleasure I received . . . was like the hallowed delight of a solitary, secret visit to the Coliseum or the Forum, when the moonbeams slept on the wrecks of three empires . . . but it was a riotous, tumultuous pleasure, which will remain in my memory, like a kind of sensual enjoyment, as long as it has vivacity enough to recall the two days I passed amidst this strange enchantment." [54]

From Granada Ticknor passed on to Malaga, Gibraltar, and Seville. In Seville he inquired about the route to Lisbon and found that the best way to protect himself against robbers while going across the mountains was to join a group of contrabandists who smuggled dollars across the border. Mounted on a mule, he met them where they bivouacked under huge cork trees near Zalamea. They were lively outlaws in a society where civil disobedience seemed the mark of the free man. Each had a gun, two pistols, a sword, and a dirk. Ticknor put his blanket on the ground and gleefully shared their food and talk. As they picked their way through the trackless mountains, he spent eight days with the smugglers "living on a footing of perfect equality and good-fellowship with people who are liable every day to be shot or hanged by the laws of their country; indeed, leading for a week as much of a vagabond life as if I were an Arab or a Mameluke." He fully enjoyed the reckless trip "in the only country in the world where I could have led such a life," safer with outlaws than under the protection of the government. The smugglers, in turn, were delighted with their "Don Jorge"; one of them even thought that Ticknor had superior powers. When the vessel in which they were crossing the Tagus River made this smuggler seasick from its continual tacking, he called to Ticknor and asked him to tell the sailors to take the vessel straight across the river.[55]

Ticknor's arrival in England, after taking the mail packet from Lisbon to Falmouth, sharpened questions that had been gnawing at his mind. After Spain and Portugal, "where all is so dead, so wretched, so abject, at least in whatever is obvious and external," England typified "prodigious activity and power — wealth and happiness." "I could hardly *feel,* though I *knew* it," he wrote, that the Spanish and Portuguese

"belonged to the same species with the people I was now among . . .
I was never so confounded with my own thoughts as in attempting to
reconcile such different opposite and inconsistent principles and characteristics in the same nature; for my senses were every moment denying
the relationship which my reason acknowledged, and I grew giddy as I
labored to satisfy both." [56]

A giddy and bewildering thought indeed; what did *progress* mean?
Judged by the tenets of a republican and protestant faith and by economic criteria, Spain was a benighted and backward despotism. Yet
somehow the real nation, the common people, was deeply reverent,
loyal, courageous, poetic, and upright. Spanish literature expressed these
conflicting qualities with unrivaled freshness and power. How could
these anomalies be designated? Ticknor's *History of Spanish Literature*
would be his partial attempt to reconcile through allegory the virtues of
Spain and the spirit of his age.

7. *Return to Orthodoxy*

When Ticknor once more stepped "upon kindred ground" in Falmouth, he "could have fallen down and embraced it, like Julius Caesar."
The packet boat had brought him back to England, the true home of
Americans in the Old World. Ticknor rode swiftly to London along the
smooth turnpike, back to the coffee houses, the libraries, the fashionable
literary society of the metropolis. Yet Ticknor no sooner arrived there
than he had to leave for Paris, the leading bookmart, to obtain works
unavailable in Spain and Portugal, or even in London. He stayed in
Paris from December 10, 1818, to January 12, 1819, buying books
for the Harvard Library and for his personal collection, which had been
steadily growing as he purchased books in each country he visited. He
also served as book agent for Thomas Jefferson. Ticknor had earlier
said that he was going to Europe for "the great means and inducements
it will afford me to study — not men but books." Like Joseph Cogswell,
later founder of the New York Public Library, he became an accomplished bibliographer and helped numerous friends in America to buy
books. This was one of his most important ways of serving as cultural
middleman between the Old and the New Worlds.[57]

Yet Ticknor was, of course, studying men as well as books. His triumphal journey had not been the traditional English grand tour, the finishing touches of a gentleman's education satirized by Pope in the *Dunciad*. His purposes were too well focused for that. Yet Ticknor relished the social triumphs which climaxed his pilgrimage. During his second visit in Paris he saw again the celebrated people he had known before and visited several new salons opened to him through his friendship with the Duke de Laval. Again France presented a hopelessly irrational political tableau to the young Federalist: the ultras berated Ticknor's republican principles and the republicans were upset about his pessimism concerning France. Ticknor met Talleyrand, too, an old man with his coat buttoned up to his throat and face obscured by a white cravat and powdered hair, standing glumly kicking the fire fender. Talleyrand had dire predictions about the fate of the French government, especially if it failed to employ the last resource: himself. Again Ticknor concluded that French society was "brilliant graceful superficial — hollow." [58]

Success in English society always meant most to Bostonians, and Ticknor returned as soon as he could to London, where he often visited Lord Holland and his circle of intellectuals. There he talked with Sydney Smith, a plump jovial man who sparkled with "phosphoric brilliancy" in conversation and who also seemed to Ticknor a just and logical man. In 1820 Smith would write an article in the *Edinburgh Review* which would anger Americans defensive about cultural inferiority. The American "must not grow vain and ambitious," Smith would warn. Every patriotic scribbler tries to persuade Americans that "they are the greatest, the most refined, the most enlightened, and the most moral people on earth." Yet a realist must ask, "In the four quarters of the globe, who reads an American book? or goes to an American play? or looks at an American picture or statue?" Smith later told Ticknor that he was one of the English men of letters most friendly to America. Ticknor never lost his high regard for Smith, perhaps because he accepted Smith's frame of reference and thought Smith's review correct. At Holland House Ticknor also met the essayist and future lord chancellor, Lord Brougham. A thin, plain man with a nervous tic, Brougham talked best in a small group where his "bare, bold, bullion talent" shone forth. In London Ticknor also visited William Hazlitt at the house where Milton had lived. On the white-washed walls of his room Hazlitt had penciled quotations of poetry and aphorisms. His conversation resembled the writing on the walls: abrupt, pointed, allusive.[59]

On his way to Edinburgh Ticknor stopped at the country house of the Marquess of Salisbury and "the splendid seat of the Duke of Bedford," Woburn Abbey. Entering the Abbey through a Roman gateway, Ticknor proceeded through a park with streams, meadows, forest and lakes to the mansion itself. It was the largest and most elegant Ticknor had ever seen, with a fine library and large picture gallery, aviary, gardens, fish ponds, and stables. While Ticknor was a guest, the duke and his fellow sportsmen had a massive hunt on the last day of the season, the duke being "anxious to have a quantity of game killed that should maintain the reputation of the Abbey, for the first sporting-ground in Great Britain." In the evening the game-keeper announced the triumphal bag of 404 partridges, rabbits, and pheasants, a report which encouraged the sportsmen to drink a great deal of wine in celebration. "It was certainly as splendid a specimen as I could have hoped to see," Ticknor wrote, "of what is considered peculiarly English in the life of a British nobleman of the first class at his country-seat. I enjoyed it highly." England was above reproach.[60]

In Edinburgh as in Geneva Ticknor found that intellectuals were highly respected and that talent "breaks down all the artificial distinctions of society . . . And it is a still greater thing to have this talent come familiarly into the fashion of the times, sustained by that knowledge which must give it a prevalent authority, and at once receive and impart a polish and a tone which give a charm to each alike, and without which neither can become what it ought to be to itself or the world." In short, scholars had a chance to become gentlemen, and gentlemen a duty to become scholars. A model, again, for Boston. Ticknor enjoyed the society of Edinburgh, where he met a young woman of such beauty — a Miss McLane — that she "has actually been followed by the mob in the street, until she was obliged to take refuge in a shop from their mere admiration." Robert Owen of Lanark was a tedious reformer who bored Ticknor "with his localities and universalities." But Scott alone justified the trip.[61]

Ticknor thought Scott as impressive in his conversation as in his novels. Scott was tall and heavy. He walked with a slight stoop, had gray hair, and showed signs of sickness — painful stomach spasms. His face brightened, though, when he talked of his favorite subjects. Sophia,

Scott's daughter, sang old Scottish ballads and played the harp. At the time of Ticknor's visit the authorship of the Waverley novels had not been disclosed, but many suspected that Scott had written them. At one party the guests asked Sophia to play the ballad Rob Roy. Embarrassed, Sophia went to her father and whispered in his ear. "Yes, my dear," Scott replied aloud, "play it to be sure, if you are asked, and Waverley and the Antiquary, too, if there be any such ballads."

Scott was at his best at his cottage on the bank of the Tweed River. As he and Ticknor tramped the hills of the Border country, they talked excitedly of the folklore of the region. For each landmark Scott told Ticknor a tradition or a ballad. Scott, for his part, was delighted with Ticknor: "a wonderful fellow for romantic lore and antiquarian research, considering his country, and free from the ignorance and forward presumption" of most Americans. Ticknor commissioned an American artist to paint a portrait of Scott, a picture which occupied the place of honor later over the fireplace in his library.[62]

On his return trip to London Ticknor visited Southey again and made a detour in the Lake Country to see Wordsworth. Southey had written ahead to Wordsworth about Ticknor's visit, and the poet welcomed the American with "Roman dignity and simplicity." Together they hiked over the mountains to enjoy the landscape and to talk about poetry. Ticknor found that Wordsworth was the patriarch of the neighborhood to whom the children took off their hats. One woman even asked him to reform her delinquent son. Wordsworth talked with respect and warmth about Scott, but bitterly about Byron, whose character he abhorred. Byron had stolen, he thought, "something of his own *lakish* manner lately, and, what is worse, borrowed some of his thoughts." [63]

After a brief stay in London and a rapid trip to Liverpool, Ticknor boarded the fast New York packet and crossed the Atlantic in thirty-seven days. When the ship encountered head winds near the shore, Ticknor grew impatient to be home and took a pilot boat at Gay Head which carried him to New Bedford. The unprodigal son, joyful to be on native soil, declared that "the little, humble, fishing-wharf where I landed is more fixed in my memory than all the wonders I left in Europe." Because of his change of plans he found himself without money; with typical self-assurance he went to the best hotel, asked who was the richest man in town, and promptly applied to Mr. William Rotch for money to hire a chaise to go to Boston. Naturally he received the money.

In the moonlight of the warm June night he set out for home. His journey was over.[64]

Not long after Ticknor reached Boston he received a letter from Thomas Jefferson asking "how has your health been affected by your European tour? how your mind? how your view of your own country, after seeing so many others?" His solicitude, based on his deep apprehension about the effects of a European education, echoed the concern of many an American parent and friend: of Elisha writing to his son; of Stephen Longfellow counseling Henry, of Andrews Norton chiding George Bancroft. Were not their fears often justified? Jefferson wrote that many a young American in Europe "acquires a fondness for European luxury and dissipation, and a contempt for the simplicity of his own country." Ticknor's answer to Jefferson was unequivocal: "What I saw of Europe only raised my own country in my estimation and attached me to it yet more." Here was final proof of his Bostonian education. Soon he would show other young men the path of the pilgrim's progress.[65]

III

The Cause of Sound Learning

Academic institutions are the more necessary with us to supply incitement to the cultivation of the spiritual man, from the circumstance that other pursuits and callings are so inviting to persons of talent and enterprise. With us, commerce, manufacture, all that is profitable, all that is mechanical, and all that is sensual, will take care of itself; and it is the rock on which the glory of America may split, that everything is calling her with siren songs to a physical, inelegant, immature, unsanctified, Carthaginian, perishable prosperity.   *John T. Kirkland* [1]

In 1819 Joseph Cogswell wrote hopefully about Ticknor's and Everett's return to the United States: "We could wish no greater good to their country than that they should be received . . . as Plato was at Athens, when he had finished his travels, and began to impart the fruits of them to his countrymen in the groves of the academy." Ralph Waldo Emerson was a student at Harvard when the two young professors began their careers. He recalled that even "the rudest undergraduate found a new morning opened to him in the lecture-room of Harvard Hall. There was an influence on the young people almost comparable to that of Pericles in Athens." Plato, Pericles, Athens — theirs was no small sense of mission. [2]

As academic missionaries, Ticknor, Everett, Bancroft, and Cogswell all returned to Harvard hoping they could show Americans the meaning of scholarship and culture. They were determined to "disprove the charge of intellectual inferiority" with which Europeans had taunted Americans since the time of Buffon. They were convinced that "mere power, unaccompanied by intellectual refinement, never failed of being a scourge, whether possessed by a despot or a republic." America was bound to become rich and strong; but was it to be an empty prosperity, "a wild and ferocious" power? In the tones of a secular sermon the new professors spoke of transplanting the culture and scholarship of Europe. Significantly, Everett called the library, not the chapel, "the life and soul of any university." [3]

These missionaries believed that Harvard was as good a place as any to promote sound scholarship. It was the oldest and the best endowed college in the country, representing the best "hope of seeing in America an university in fact as well as in name." Perhaps in Cambridge the four returning scholars could find colleagues eager to join them. "I have pondered what you and Mr. Ticknor have written about our education and literature, and college," President Kirkland had written to Edward Everett in 1816. "I am trying, feeling round, watching, praying in a quiet way to enable us to realize some of the improvements . . . I want you to tell me what you would do with our University and how you would do it, if you had money enough." Kirkland asked young Everett to send him an article on universities for the *North American Review* which "I will adapt and alter — and . . . pass it off for my own compiled with the help of your correspondence that the pride in this business may be partly saved and I get some factitious credit." This Kirkland did in an article published in 1818, "Literary institutions — University." [4]

Bolstered by Kirkland's request for a blueprint for reform, by the comparison of their role to that of Plato and Pericles, and by their own strong convictions, Ticknor and his friends returned to Harvard with great expectations. Bancroft remained one year, Cogswell two. Everett stayed only until 1825, when he left to pursue a political career. Ticknor alone remained at Harvard to fulfill the original mission. When he resigned in 1835, he confessed that he had failed in his aims everywhere save in his own department.

Ticknor's analysis of Harvard and his prescription of remedies for its weaknesses bared some of the most important issues in American higher education, then and since: the relation of general education to specialized education; prescription as opposed to election of courses; the role and status of the professor; the question of whether laymen should make educational policy; and the connection between higher education and leadership in the larger society. But Ticknor was "a reformer fifty years in advance of his time," as his nephew Charles William Eliot later declared.[5]

1. *The Professor in Boston*

On August 10, 1819, Ticknor was formally inducted as Abiel Smith Professor of the French and Spanish Languages and Literatures and Professor of Belles Lettres. He had previously defined his duties in correspondence with President Kirkland. He was, they agreed, not "to be expected to teach any language as such." Harvard gave him funds to purchase enough books in French and Spanish literature to allow him to prepare scholarly lectures and to conduct tutorial with advanced students. He was also to live at home in Boston rather than in Cambridge. By this agreement Ticknor avoided two of the most onerous tasks of college instructors at the time: giving recitations in the rudiments of language; and serving as a parietal officer in the dormitories or as a member of the professorial police force at Harvard.

This definition of his role profoundly affected Ticknor's experience at Harvard. Like some of the other nonresident professors, who gave lectures but who pursued independent careers as professional men or scholars, Ticknor had time to follow the bent of his own intellectual interests. He could achieve a scholarly identity independent of the college. Free from the ignominious task of policing dormitories full of ingenious delinquents, he could become a Bostonian gentleman as well as a Harvard scholar. He would not need the cloak and dagger equipment of the parietal officer: a dark lantern with a slide on the side which could be opened suddenly in the Harvard Yard at midnight to identify an unsuspecting junior making catcalls outside a tutor's room. He would not need to sit through interminable recitations while students butchered Racine or rattled their tongues like the clapper of a bell giving rules governing the subjunctive mood. He would not experience the teacher's feeling of isolation from mature society and estrangement from youth. He would not look on the lay members of the Harvard governing bodies, the Corporation and the Board of Overseers, as alien snoopers, but would know them intimately as neighbors and friends.[6]

It was not that Ticknor was lax about his teaching. Far from it; he worked diligently on his lectures and petitioned Kirkland to allow him to give them in the evening three times a week so that he would have his mornings free for study. He described his ambitious schedule of study and teaching in a letter to Jefferson and added that "when I have finished the whole, I shall look about for something else to do, as I have no idea that a Professor should ever be doing anything but preparing to teach." Still, Ticknor's light teaching load — three lectures on Monday, Wednesday, and Friday evenings, occasional supervision of elementary instruction in French and Spanish given by Francis Sales, and an infrequent tutorial with advanced students — constituted a radical departure from the normal instructor's schedule.[7]

On his return to Boston in June of 1819 he had entered a closely knit society quick to resent any foreign affectation or dilettantism, but ready to appreciate the learning, anecdotes, and refined manners he had acquired in Europe. Many of the qualities of intellect and character which had won him recognition in Europe served him well in Boston. A portrait of Ticknor painted by Thomas Sully in 1828 clearly delineates his self-confidence, his earnestness, and his strong will. Ticknor sits in an easy chair in his study with manuscript in hand, an attractive, slight, relaxed figure, with abundant black curly hair and ruddy face. His prominent nose and chin and his firm mouth suggest a determination and self-discipline which Sully glossed over in his romantic, almost Byronic, interpretation. Sully also flattered Ticknor's crooked nose, which looked, Ticknor's young friend Samuel Ward said, much like that of Lorenzo de' Medici "and Lorenzo was no beauty."

To a generation which paid homage to Longfellow's "Psalm of Life," Ticknor's high seriousness had great appeal. Many of the foremost men of New England, both intellectuals and men of affairs, valued his friendship: Daniel Webster, senator from Massachusetts, Presidential hopeful, and Secretary of State; Joseph Story, brilliant Supreme Court justice and teacher, and author of several influential books on constitutional law; the Prescotts, father and son; William Ellery Channing, Ticknor's minister and patron saint of Unitarianism; George Bancroft; Jeremiah Mason, a blunt Federalist, one of the best lawyers in Boston, though he looked like a New Hampshire farmer; Nathaniel Bowditch, the self-made navigator and scholar, a frank, precise, and public-spirited New Englander on a classic Roman model; Jacob Bigelow, a physician and Harvard professor, witty and cultivated; Joseph Cogswell; Andrews Norton, Ticknor's brother-in-law, a formidable defense attorney for Unitarianism and prosecutor of Transcendentalism; Edward and Alexander Everett; Jared Sparks, editor in the 1820's of the *North American*

Review and later the president and first professor of history at Harvard; Washington Allston; and many other notable New Englanders. All respectable Europeans seemed to come to Ticknor with letters in their pockets — and how could he complain? [8]

Though Ticknor prided himself on his friendships with men of affairs, including all the members of the Harvard Corporation, he especially enjoyed the company of intellectuals — men like Prescott, Sparks, Cogswell, Bancroft, and the two Everetts. At small suppers of venison or roast chicken and brown bread, well lubricated with whisky punch made according to Walter Scott's recipe, he and his literary friends talked about Harvard affairs, travels, diplomacy, and, of course, literature. Ticknor excelled in such conversation. Maria Edgeworth, who had heard Sidney Smith, Talleyrand, Scott, and many other famous talkers, declared that "Mr. Ticknor's conversation appeared to me fully on an equality with the most admired, in happy, apposite readiness of recollection and application of knowledge, in stores of anecdote, and in *ease* in producing them, and in depth of reflection not inferior to those whom we have been accustomed to consider our deepest thinkers." "Society was to him," Henry Adams commented, "one of the minor fine arts, of which the practice was its own reward . . . and in a community quite without any real taste for society, Mr. Ticknor's example had a positive value in showing what a pleasant thing it might be." [9]

In Europe Ticknor had met many beautiful and cultivated women. His journal often told of dancing till midnight with Spanish and English ladies or talking in Paris and Rome with gifted women who adorned the salons. On his return to Boston, believing that "in any country, and most of all in America, marriage is a *sine qua non* to happiness," Ticknor sought a wife. One young woman especially attracted him, Anna Eliot, Samuel's lively and cultivated youngest daughter. Together they danced at Boston balls, and talked of art, literature, and Ticknor's adventures in Europe. After their engagement they accompanied Anna's sister and her husband Andrews Norton on a gay trip to New York, Lake George, and back through the Green Mountains of Vermont to Hanover. On September 18, 1821, Anna and George were married.

Anna Ticknor was an intelligent woman who fully shared her husband's taste for letters and society. Beneath a conventional facade, she was an independent and witty spirit, with a pungent style of writing and conversation and ready affection. She impressed persons as diverse as

John Calhoun, Charles Sumner, and Maria Edgeworth. Delighted with their own marriage, the Ticknors tried to persuade their friends to follow suit. Ticknor counseled George Bancroft "as one experienced in such matters, to get married as soon as you can . . . You may write a little less poetry and talk a little less Romance; but the good substantial prose of sympathy, support, and cooperation is worth all the imaginings that ever came into an unwed lover's fancy." Anna told Bancroft of the "delight" and "assimilation of . . . characters" in marriage and teased him about missing the fine ball at their house: "such an assemblage of beauty, grace, brilliancy, and fashion, as graced Mrs. Ticknor's rooms that night, is hardly to be conceived, much less to be described." [10]

Anna's inheritance of $84,394.50 from her father, coupled with George's modest legacy from Elisha, who died in 1821, enabled the Ticknors "to live at ease, with unpretending elegance." Francis Grund, who wrote a satirical study of American "aristocracy," noticed that it was common in Boston for literary men to be "in easy circumstances," and asked a rich merchant why. "They marry rich women, who can afford paying for being entertained," replied the businessman. "They show their common sense in that. It's quite the fashion for our rich girls to *buy themselves a professor*." In Boston marriage often did link commerce and culture: witness the marriages of Edward Everett and Charlotte Brooks, daughter of Peter C. Brooks, the richest man in Boston; Longfellow and the rich and beautiful Fanny Appleton; Bancroft and the daughter of the wealthy Jonathan Dwight of Springfield; and Ticknor and Norton to Anna and Catherine Eliot. All these professors were men of modest means; all of their wives were wealthy.[11] Happily married, at home in the fashionable society of Boston, respected by the most eminent men in New England, Ticknor had good reason to be pleased with his life. But it was a quite different sphere he entered when he took the long carriage ride to Cambridge.

2. *A Well-disciplined High School*

From the first, Ticknor and Everett opened "a new morning" to Harvard students and gave many of them a sense of the constriction of Harvard's archaic curriculum. At the age of thirty-five, cured of his adolescent hero worship of Everett, Emerson still admitted that "Everett has put more stories, sentences, verses, names in amber for me than any other person." Students admired Everett's handsome face with its heavy eyes and "marble lids," his richly melodious voice and delivery that became a model for young orators all over New England: "not a sentence was written in a theme," Emerson observed, "not a declamation attempted in the College Chapel, but showed the omnipresence of his genius to youthful heads."

Ticknor, too, brought literature to life so that all could share vicariously in cultures they had never known. Young Josiah Quincy and Emerson marveled in almost the same words at the magic strokes with which Ticknor transformed the scholarly subject of French philology into a pageant of clashing peoples and tongues. "There is something very pleasing," Quincy remarked, "in his style and delivery . . . But independently of this, there is a melody in his voice truly delightful. When describing the softness and beauty of the Provençal, it seemed as if he spoke in that delicious language. When he said of St. Louis, 'whether he desired his canonization or not, he certainly was one of the truest patriots, one of the bravest knights, and one of the noblest gentlemen who ever lived,' it seemed as though his eulogy was complete." Ann Storrow, a Cambridge girl who attended his lectures, admired Ticknor's "unbounded enthusiasm and personal knowledge." She was impressed with his modesty when, in discussing Madame de Staël, he did not speak of the "intimate intercourse with Madame de Staël's family and friends which we all know that he had." As Madame de Staël's daughter observed, Ticknor had more pride than vanity.[12]

Though Ticknor was doubtless pleased with the warm response of his students to his lectures, he was convinced that eloquence alone does not teach. He believed that students should attend his lectures only after previous study in modern languages and should use the lectures as guides for independent study, as he had in Germany; to this end he wrote a detailed syllabus to accompany his lectures in Spanish literature. He impressed some of the students as a more earnest teacher than the rhetorical Everett. Ticknor's brother-in-law, Samuel Eliot, wrote Bancroft that "Ticknor continues to deliver the most admirable and interesting lectures; by far the finest course we have ever had here on any literary subject . . . Everett's are of a different and . . . far inferior character. They are crowded with all sorts of useless erudition . . . and are rather calculated to set forth the amount of the professor's studies than to do any particular benefit to the students." Emerson at length concluded that Everett's fame "was a mere triumph of rhetoric . . . He had no thoughts." [13]

Ticknor was remarkably successful in communicating "a sort of undefined and indefinite feeling, respecting books and authors" that "gives life to the dead mass of inefficient knowledge and vigor and spirit to inquiry." He was also fascinated with the problems of teaching modern languages; his "Lecture on the Best Methods of Teaching the Living Languages," delivered in 1832, contains sound advice about the merits of oral instruction and the best ways to study grammar. Throughout his career at Harvard Ticknor insisted that the college employ native speakers to teach the foreign languages and kept a close eye on their work. He and his colleagues produced a number of useful elementary language texts and readings for use in beginning classes. He never lost sight of the fact, either in his own teaching or in his suggestions for institutional changes, that "there is one point that . . . must be made a sort of cynosure, when beneficial changes are undertaken, both at Harvard and at our other colleges; and that is, the principle of thorough *teaching*." [14]

Writing in 1825 to a friend, Ticknor claimed that when he began teaching at Harvard he had "no misgivings about the organization and management of the College . . . I went about my work, therefore, with great alacrity and confidence . . . according to the established order of things which I was urged to adopt as my own, and which I did adopt very cheerfully." Yet even before he had arrived at Harvard, on February 13, 1819, Ticknor had written to Jefferson about the "indolence" of the Harvard faculty and the need for Harvard to have a rival in the University of Virginia, then in the planning stage. It was true that he venerated Harvard as an ancient and honorable institution, but he never had patience with "the established order of things" there.[15]

During his tenure Harvard was a small college, averaging about 225 students and about thirty professors, instructors, and tutors. Admission requirements, in a day when colleges were competing for the small number of applicants, were fairly slack — one reason why so many boys were admitted at an early age of thirteen or fourteen. Candidates were examined on Latin and Greek grammar, Cicero and Virgil, some simple Greek texts, some mathematics, and a smattering of geography; the subjects required were important, however limited, but the standards were not rigorous. When Prescott took his entrance examination he found it not half so formidable as he had feared. President Kirkland brought the candidates a dish of pears, and the faculty treated the students "very much like gentlemen."

Once admitted, the students were divided alphabetically into recitation sections. The bulk of the prescribed curriculum, which all took in a rigidly ordered sequence, was Latin, Greek, and mathematics. Complementing these basic subjects in 1820 were English composition, history, logic, natural and moral philosophy, and modern languages. The only opportunity for students to elect courses came in the junior year when they could substitute for Hebrew additional work in Latin, Greek, or mathematics or begin the study of French; later students were allowed a slightly greater degree of latitude in their choice.[16]

On paper the curriculum had a fair scope, but the methods of instruction vitiated its promise. The predominant mode of teaching was recitation, an exercise in which a teacher, customarily a young and inexperienced tutor, policed the students by hearing them repeat the lesson they were supposed to memorize from the textbook. As Ticknor soon bewailed, students tended to study a given book rather than a subject. Their rank in class depended on how well they were able to parrot its contents. "No attempt was made to interest us in our studies," complained James Freeman Clarke of the class of 1829. "We were expected to wade through Homer as though the Iliad were a bog, and it was our duty to get along at such a rate *per diem*. Nothing was said of the glory and grandeur, the tenderness and charm of this immortal epic." Clarke contended that the system of ranking students stultified the entire program: "the teacher was there, not to teach, but to give marks to each student . . . Pencil in hand, he listened in silence to the student's translation or solution of a problem, and having affixed the proper number to his name, went on to the next." [17]

Given this judicial view of teaching, it is not surprising that there was a social barrier between faculty and students despite the small size of classes and the intimacy of a residential college. If a student visited a tutor's room voluntarily, he kept it a secret. Students considered it high treason to enter a recitation early or to ask a teacher questions — this was apple polishing and obviously could be done for only one reason: a higher number in the rank book. The system depended on competition, but the student mores effectively sabotaged it.

The more able and less docile students — men like Thoreau and

Emerson, for example — chafed under the mechanical academic book-keeping and gained their real education in independent study. In Thoreau's senior year President Quincy wrote to Emerson that Thoreau had "imbibed some notions concerning emulation and college rank, which had a natural tendency to diminish his zeal, if not his exertions." In reply to a comment that Harvard taught all the branches of learning, Thoreau quipped, "Yes, indeed, all the branches and none of the roots." A bright student could easily pass with two or three hours of study a day, which left a good deal of time for informal education.[18]

At six o'clock in the morning in summer and one-half hour after sunrise in winter students went to morning chapel; this outing was a particularly Spartan custom in the bitterly cold winter mornings. Before their meager breakfast of coffee and rolls they attended a recitation. Two or three more recitations or lectures followed, interspersed with rowdy meals in the new Bullfinch building, University Hall. Evening prayers at six in the evening closed the day.

Students came to Cambridge from near and far. Many young men from the South attended Harvard during Ticknor's years — Carolinians dapper in their swallow-tailed coats and calfskin boots, Virginians with cavalier manners, sophisticated boys from New Orleans — and helped to substantiate the charge that the college was a haven for aristocrats. Students had ample time for mischief and for the literary and social clubs that sprouted like radishes on a warm summer day. One of the rowdiest societies was the Navy Club, composed of all the seniors who failed to win parts in the commencement. "The 'Lord High Admiral,' jolliest of all 'jolly blades' in the class, organized his staff, consisting of the Vice-Admiral (the poorest scholar), the Rear-Admiral (the laziest), the Chaplain (the most profane), the Boatswain (the most obscene), and so on down to powder monkeys." It was a golden era of high jinks and low escapades.[19]

When Ticknor came to Harvard, the college had an institutional structure which would have been appropriate in 1800, or for that matter in 1700. By 1820 it was obsolete because of greatly enlarged academic resources. Under President Kirkland's regime from 1810 to 1828, fifteen professorships were added to the college. Thus, alongside the traditional recitation system and the prescribed curriculum, there arose a series of lectures which bore little relation to the rest of the course of study. The college suffered from a severe case of academic indigestion.

According to the *Course of Instruction* of 1820 the students were "to be frequently and regularly examined by the Professors on the subjects treated in their lectures." Yet the real problem was that these lectures for juniors and seniors became, in effect, extracurricular. They were, Ticknor lamented, "attended by whole classes, whether the individual members were prepared for such instruction or not; no notes were taken; and a law passed a few years since, requiring examinations, was not executed. The lectures were simply read, and then the students dismissed." In his early years of teaching Ticknor could not control attendance or set standards of performance. In exasperation he complained in 1822 to President Kirkland that since "all control and knowledge of the persons who may attend my lectures this year is taken from me . . . I am, of course, happily relieved from all responsibility . . . it will be a total waste of my own time." [20]

Ticknor denounced the failure of Harvard to use the time and talent of its professors. He discovered that four tutors, whose aggregate income was $4,300, gave 2,364 exercises annually, while eleven other instructors, whose salaries totaled $14,382.76, gave only 824 exercises yearly, "a number less than is often given by a single professor in Europe." His own light official duties were typical of those of most of the other professors. Beyond the bare minimum of recitations on required subjects, which largely determined a student's rank in class, a student could, it was true, benefit from lectures on many subjects or take tutorial with men like Ticknor and Everett; but only an exceptional student would be likely "to take advantage of the facilities that existed on paper." One of Ticknor's strongest motives for proposing institutional changes at Harvard was his conviction that his own lectures were anomalous in the existing system, only a way for a schoolboy to occupy an idle hour.[21]

In time Ticknor would press for far-reaching reforms to correct this institutional lag. Yet the first of Harvard's faults to provoke his zeal for reform was laxness of discipline. Before the college could undertake any major changes it must at least do its avowed tasks well. Harvard claimed to produce Christian gentlemen, but early in his teaching Ticknor discovered that students had fallen into habits of sloth, extravagance, and immorality which were either unknown or ignored by the Immediate Government of the college — a disciplinary and academic board composed of the president and most of the resident faculty. Ticknor scornfully commented that "with Christo et Ecclesiae for our motto, the

morals of great numbers of young men who come to us are corrupted."
From students and from his own observation Ticknor learned that under-
graduates were playing billiards at Lechmere Point, drinking brandy in
the morning at the Marlboro Hotel in Boston, and contracting venereal
disease by consorting with women of ill repute. When Yale's president,
Timothy Dwight, had visited Harvard in 1810 he warned that the college suffered from its proximity to Boston: "The allurements of this
metropolis have often become too powerfully seductive to be resisted
by the gay, and sometimes even by the grave youths." [22] Ticknor believed that Harvard should stand *in loco parentis* for its regular students
— should be, in a sense, an extended family for its Brahmin youth and
aspiring poor scholars — and thought that the college was not discharging its parental obligations adequately.

After setting a stony face against the temptations of Europe, Ticknor
was of no mind to treat these vices casually, nor were Andrews Norton
and Henry Ware, both professors of theology. Ware, the kindly and
dignified father of nineteen children, was appalled by the luxurious tone
of the college. The mortifying state of Unitarian Harvard, Norton wrote
to William Ellery Channing, "concerns the credit of rational Christians
. . . The College is becoming an institution for the rich and for the poor
supported by its charity." If Harvard could not even curb vice and
extravagance among its students, if it could not even provide reasonably
efficient instruction within the confines of its prescribed curriculum, how
could it hope to be a university? [23]

Ticknor was constantly frustrated in discussing these matters with
President Kirkland. With the approval of Norton and Ware he presented
his complaints in 1821 to his friend Judge Prescott, then a member of
the Corporation, in a long letter which exposed the defects of the college
and proposed remedies. Ticknor's disillusionment had convinced him
that Harvard was not ripe for extensive reform. Instead he urged Prescott and the Corporation to tighten the college into a *"well-disciplined
high school"* in which young men would receive sound training of character and intellect.

I most sincerely wish that . . . [Harvard] were now in a condition to be
raised above the highest wants felt among us, and to prevent so many of our
young men from seeking in solitary unaided exertion, and in foreign countries, the degree of Instruction, which we cannot offer them. — But this does

not seem to be possible. If we can ever have a University at Cambridge, which shall lead the intellectual character of the country, it can be I apprehend only when the present college shall have been settled into a thorough and well-disciplined high school, where the young men of the country shall be carefully prepared to begin their professional studies; and where in Medicine, Law, and Theology, sufficient inducements shall have been collected around and within the college, aided by regular courses of instruction in the higher branches of general learning and science, to keep Graduates there two years at least, and probably three. As, however, we are not arrived at this desireable condition, and cannot very soon hope to arrive there, the first thing to be done, in order to satisfy the reasonable demands of the community, is, to take measures to make the college *a well-disciplined high school,* in which the knowledge preparatory to a professional education, shall be taught *thoroughly,* and the habits and character of the young men fitted for the further intellectual exertions to which they are destined.[24]

Ticknor then proposed a thorough revision of discipline and instruction within the existing framework of the college. The pamphlet of disciplinary regulations given to the students, he complained, contained obsolete, unenforced, and unenforceable provisions; its wording was too often argumentative rather than imperative. The Immediate Government was too large a body to exert effective discipline, and its rulings were apt to be contradictory and partial. Instead, Ticknor argued, a three-man tribunal should judge all disciplinary cases and its members should be given additional time and compensation.

Ticknor was as concerned with moral reform as with academic. He advocated a requirement that all Harvard students wear a uniform, both to cut expense and as "part of a general system of Discipline." With Ticknor's advice and encouragement the Corporation passed a law requiring that students should wear a coat "of black-mixed, single breasted, with a rolling cape square at the end and with pocket flaps . . . three crows feet made of black silk cord . . . pantaloons of black-mixed or of black bombazet . . . The buttons . . . must be flat . . . not more than eight or less than six in the front of the coat and four behind." Every student had to wear this costume all the time he was in the state of Massachusetts, even during vacations, under penalty of dismissal from the college. Now, were Harvard students so errant as to play billiards at Lechmere Point, all would be sure to notice. Thus far were Ticknor and his fellow reformers to go in purifying the moral atmosphere at Harvard. Ticknor hardly proposed for Harvard the complete freedom of the German student.[25]

This was to be a "high school" indeed. Little wonder that students became casuists. Charles Sumner began his career as a moral crusader by insisting that his buff-colored waistcoat was white when the Immediate Government summoned him for "illegal dress." Sumner told the Board that his coat "might need the manipulations of a laundress, but it was worn for the lawful color." After several hearings the professors wearily voted "that hereafter Mr. Sumner's vest be considered by this Board white." [26]

To improve the "poor state of intellectual . . . discipline" Ticknor urged that the hurried and farcical entrance examinations be stiffened. He proposed that students take several days of oral and written examinations, and that those who passed should spend a probationary period of one term during which the dull and dissolute would be weeded out. The recitation system Ticknor dismissed as a failure. In the crowded classes each student recited only four minutes a day on the average; some of the schools preparing students for Harvard required more than this. As a remedy Ticknor suggested that students be selected according to ability and ambition and placed in classes of no more than fifteen where they could proceed at their fastest pace. This arrangement would be far better than the existing alphabetical division of classes, a Procrustean bed in which the interest of the bright was amputated and the wits of the dull unduly stretched. Real teaching was not policing: the instructor should illustrate the text by examples, commentary, and imaginative questioning. Each year the work load should increase so that the devil would not find play for the idle juniors and seniors. Last, the examinations at the end of courses should be rigorous, with distinguished outside visitors invited to judge the students — and, indirectly, the faculty.[27]

Perturbed by Ticknor's contention that Harvard was corrupt, the Corporation sent a questionnaire to the members of the faculty to probe the condition of the college and to request suggestions for improvement. Most instructors replied that they were content with the *status quo;* it was clear from their answers that they resented Ticknor's meddling. Kirkland, too, considered Ticknor a thorn in his side — Ticknor had, for example, pointed out that two notorious drinkers had been honored at commencement. When the president in his amiable way suggested that

Ticknor had been stirring up ill will against Harvard in New England, Ticknor angrily replied, "This I deny in toto. Ever since I returned from Europe, I have been in the habit of hearing this [unfavorable] opinion [of Harvard] expressed; but it is only since last winter, that I have believed it to be well founded . . . But in truth, if you . . . knew the state of public feeling in New England and . . . at the south, you would never have thought of me in the case. I have no means to move such a mass as is now likely to come down upon us." Ironically, only four years before, Elisha Ticknor had written Kirkland, asking the president and Corporation "to remember . . . [George's] youth and inexperience and not forget that he will often need . . . advice and incouragement." After discovering the conservative temperament of the faculty and its undercurrent of resentment, the Corporation did little save making regulations concerning dress and reduction of expenses. But the charge that Harvard was a school for the idle and dissolute rich persisted.[28]

Two calamities in 1823 and 1824 forced the governing boards to take a second and closer look at the reforms which Ticknor had proposed in 1821. The class of 1823, already notoriously rowdy, with a long record of clandestine parties, battles in Commons, explosions, and ingenious vexing of tutors and professors, erupted in the spring of their senior year in a "Great Rebellion" so severe that the college expelled forty-three out of a class of seventy. During the following winter the lower house of the Massachusetts General Court, "almost without discussion and with a unanimous vote," as Andrews Norton grimly reported, refused to renew the $10,000 annual grant which Harvard had enjoyed for the last ten years.[29]

It was at this juncture, when both Harvard's prestige and finances were imperiled, and when the community at large was convinced that reform was imperative, that Ticknor concluded that he should go beyond the modest changes he had earlier advocated, and should press reforms "with the purpose of opening the College and making it a University." Now was the time for a "beneficial compromise" between the American college system and the "most liberal conception that would be demanded by one of the merely free and philosophical Universities of Europe." Such a hope had been on his mind for some time. "I pray you to consider," he had written Kirkland in 1822, "whether it will not be possible, and even easy, to remodel the old Building [Harvard], which we all so much

venerate, without absolutely pulling it down and erecting a new one." [30]
Ticknor had learned much from other models of higher education. Now
was the time to draw his blueprint for reform.

3. Models

"I care not three straws," Ticknor told Bancroft in 1824, "about any
of the *theories* [of education] from Plato and Quinctilian down to Rousseau. Show me what has been *done,* and I am ready to believe and trust
and imitate." Once when a friend asked his advice on education, Ticknor replied that he had "always had two fixed ideas about young men:
first, that they should be substantially educated in the country where
they are probably to live; and second, that not a small part of the
value of a university or public-school education consists in adjusting a
young man, during the most flexible period of his life, to his place among
the associates who can best help him onward." Here was no wild-eyed
visionary. As a reformer Ticknor prided himself on his common sense,
his recognition of the practical limitations and opportunities inherent in
Harvard. He always justified his suggestions by pointing to successful
practice elsewhere. He contended that his notions about teaching were
those of "Cardinal Wolsey and Roger Ascham, Milton and Locke, and
. . . the vast majority of skillful teachers in those parts of Europe
where Education at the present time is best conducted and advanced the
furthest." [31] He strongly believed that the republic of education should
be pluralistic rather than monolithic: only thus could institutions benefit
from each other's innovations.

Ticknor concurred with Cogswell that "adaptation to the country
where the [educational] institution is, constitutes the first point of excellence." Recognizing the differences between German and American
society, Ticknor did not intend to make Harvard a carbon copy of
Göttingen. He realized that, compared to German scholars, Harvard
professors were poorly trained and had little zeal for research. Even if
they had been ardent investigators, with ample time for investigation,
the meager library and laboratory facilities of the college would have
stymied scholarship. The students were younger and less informed than
those in Germany. Parents assumed that the officers of the college would
keep a close watch over their sons. Most professors knew only the tradi-

tional prescribed curriculum, and preferred it on theoretical as well as practical grounds.

Above all, higher education in America bore a different relation to success after commencement. Francis Grund reported the opinion of a Boston apostle of common sense: "I have brought up my sons to become merchants and manufacturers; only Sam, the poor boy who is a little hard of hearing, and rather slow of comprehension, shall go to college. Our merchants, sir, are the most respectable part of the community." Grund, astonished, asked him where he planned to send poor Sam. "I shall send him to Harvard University," he replied, "the oldest literary institution in the country." In Germany students had a compelling motive to learn despite great freedom. Cogswell pointed out that the success of the German university depended on the fact that only successful graduates could gain access to the professions. "Where all instruction is given by lecturing and attendance entirely voluntary, there is great danger that young men will be wanting in active diligence, and grow remiss. But the German system guards against this evil, by closing every avenue to advancement in professional or public life, to all who cannot pass the ordeal of a rigid examination." No wonder that the German student rarely wasted time, Cogswell observed, whereas Americans dissipated the greater part of the four years they spent in college, to the point where a diploma became more a certificate of residence than a seal of competence.[32]

Was German education irrelevant then? Surely not, in Ticknor's opinion, but in characteristic eclectic fashion Ticknor selected only those elements which could thrive in American soil. He believed that lectures in the German style, coupled with private tutorial and directed readings — as in his *Syllabus of Spanish Literature* — could give students a broad philosophic grasp of subjects. Certain practices of the gymnasium — grouping students in small classes by ability, and more searching questioning, for example — could reform the American recitation system. Ultimately Harvard might develop a graduate school comparable to the German "philosophical faculty" for advanced work in the liberal arts and sciences to prepare teachers for colleges and secondary schools. He thought Harvard should divide its block curriculum into broad departments, as in German universities. But these interrelated changes would only work at Harvard, Ticknor believed, if they could successfully be grafted to the basic structure of the college.[33]

Ticknor did not need to go beyond the borders of the United States to find object lessons for Harvard. Since his Dartmouth classmate, Sylvanus Thayer, was the head of West Point, Ticknor had several opportunities to see the military academy at first hand. In an article in the *Boston Daily Advertiser* on August 7, 1821, Ticknor wrote that the cadets "are a body of *Students,* who are constantly devoted to an intellectual discipline much more severe than their military discipline — who are much more thoroughly taught, what they pretend to learn, than any of the young men, who are sent to any of our colleges." The entrance examinations were *"much more rigid and effectual than any we practice,"* the intellectual rivalry keener, the students more orderly, industrious, and exact, than at other colleges. Ticknor was convinced that West Point produced the best scientists and engineers in the country.[34]

Ticknor knew another school which he felt produced better scholars than Harvard. This was the Round Hill School in Northampton, Massachusetts, founded by his friends Cogswell and Bancroft. Cogswell had spent two years at Harvard as Librarian and Professor of Mineralogy and Geology but soon grew restive "under [the] control of others" in a college which seemed archaic after Göttingen. Bancroft spent a disastrous year during 1822–23 as tutor of Greek at Harvard. The steward of Harvard, Stephen Higginson, wrote that Bancroft's "manners, style of writing, Theology, etc., [are] bad, and as a tutor [he is] only the laughing butt of all the College." Students used to gather outside his window and taunt him by calling, "This is the way we do it in Germany." He was relieved to flee the scene of failure. Ticknor, sorry to see his allies go, felt that "their discontent with their situation in Cambridge" would lessen with time, but he was delighted with the school they established on the model of a gymnasium. He visited the Round Hill School during the summer of 1824 and "saw things just as they happen every day and lived with them just as they all live. I ate with them, taught with them, and frolicked with them as if I had been part and parcel of the establishment." He found that the thirty-two boys were busy and happy and "thoroughly and judiciously taught — and that the whole arrangement of things is easy, cheap, and *practical*. It was on the last item that I was most pleasantly disappointed, for there was no theorizing about any thing. All was orderly, exact, useful, and, at the same time, very pleasant." Though it was technically a secondary school, Ticknor did not hesitate to say that it gave better instruction than Harvard; and he recommended it to his friends.[35]

Not content with making invidious comparisons of Harvard and these schools, Ticknor compounded his indiscretion by praising Harvard's new rival, the University of Virginia. He and Jefferson had talked and corresponded about this exciting experiment. Jefferson had tried to lure him away from Harvard by the offer of a Professorship of Belles Lettres with a salary of two thousand dollars and a house on the beautiful new campus he had designed. Although Ticknor refused the professorship, he followed with keen interest "the first truly liberal establishment for the highest branches of education, that has been attempted in this country."

In December of 1824, with Jefferson as guide, Ticknor toured the new university — its large library modeled on the Pantheon, its fine lecture rooms, its rows of students' apartments and professors' houses — which was located on a high plain affording striking views of the Virginia countryside. Ticknor thought it "a mass of buildings more beautiful than anything architectural in New England, and more appropriate to an university than can be found, perhaps, in the world." He found Jefferson's educational plan "more practical than I feared, but not so practical that I feel satisfied of its success . . . It is, however, an experiment worth trying, to which I earnestly desire the happiest results." [36]

In drawing the blueprints for an entirely new institution, Jefferson had no need to remodel an old one. His plans were more radical than anything Ticknor contemplated. He tried to combine in one institution instruction of the highest caliber in the established disciplines of the liberal arts and sciences with instruction in utilitarian subjects. He established eight independent "schools": moral philosophy, mathematics, natural history, natural philosophy, law, anatomy and medicine, ancient languages, and modern languages. Abandoning the traditional division of students into four classes, he also abolished the B.A. degree. Students could elect any subject, while each "school" could award its own diploma based on successful completion of standards it set.[37]

Jefferson and Ticknor may well have influenced each other's ideas: Jefferson's concept of "schools" resembled Ticknor's departmental system, and both men believed in election of courses, though Ticknor was to propose a far less radical departure from the prescribed curriculum than Jefferson. At least, as Ticknor assured Jefferson, it was useful to have a rival to stimulate sluggish Harvard; and Jefferson, sage politician that he was, warned Virginians that unless his state had an outstanding university, "Harvard will still prime it over us" and teach our youth "the lessons of Anti-Missourianism."[38]

During Ticknor's efforts at reform, there were, then, a number of models and competitors to which he could point. But during the debates that ensued, no member of the Harvard faculty wrote a clear and reasoned justification for the traditional liberal arts college, though most of them still believed in it. It fell to the faculty of a rival college, Yale, to give a full exposition of the views expressed only partially and hesitatingly by their colleagues in Cambridge. In 1828, in response to the demand for a reappraisal of higher education which was sweeping the country — a demand to which Ticknor gave impetus — the Yale president and faculty defended the prescribed curriculum in a classic and influential report.

The Yale faculty stood ready to repel barbarian innovation. Basil Hall, an English Tory who found little to admire in America, was delighted with the college: "It was extremely agreeable to see so many good old usages and orthodox notions kept up as vigorously . . . as possible. How long the able and zealous professors . . . will be able to stem effectually that deluge of innovation and would-be improvements in doctrine, discipline, and pursuits . . . I cannot pretend to say." Jefferson had a different opinion of conservative professors: "the spirit of that order is to fear and oppose all change, stigmatizing it under the name of innovation, not considering that all improvement is innovation." Still, the Yale faculty knew that change could bring ruin as well as progress, and they feared that reform would result in superficiality.[39]

They believed that the rise of new institutions, usually called academies, threatened to undermine the rigorous character of the liberal arts colleges, which were doing a modest, but important, job thoroughly. In particular, the central position of the classics in the traditional college was under attack because of growing insistence on more "useful" subjects such as surveying and accounting.[40] Cogswell had assailed the academies in an article in *Blackwoods' Edinburgh Review,* asserting that "Americans take a strange delight in high-sounding names, and often satisfy themselves for the want of the thing, by the assumption of a name.

These academies are not always exclusively classical schools; some are partly appropriated to education for the counting room; and as far as this object goes, there is no striking defect in them; it not being a very difficult matter to teach a lad to count his fingers . . . But in . . . classical learning, they are totally deficient." At this time Americans tended to use the terms "seminary," "college," "academy," and "university" interchangeably (though "university" had the greatest prestige). This confusion of terminology betrayed confusion of thought. Names were chosen for prestige, not accuracy. The Yale faculty wanted to give a distinct definition of the character of their college lest it be submerged in the faceless crowd of new institutions. If the public wanted superficial education in the academies, that was its business. But as for Yale, it did not intend to "abandon the ground which, for thirty years past, we have been striving so hard to gain." [41]

It would have been equally absurd for Yale to emulate the German university with its different purposes and incomparably greater resources. "We hope at least that this college may be spared a ludicrous attempt to imitate them, while it is so unprovided with the resources necessary to execute the purpose." Furthermore, parents would never tolerate a college "in which there should not be even an attempt at discipline, farther than to preserve order in the classroom."

If, then, Yale should not try to perform the functions of an academy or a genuine university, what should be its purpose? "The two great points to be gained in intellectual culture," the report stated, "are the discipline and furniture of the mind; expanding its powers, and storing it with knowledge." The professors believed that the mind contained certain faculties which were developed by mental exercise. It was necessary to balance studies to prevent students from becoming mentally musclebound: "Those branches . . . should be prescribed . . . which are best calculated to teach the art of fixing the attention, directing the train of thought, analyzing a subject proposed for investigation; following, with accurate discrimination, the course of argument; balancing . . . evidence . . . awakening . . . the imagination; arranging with skill, the treasures which memory gathers." Such training of the faculties did not complete a student's education but laid *the foundation of a superior education*," whether the student went on to a professional school or continued his self-education. [42]

Adroitly, the Yale "Report" made a virtue of necessity, for it insisted that the subjects best calculated to exercise the faculties were precisely those taught at the college. Thus even if Yale had greater resources, there would have been no reason, in theory, for it to alter its curriculum. It already taught the subjects which were indispensable for mental discipline and for the liberal education of a gentleman. "But why, it is asked, should *all* the students . . . be required to tread in the *same steps?* Why should not each one be allowed to select those branches of study which are most to his taste . . . best adapted to his peculiar talents, and . . . most nearly connected with his intended profession? To this we answer, that our prescribed course contains those subjects only which ought to be understood . . . by everyone who aims at a thorough education."

The Yale faculty also justified other features of the traditional liberal arts college. Creative scholarship was all well and good, but the way to make sure that the student was learning was to assign him a textbook and hear him recite. Only thus "can the responsibility be made sufficiently definite . . . we know of no method which will more effectually bewilder and confound the learner . . . than to refer him to half a dozen authors." Since students were young "and exposed to the untried scenes of temptation, it is necessary that some faithful and affectionate guardian take them by the hand, and guide their steps." Punishment was necessary for those who bit the hand that led them, for there "may be perverse members of a college, as well as of a family." It was inevitable that the student had to plow through "the rugged and cheerless region of elementary learning"; it was inevitable that the college should exercise *"parental superintendence";* but the end justified the means. The well-disciplined college graduate was essential to the republic. "The active, enterprising character of our population, renders it highly important, that this bustle and energy should be directed by sound intelligence . . . When nearly all the ship's crew are aloft, setting the topsails and catching the breezes, it is necessary that there should be a steady hand at the helm." [43]

With many of the opinions of the Yale professors Ticknor would not have quibbled. Like most teachers at the time he believed that exercise of the "faculties" prepared students to think; in fact, one of his objections to the mechanical recitation system at Harvard was precisely that it stultified the "intellectual faculties for purposes of reasoning." Ticknor was too thorough a scholar to wish to dilute the curriculum to meet transitory utilitarian demands. Although "commercial Spanish" like that taught in the academies may have been in Abiel Smith's mind when he founded the Smith Professorship, such a purpose was antithetical to Ticknor's. He believed that a college could serve the community yet retain high scholarly standards. He considered certain subjects so important that they should be prescribed for anyone earning a degree. An ardent classicist, he would have been the last man to desert Latin and Greek, as his friend, the master linguist John Pickering, knew when he wrote to Ticknor ironically about the opponents of the ancient languages: "I do not see but you may dispense with a new Latin professor at Cambridge; and, as to *Greek,* what a lucky man I am to have got rid of the Lexicon as soon as I have! I shall now be better off to keep to the *LAW*." [44]

In what respects, then, did Ticknor disagree with these advocates of the traditional college, whose arguments so closely paralleled those of the conservative Harvard faculty? Basically what he wished to do was to "open up the college," to incorporate the disparate new elements of education at Harvard into a system which would employ existing resources to full advantage. In this way Harvard could profit from models elsewhere "to keep even pace with the increasing demands of the community, without any further alteration in its essential plan." [45] Previously inevitable, the prescribed curriculum was no longer necessary. New subjects, such as modern languages, should not be treated as anomalous accretions but as integral parts of the course of instruction. By 1823 his plans for reform had matured. Now was the time for action.

4. *The Strategy of Reform*

After the "Great Rebellion" of the senior class in the spring of 1823 public interest in Harvard ran high. This disgrace could trigger reform if only someone would take the lead. Leadership of the sort Ticknor wanted was scarce at Harvard. Under the stimulus of Everett and Ticknor, President Kirkland had called in 1818 for changes strikingly like those Ticknor now wanted. "Our institutions for training the young . . . and advancing lettered knowledge, must be expected, like our state of society, to wear a progressive cast," Kirkland had announced, "and be subjects of experiment and change." The president then urged that

Harvard become a true university by enlarging its library, seeking new professorships, and raising its entrance and examination standards. He deprecated, almost in the same words that Ticknor used, "the Procrustes bed of a miscellaneous class, waiting for the idlers and the dunces to catch up," and the fallacy of trying to teach subjects by "repetitions or recitations from a printed text-book." "I am sorely troubled at the loss of time, produced by our system or no system," Kirkland had written Ticknor in 1816.

President Kirkland was ex officio member of the Immediate Government — or resident faculty — the Corporation, and the Overseers, all three of Harvard's governing bodies. Thus he would have been the logical person to lead the reforms he had earlier suggested, but by 1823 Kirkland was preoccupied with the internal problems of the college — especially discipline and funds — and worried about dissension among the faculty and the governing boards. The kindest of men, dignified in manner, so tactful that he could make a reproof sound like a benediction, Kirkland was much loved by the students and faculty and by the powerful men of Boston who had enriched Harvard during his administration. But he was not made to lead in times of stress and strain. He hated controversy, and took pride in the fact that in his days in the pulpit no one could tell for sure whether he was a Unitarian.[46]

If Kirkland would not lead the college into reform, could Ticknor find powerful allies on the faculty? By the summer of 1823 Cogswell and Bancroft were gone. Of the four "new Americans" who had studied at Göttingen, only Everett remained to help Ticknor. Everett had written glowing letters from Germany about the virtues of the continental university and published an article in the *North American Review* in 1820 deprecating the fact that there were no true universities in the United States. Yet Everett — the golden boy who had been told that he resembled a bust of Apollo, who had won early fame as a scholar and preacher, who had made a triumphal tour of Europe — would not lead. Everett's brother-in-law, Charles Francis Adams, later called him "stuff not good enough to wear in rainy weather, though bright enough in sunshine." Accustomed to seeing himself reflected in the mirror of an admiring public, he early decided that a professorship would not satisfy his ambitions. "From the first week of my return here," Everett wrote Judge Story in 1821, "I saw that our university . . . would furnish me little scope . . . The whole pursuit, and the duties it brings with it, are not respectable enough in the estimation they bring with them, and lead one too much in contact with some little men and many little things." Emerson observed that Everett "had no warm personal friends. Yet his genius made every youth his defender and boys filled their mouths with arguments to prove that the orator had a heart." Everett's ambitions lay elsewhere than in reforms at Harvard. Soon he would resign his professorship to go to Congress.[47]

Even after the "Great Rebellion" a majority of the faculty opposed innovation. A few professors shared Ticknor's opinion that change was necessary, although they differed with him on the type of reform required. They did not share his vision of an open university. Andrews Norton and Henry Ware were still alarmed at the moral decay of the college and the public response to the riots: this threatened the prestige of liberal Christianity, already under severe attack from orthodox Christians. In July, 1823, Norton and Ware raised the subject of the college at a religious club to which they and Ticknor belonged, and for three evenings the group heatedly discussed reform. On the fourth night the club members decided to refer the issue of reform to a selected group to meet at Ticknor's house. Ticknor approved this proposal "because some of the members of the club were not, in my estimation, the right persons to discuss it at all." Such a group might give an initial leverage for reform, but one had to be careful not to display Harvard's dirty linen too publicly.[48]

At nine o'clock on the morning of July 23, nine men assembled at Ticknor's house to discuss the destiny of Harvard. At the suggestion of Norton and Ware, no resident instructors were invited, but George B. Emerson and John Gorham Palfrey, who had recently been tutors, were asked to come to provide inside information. Perhaps Norton and Ware believed that a group which did not include resident faculty could be more objective, or that inviting some professors and not others would seem invidious. Whatever the reason, later events proved that the decision to exclude resident faculty members was a tactical mistake. Ticknor and Dr. James Jackson, Hershey Professor of the Theory and Practice of Physick, represented the nonresident professors. Of the other five, four were presently members of the Board of Overseers — Judge Joseph Story, John Pickering, Rev. Charles Lowell, and Richard Sullivan — and Ticknor's legal mentor, William Sullivan, was a former overseer. Judge Prescott and Harrison Gray Otis, both members of the

Corporation, were invited, but had to attend a Corporation meeting on the same day.

From nine in the morning until six at night the discussion at Ticknor's house continued, even through dinner — New Englanders did not come to hasty conclusions. The group had prepared over twenty questions for consideration, but the bulk of the day they spent discussing a clear and ingenious plan for reform which Ticknor had written beforehand. Here at last was a chance for Ticknor to present the ideas which had slowly taken shape in his mind. He was convinced that some of the reforms he had advocated earlier — when he wrote to Prescott about turning Harvard into a good secondary school — were still necessary: better entrance and final examinations; more thorough teaching, especially in the recitations; and stricter and more efficient controls over student conduct.[49]

He added to these suggestions a plan to revise the anachronistic structure of Harvard, to "open up the College." The new demands of the community, the great expansion of knowledge in traditional subjects and the appearance of new academic disciplines, the stimulus of successful schools elsewhere, the inefficient use of Harvard's existing resources — all these, Ticknor declared, made it imperative to alter Harvard's academic organization. This he wished to do through four logically related proposals. The first was to group students in courses by proficiency rather than by the alphabet. This he had suggested earlier, but now he extended the proposal by grouping students solely according to ability, without reference to the college class to which they belonged (i.e., freshman, sophomore, junior, and senior). Second, he advocated that the college be divided into academic departments. Third, he recommended that students be allowed to elect certain courses over and above the minimum of the prescribed curriculum. And last, he believed that Harvard should open its doors to students who were not candidates for a degree but who wished to take certain specialized courses. What he was campaigning for, ultimately, was "the abolition of the classes at College, making the only division in each branch a division according to merit. A minimum could then be fixed for admission; a minimum for a degree; a minimum for the length of time to be passed at college; and a maximum for the choice of studies."

Assignment of students to classes by proficiency would offer advanced placement to able and ambitious students. By existing college regulations students could gain advanced standing in one of the three upper classes by taking examinations on all the books covered in the previous years and by paying additional tuition. But now under Ticknor's proposal a student could earn advanced placement in any subject in which he could show suitable achievement. This was one important way to break up the academic lock step of the uniform curriculum which proceeded pace by pace, college class by college class. Ticknor thought that it would also produce a healthy academic rivalry and help to disintegrate cliques, which created discipline problems. Division according to proficiency was basic to all the other reforms: "it is a plain injustice . . . to give a young man of high powers and active industry no more and no other means of improvement than are given to the idlest and dullest in a class of sixty or seventy . . . it is a right of which no man will permit himself to be easily defeated, when he is afterwards entering into his profession or into the business and interests of the world." Just as Ticknor wanted professors to be paid, in part, according to the number of students they attracted, so he wanted a system of free academic enterprise that would allow the fittest pupils to rise rapidly to the top.

Ticknor believed that division of the college into academic departments would facilitate placement of students in courses by proficiency, since each department could examine students separately. A departmental structure would also encourage the student to study subjects, not simply a textbook, and would allow a more carefully regulated sequence of courses. A requirement that the professors in each field oversee the instruction and assist the tutors in their department would assign clear responsibility "for its management and success." Coupled with rivalry between departments, this would make professorships less of a sinecure. With such a flexible institutional structure the college would be able to add new departments or expand old ones without changing the system. It would also make it easier for part-time or graduate students to obtain a thorough grounding in individual subjects of particular interest or usefulness to them.[50]

In turn, departments would control election of courses. The vast increase in knowledge and the need to prepare students for new types of careers made election of courses necessary, Ticknor told the guests at his house. "It cannot be expected to give more than the most superficial view of the many important subjects even to those who would most gladly investigate them thoroughly; because, they must keep up with the class to which they are bound, and hurry on from a Teacher and a subject to which they have . . . important reasons for being attached, to another teacher and another subject, wherein their present dispositions and final pursuits in life, make it impossible to find any interest." At the same time, students' interest was not the best or the only guide. It was true that the prescribed curriculum "has been carried too far by a persevering adherence to the earliest organization of the College," but in some subjects it has "its peculiar advantages . . . The majority of young men who come to Cambridge, should not be left entirely to themselves to choose what they will study; because they are not competent to judge what will be most important for them."

Here as elsewhere in his blueprint for reform Ticknor advocated compromise: namely to require students to study in some departments and to allow them to elect others. Ticknor and his friends concluded that the indispensable departments "for all who receive the degree of Bachelor of Arts" should be Greek, Latin, moral and political philosophy, rhetoric, mathematics, the physical and exact sciences, and history — those which the Yale faculty had most ardently defended as the backbone of the required curriculum! The elective departments should be Hebrew, chemistry, anatomy and physiology, botany and zoology, mineralogy and geology, applied sciences and modern languages. In addition to prescribing the students' general education, the departments would further restrict the scope of electives. Ticknor believed that if a student chose to study any subject, the department should not allow him to drop it until he had become reasonably proficient. Ticknor would have no dilettantes if he could help it. After his unhappy experience with giving lectures to groups of students over whose admission and performance he had little control, Ticknor would welcome the opportunity as chairman of the Department of Modern Languages to supervise instruction, even though it would increase his own labors.

Eagerly, Ticknor anticipated the day when Harvard would open its doors to large numbers of students who were not candidates for a degree but who desired specialized training. "Let no one come seeking for instruction in vain." A college as well-endowed and large as Harvard "has no apology for . . . embarrassing and restricting its usefulness." "It should open its doors to all; for, if its resources be properly and efficiently applied, it has means of instruction for all." Harvard should place the Commonwealth under obligation, instead of earning a reputation as a school where aristocrats might gain a Mandarin education.

All through his life Ticknor insisted that the opportunity to learn be open to all. He later proposed that Harvard give extension courses in Boston. This plan was not adopted, although he did give public lectures there on his own initiative. There seems little question that Ticknor also hoped that college graduates would come to Cambridge for advanced work in the liberal arts and sciences, since he believed it unfortunate that Americans had to go to Europe for such instruction. At the moment, however, he was chiefly interested in reorganizing the college.[51]

Ticknor's vision of a new Harvard caught the imagination of his guests. Before they left his house at six o'clock they had already planned their strategy. They knew that the Overseers would meet tomorrow. Story would raise the question of reform with them "to have a committee of the Overseers appointed, — if we could compass it, — with full powers to examine into the whole condition of the College. This we knew would be agreeable to Mr. Prescott and Mr. Otis, who thought the work could not be carried on without the intervention of a larger body than the Corporation, and a stronger action of public opinion that such a body could produce." [52]

The Corporation was a self-elected group composed of the President, the Treasurer, and five "Fellows," usually merchants and professional men. Its functions were for the most part those of a board of trustees. This body managed the funds of the college, appointed instructors, and made laws governing the college. All important actions of the Corporation went to the Board of Overseers for final approval. Normally the Overseers took little interest in the day-by-day details of running the college, but it was a large body of influential men who could now shift the balance of public opinion towards reform if it so chose. The Board included fifteen of the most important ministers in the Commonwealth, the Governor and Lieutenant Governor, the Governor's Council, the Senate, the Speaker of the House of Representatives, and fifteen laymen elected by the Overseers — it was a powerful assembly and indicated the mixed private-public character of Harvard at that time.

At the meeting of the Overseers on July 24, 1823, Judge Story and his allies called for an inquiry into the college. After discussion the Overseers elected Story, Charles Lowell, Richard Sullivan, Henry Ware, and three others to constitute a committee to examine the university and report at the next session what changes, if any, the Overseers should recommend to the Corporation. The committee was packed with Ticknor's friends — advocates of reform — and the ubiquitous Story, whose cherubic face and flowing conversation belied his canniness, was, of course, chosen chairman. Shortly he would appear on the Corporation at just the right time to stiffen the backbone of that group.[53]

On May 4, 1824, after consulting with a subcommittee of the Corporation, the Story committee made its report. Almost all of Ticknor's proposals were there: talk of "the spirit of the age," the need to change an antiquated system, grouping of students by proficiency, the departmental system, elective courses, more thorough teaching, and admission of candidates not seeking a degree — almost in Ticknor's own words. But despite a tactful introduction, the tone of the report, in parts, resembled a memo to stockholders of a cotton mill on plans to make the mill operate more efficiently, especially ways to get more work from the superintendent, foremen, and operatives. The president, said Story, "shall be the real, effective Head of the University, having general superintendence of all its concerns . . . complete visitatorial authority with respect to . . . the Professors . . . an independent and responsible negative upon all the acts and proceedings of the other Boards and Departments in the University." Like the president, the professors were to tighten things in their own domains, supervising instructors under them and making quarterly and annual reports. Some officer of the college was supposed to visit the room of every student at nine o'clock in the evening, to make sure he was there and not misbehaving.[54]

Story admitted, at the close of his report, that some "of the proposed alterations may be thought in some degree to affect the real or imaginary rights of some of the Professors . . . It is far from . . . [the committee's] wish to give any pain or uneasiness to any of these gentlemen, or to forget that scrupulous delicacy, which their situation demands." No doubt Story was getting word of grumblings in Cambridge. President Kirkland sat on the report for two months and returned it without comment, but privately he was unhappy about the inquiry. One of the members of the Story committee, John Pickering, wrote Ticknor that Kirkland thought the failure of one of its meetings "a good joke against us" and added, with a conspiratorial air, that the "lead must be taken by some Boston men whose property and rank give them the influence necessary to effect something useful, or will secure them (in case of ill-success) against the unpleasant consequences to which persons in different circumstances would be exposed . . . for myself, I ought not, in duty to my children, to hazard the consequences of being held up as the leader of a faction." [55]

Kirkland and Pickering might not want to speak up, but Andrews Norton was not one to mince words. Stiff and fine-grained as an oak, he gave a speech before the Overseers in which he tried to express the frustration, puzzlement, and anger of the resident faculty at the endless inquiries and proposals for reform. He was in favor of raising the moral tone of the college but not in favor of major changes imposed by outsiders. Between the May and June meetings of the Overseers in 1824 he printed a pamphlet primarily opposing not the idea of reform, for he had long advocated changes, but the manner in which change was being foisted on a reluctant faculty. Norton held that the system of minute inspections and reports, of a presidential veto on faculty decisions, would only create a despotic bureaucracy "foreign from the whole spirit which breathes around us in our republican habits and institutions; and is such as no man of proper feelings would submit to, unless the necessity of a family compelled him to make a choice between different duties, his duty to himself and his duty to those dependent upon him." It was like being served a notice of "compulsory good behavior." The Story report gives "no settled and distinct conception of the character which it is proposed to give to the College." If it should be a university, why the minute superintendence of students? If a high school, then why admit advanced students, or admit no student under the age of sixteen? "No error is more likely to be prejudicial than a rash adoption of modes of education which have been found to work elsewhere, without regard to the peculiar circumstances of the institution in which they are copied."

Partly as a result of Norton's slashing attack on Story's report, the Overseers voted after public debate in the Senate chamber on June 1, 1824, to appoint another committee to look into the condition of the college and to compile a report which would be examined, together with the Story report, at the next meeting of the Overseers on January 6, 1825. [56]

Another reason for postponing action on the Story report was a related new issue raised by the faculty: their right to be Fellows of the Harvard Corporation. They were upset about all this innovation without representation. After all, they were still the persons who had to teach the students, trap them in the Yard at night with their black lanterns, and break up riots in the sophomore mess at University Hall. Norton had mentioned one day to Everett his opinion that only resident teachers should be members of the Corporation. Shortly afterwards Everett replied that he had discovered some legal papers in the president's office convincing him that a Corporation composed of laymen "was not only an impropriety but a Usurpation." [57] The battle was on.

During the early years of Harvard it was assumed that the Fellows of the Corporation would normally be regular faculty members, as in the English universities. But in time practice changed, and by the 1820's the natural course of events would have been to elect a non-teacher to the vacancy that occurred in 1823. Tired of being pushed around, nine of the resident faculty joined Norton and Everett in presenting a memorial to the Corporation in the spring of 1824. In this statement they claimed that only resident faculty were rightfully eligible for the Corporation. In this plea and in pamphlets published by Norton and Everett the faculty expressed their deep sense of concern over the erosion of their prestige and autonomy. When the Corporation declined jurisdiction over such a radical move, the resident faculty took their case to the Overseers. [58]

Norton now suggested, in effect, that the Corporation should be abolished, with the Immediate Government, or key faculty, running the college and the Overseers exercising a general supervision on behalf of the public. This would remove the imputation, he said, that the faculty is incapable of running its own business since a lay corporation does this instead: the members of the Corporation presently "are . . . [the college's] governors. The resident instructors have been called their servants; and the name, perhaps, may express the relation which naturally exists between these two bodies; but certainly does not correspond to the state of things which ought to exist." If the resident faculty had total responsibility, and were not beset by outsiders, their pride would demand that they constantly improve the college. As it was, the low status of professors discouraged men of the highest talents. The best way to reform the college, Norton insisted, was to dignify the office of teacher. Instead, the Story committee bypassed faculty "without asking even for their cooperation, which, on the contrary, has been treated as something to be carefully shunned. It would be a strange anomaly, if it were not for the consistency with the whole course of things for some time past." Teachers don't meddle with merchants' affairs; why do merchants assume that they are experts in education? In his peroration to the Overseers Norton cried out, "You, surely, will not suffer this most important institution, intrusted to your care, to be irregularly acted upon by uncertain or accidental impulses from without; you, surely, will not suffer to be forced on its governors or instructers, any new theoretical system, the work of unauthorized, unapparent, irresponsible individuals, however respectable they may be." [59] This last remark may well have been aimed at Ticknor, as well as at Story and his committee and the Corporation. Norton now probably realized that excluding resident faculty from the meeting at Ticknor's house had been a strategic mistake.

The issue was now drawn; the immediate question was not what reforms, but who should direct the reforms, if any. Appropriately, both Story's report and the issue of faculty representation on the Corporation came up at the same time before the Overseers. On January 6, 1825, the Board of Overseers accepted Story's report, embodying most of Ticknor's basic reforms, rather than Lowell's committee report, which contained only the small changes the faculty wanted. The next blow to the faculty came on February 4, the day after Norton and Everett had made a lengthy and eloquent plea for the right of the resident faculty to sit on the Corporation. At that time the Board of Overseers voted unanimously against the faculty's legal and moral contention, and resolved that it was not expedient "to express any opinion on the subject of future elections" to the Corporation.[60]

By now Ticknor saw that he had helped to open Pandora's box by turning to the Overseers a year and a half ago. In February of 1825 he sent a description of the present state of college affairs to Daniel Webster and Joseph Story which showed "in what an awkward position we stand." The next month he confided to Jefferson that "there is a good deal of difference of opinion between the different boards . . . and this is likely, I fear to produce more and more bitterness. I am much afraid, that for a long time, we shall not be able to put things in the condition we desire." Nonetheless, the Corporation and the Overseers finally agreed in June, 1825, to a new set of laws embodying at least the germ of each of Ticknor's key ideas: grouping by proficiency, the departmental system, the admission of candidates not seeking a degree, and at least a beginning at an elective system. Ticknor also welcomed a shortening of vacations and other regulations affecting discipline.

In an eloquent pamphlet called *Remarks on Changes Lately Proposed or Adopted in Harvard University,* Ticknor reviewed the causes of dissatisfaction with the college and defended the new laws. Later he claimed that this pamphlet had "tenderly explained and a good deal smoothed over" the real defects of Harvard, but at the time it was a bombshell. The newspapers largely agreed with Ticknor's diagnosis and prescription. The *Boston Courier* of October 27, 1827, applauded his *Remarks* and added that:

It is true, we have been able, from having noticed the frequent appearance of students at the theatre and their feats of horsemanship in the streets of Boston — from the apparent leisure and unconcern with which the President and Professors visit our metropolis . . . from the bill of performances on commencement days — we say, from these circumstances, we apprehend that we have been able to form a tolerably accurate conjecture of the discipline, mode of instruction, and progress in literature and science which gave Harvard College a claim to be considered the first literary institution of the country, and rendered it the object of never-ceasing munificence of a rich state and still richer individuals.[61]

Little wonder that some of Ticknor's colleagues thought him a traitor in their ranks. In a powerful counterblast to Everett and Norton in his *Remarks* Ticknor defended the new laws and attacked the notion that resident teachers should compose the Corporation. Not only on legal grounds — with a brief ably prepared by Judge Story, Daniel Webster, and Judge Prescott — but also on grounds of expediency, Ticknor maintained that it was improper to recruit the Fellows from the resident teachers. "Such a body of men would hardly fail, in the course of a few generations, to make a college, as much, and as truly a monopoly for their own benefit, as any thing in the English universities." The college "already has a clear and purchased right to all the time, all the powers, and all the experience of its resident teachers." As influential men of affairs eager to advance Harvard, lay Fellows could serve its interests in the wider community.[62]

Ticknor was obviously deaf to the *cri de coeur* of his colleagues who feared becoming hirelings dictated to by meddlers. Ironically, Ticknor had recognized that German professors profited from their freedom from outside dictation, and that the chancellor of the university could do little or nothing without the active support of professors. Firmly convinced that an impetus from outside the college was needed to push reforms through a myopic faculty, he had underestimated the frustration, annoyance, and saboteurs' skill of the Harvard teachers. With what Longfellow called "his confounded positive way about everything," he had assumed that the patient would swallow the doctor's prescription, but he was sadly disappointed.[63]

5. *Sabotage*

"They want to legislate," President Kirkland commented sadly to Jared Sparks about the governing boards, "that professors shall be amiable, tutors popular, and students loving, but these things are above legislation." Although the president and instructors might by compelled to comply with the forms of this new Harvard — quarterly and yearly reports, stricter examinations, police work, and all the other tedious duties — they could hardly be expected to embrace the reforms with enthusiasm. Why shouldn't the resident instructors resent Ticknor? Aloof in Boston, far from the scene of riots, Ticknor was advocating that college officers visit the rooms of students daily. He was calling for thorough teaching, as if this was not what they had been doing all along. He was applauding shorter vacations — abridging their freedom. He was insulting their examinations as a "miserable farce." He was siding with laymen of the Corporation and claiming that if professors were Fellows, Harvard might become as corrupt as Oxford and Cambridge. With his abundant free time, his fine education, and his resources, Ticknor might be a scholar; but what good did it do to talk of a philosophical approach, of scholarly research, if a professor was chained to a pedagogical treadmill? Besides, most of the Harvard faculty probably agreed with the rationale of the Yale "Report," and accepted the view of Professor Ware that the purpose of Harvard College was to provide a "general cultivation of the faculties and an elementary knowledge of many things preparatory to future usefulness." [64]

Stripped of the ability to make laws themselves, the professors became adept at sabotaging the laws passed by the Corporation. Ticknor had hoped that if the new laws were "carried through with alacrity, perseverance, and energy by the officers to whom they are now committed

. . . [they would] do much to raise the tone of the higher branches of education among us." Instead he bitterly watched his reforms ruined. "Ticknor (tho' you may not now be able to believe it)," Edward Everett wrote to his brother, "is surcharged with gall." [65]

The division of classes by proficiency — which Ticknor called the "broad cornerstone for beneficial changes" — proved instead the rock upon which the reforms were shattered. Ticknor's friend, the Overseer Richard Sullivan, had warned him of this: "I have heard but one opinion from gentlemen entitled to attention and that in favor of a subdivision according to merit. Most of them, however, think it inexpedient to attempt it at present — they fear that it would disaffect the mass of parents and scholars and injure the college." A unanimous petition of the freshman class in 1823 had forced Bancroft to abandon his practice of sectioning according to ability in his Greek classes. In the first year of the new laws, 1825–26, an unsympathetic professor did not have to stretch himself to make the practice unpopular: Professor Hayward, for instance, tried to undermine the law by making an unpleasant show of dividing his classes and then assigning identical lessons to each. Later he changed his tack for fear of losing his job when he learned "the Corporation were acting with determination"; and, by following Ticknor's example of adjusting the work load to the capacity of students, he obtained successful results. But division according to proficiency became only "an odious farce," Ticknor complained, because the instructors made it so. The plan would have increased their labors and apparently struck them as an invidious intrusion upon their familial institution. Apathetic professors also sabotaged the departmental system, Ticknor held, because they shirked the "laborious, anxious, and trouble-some duty" of being active chairmen. Only in modern languages had these two reforms succeeded, since only there were they fairly tested. The policy of admitting candidates who did not desire a degree fared little better, for "the young men who have entered on this plan, have been so trammeled, that the whole amounts to nothing." [66]

Caught in the midst of this academic civil war, President Kirkland became sick of controversy. Although he had been given new powers by the Corporation to superintend instruction and to lead reform, he straddled the fence, neither openly supporting nor opposing the reforms. Ticknor had foreseen Kirkland's inertia when he wrote to Story that he believed "that this Report will give the President all possible opportunities and means to make the College what you desire. Your plan is not laid down so distinctly but that it *may* still be made something quite different. Perhaps, it is better the whole matter should thus be left to rest finally with him, and he be held responsible for the result." Beset by watchdogs on the Corporation and the Overseers, beleaguered by complaints of parents, students, and faculty, feeling old and rheumatic, Kirkland sighed to Sparks "with his accustomed good humor, 'Ah, these senators' chairs, they are not so easy to sit in, as some people think.'" Ticknor's constant criticisms of Harvard, and his praise of other schools, finally drove the exasperated president to beg him to communicate his opinions "with as little of direct reflection on what has been done or proposed by others as you think you can justify to yourself." [67]

Resentment against Ticknor mushroomed in Cambridge. When the Corporation started a drive for economy at Harvard, Ticknor offered to resign. Kirkland "let fall a word or two which . . . [indicated] that he was hostile to Professor Ticknor, and that he would willingly have accepted his resignation." When the resident faculty were asked how expenses could be cut, they suggested that the salaries of nonresident professors be reduced and that Ticknor be required to give elementary instruction in French and Spanish — a suggestion which they knew he would abhor.[68]

Ticknor found an aggressive new ally on the Corporation in 1826 in the newly elected Nathaniel Bowditch. Ticknor and Bowditch were convinced that Kirkland had manipulated the college to defeat the reforms. Bowditch accused the president of duplicity in speaking favorably of subdivision of classes according to merit to friends of the measure while working secretly with the faculty to repeal it. Once, as a meeting of the Corporation was ending, and Bowditch had on his overcoat and was waiting together with the other members of the Corporation in the entry, "the President observed, — Gentlemen, as there is now a meeting of the Corporation, we may as well decide on the business of the abolition of the division of the classes into sections. I inquired what this meant, supposing from the manner in which this had been introduced it was some trifling affair, and found that the President had made up his mind fully that the very important step of the division of the classes according to proficiency, which had been so fully argued before the Overseers . . . ought to be abolished." Bowditch noted that

Judge Story, the most forceful advocate of the measure, was missing from that meeting of the Corporation, and concluded that it all "had the appearance of *management* to decide on it in *his absence*." Bitterly, Ticknor wrote in his "Report to the Overseers on the State of the University for the Academical Year 1825–26" that "those who have the management of College involve its affairs in as much mystery as possible." [69]

The whole attempt to reform Harvard had been dispiriting. After avoiding politics because of his dislike for contention, Ticknor found himself embroiled in academic infighting. The life of the scholar was not so aloof and impartial as he had hoped. His friend James Marsh, soon to become an equally disillusioned reformer at the University of Vermont, expressed his regret that the dispute "should have occasioned so unnecessary a disturbance in your social and literary circle." Marsh was referring to the hostility which had arisen between Ticknor and his friends Everett, Norton, and Jared Sparks. To Everett, who had deserted Harvard for a seat in the Congress in 1825, Ticknor was barely civil. With Sparks he wouldn't speak, for Sparks — as editor of the *North American Review* — had solicited his article on the college controversy (later published as the *Remarks*) only to reject it because it seemed too one-sided. Sparks was loyal to his friend President Kirkland, who had subsidized him when he was a poor student at Harvard. Alexander Everett was shocked to learn that Ticknor had stopped contributing articles to the *North American Review* and was writing instead for a Philadelphia journal, the *American Quarterly*: "This is owing I suppose to your Brouilleries with Sparks and Edward; but I see not why you should allow them to influence your public proceedings. We are all laborers in literature as well as politics for the honor of Old New England . . . There is no harm in pouting a little occasionally provided you make up before you do each other or the public any mischief." But Ticknor never again wrote an article for the *North American Review,* nor did he soon forgive his grudges against his former friends.[70]

Disgusted with the fate of reform in the college as a whole, Ticknor was reduced to cultivating his departmental garden. This he did with consummate skill until his retirement in 1835. Even after the rest of the faculty had abandoned division by proficiency and after the departmental system elsewhere had rusted away, he continued to demonstrate what could be done by true believers. In his "Report for 1825–26" he boasted that 227 students out of a possible 240 had elected to take modern languages, and had thrived in classes grouped according to ability. The fastest freshmen had read 500 pages more than the slowest, and in a carefully organized and supervised sequence of course students advanced to Cervantes, Molière, Dante, and Goethe. Ticknor thought that the success of the modern language department vindicated the new laws.[71]

6. *The End of the Kirkland Era*

Ticknor concluded this acid annual report on a note of financial concern. He pointed out that Harvard had ended the year with the alarming deficit of $4,182 and that the number of students was declining. Harvard's "funds and means are to be administered chiefly for the benefit of the publick," he warned, "and not chiefly for the benefit of the incumbents in its offices." An investigation of college finances next year, led by the supreme calculator Nathaniel Bowditch, revealed shocking inefficiency in the management of college funds. Kirkland, who was just emerging from academic battles, now confronted the implacable Bowditch and the "Salem administration," a Corporation dominated by two Salem men, Story and Bowditch.

The legislature's refusal to renew its $10,000 yearly appropriation had ended the days of easy financial virtue, when accounts could be approximate and the president could slip a few dollars to needy students — and to some not so needy, according to Bowditch — out of general funds. Slipshod accounting was heresy to the self-made Bowditch, who disliked the fashionable tone of the school as well. Like Ticknor, he suspected that the college was a nest of sinecures. When he discovered that the treasurer, Judge Davis, and the steward, Stephen Higginson, were as lax with money as Kirkland, he pursued them with inquiries and accusations until they resigned. Bowditch discovered that Kirkland owed the college substantial sums; that Davis had made errors in his accounts amounting to $120,000; and that Higginson had lost $21,000 worth of receipts. These disclosures did not surprise Ticknor. Now he hoped that the exposure of cronyism and sloppy administration might clear the way for wiser use of the college's resources.[72]

In the feud between Kirkland and Bowditch, public sympathy was on Kirkland's side, hard common sense on Bowditch's. Kirkland's liberality, now under attack, had permitted Everett and Bancroft to study abroad and Ticknor to collect books for the Harvard library. The achievements of Kirkland's presidency had been signal: he had strengthened the professional schools; he had added fifteen professorships to the ten existing in 1810 when he took office; he had helped to raise the funds for the library, scientific collections, and University and Holworthy Halls; and he had won the deep esteem and affection of generations of students, alumni, and friends of Harvard. What did it matter if he kept records of the Corporation meetings in an undecipherable scrawl on odd-shaped bits of paper — when he kept records at all? What did it matter if he forgot to inform Chief Justice Marshall of the award of an honorary degree? What did it matter if he tried to cancel afternoon chapel so that he could eat dinner at three o'clock with friends in Boston? These were amiable faults, or so it seemed to his friends. When Kirkland resigned in the spring of 1828 under pressure from Bowditch, it shocked many.[73]

Kirkland's resignation followed an affair involving both Bowditch and Ticknor. Ticknor had petitioned the Corporation to allow him to use the top floor of Hollis Hall for his department. Kirkland refused to support Ticknor's request when a student who occupied one of the rooms swore at the janitor sent to evict him, saying "that he would be d----d if he would move." This was the last straw for Bowditch. He criticized Kirkland sharply. Kirkland's wife, "a masterful Cabot," prompted her husband to resign. Rumor spread — and was denied by Bowditch — that "the Salem sailor" had called Kirkland *imbecile, and unfit for his office, and that if he had any regard for his own dignity he would resign.* The public press denounced Bowditch and called for his resignation; John Sibley recorded in his journal the common opinion that he was "only a man of dollars and cents" who had bullied the sickly and lovable Kirkland. But another man of dollars and cents, who knew how to run a profitable cotton mill, Amos Lawrence, reflected that where "a good-natured carelessness is apparent in the head, the subordinates are likely to become equally so, and no institution can sustain for a great length of time, such want of fidelity in the person who administers it." Finally the excitement died down, partly dampened by Bowditch's threat to publish his manuscript, "College History" — which revealed incredible mismanagement — if the malicious rumors were to continue.[74]

Now the choice of the next president became an important topic of conversation around Boston and Cambridge dinner tables. Everett, who made it his business to know about such matters, wrote Sparks that the Corporation was "strongly disposed to choose Mr. Ticknor," but that the Overseers preferred "another candidate" (himself). He told his brother that the "public sentiment is very strong" against Ticknor. "I believe that the contest is supposed to be between T.'s friends and mine . . . An attempt will, I think, be made to remodel the edifice, so as to unfit it for any body but him." Cambridge gossip, Ann Storrow told Sparks, had it that the Corporation was delaying the choice of a new president in order to prepare the public mind for Ticknor. Charlotte Everett confessed to her husband that "I have but one reason for wishing you to have the place — that is a most malicious and wicked one — it is merely to torment Ticknor, who means if possible to be Pres. himself." [75]

Tasting the prestige of politics for the first time, Everett had no desire to return to the maelstrom at Harvard. Ticknor hoped for an administration friendly to reform — he wrote to Bancroft just before Kirkland's resignation that "nothing beyond preparation for change can be made while the present administration continues, but the preparation is making with diligence and the changes will certainly follow." In July of 1828 he wrote to Nicholas Biddle that the likely candidates for the presidency were Edward Everett, Cogswell, John Pickering, and "one or two Unitarian clergymen." His unhappy embroilment in academic politics thus far seemed to have choked any ambition he might once have had to be president. He knew that he would have faced a faculty hostile to his ideas, and, to an extent, to himself personally. "Sally has heard that T. has disclaimed being a candidate," Everett wrote in September to his brother Alexander.[76]

In the end bluff old Josiah Quincy was chosen president — an energetic and efficient man not committed to any particular faction. Quincy was a striking contrast to Kirkland. A lawyer, former Congressman, former mayor of Boston, he was primarily an administrator, not a paternal and kindly minister and gentleman of letters. Abrupt in manner, he could never remember students' names. "Old Quincy, with all his worth and a sort of violent service he did the College, was a lubber and a grenadier among our clerks," Emerson said. Judge Story wrote Ticknor in February of 1829 that "the choice of Quincy goes well (I hear) with the public. It is an evidence of the discernment of good men, and justifies a reliance on their good faith in perilous times. I doubt not that he will make an energetic, firm, and honest President . . . I take it for granted, that he is a stout reformer." [77]

He was indeed a stout reformer; but he moved in quite a different direction from the thrust of Ticknor's reforms, although he liked and respected Ticknor and gave him autonomy in his own department. He riveted a "Scale of Merit" system on the college which made the recitations even more mechanical. Every recitation was marked on a scale of eight and every declamation and written exercise was graded on a multiple of eight, with suitable deductions for absences. Quincy took great pride in auditing weekly all instructors' accounts of the students' performance. So obnoxious was the grading system that Richard Henry Dana, Jr., was delighted when his participation in a student rebellion resulted in his rustication to Andover: "I can hardly describe the relief I felt at getting rid of the exciting emulation for college rank, and at being able to study and recite for the good of my own mind, not for the sixes, sevens, and eights, which, at Cambridge, were put against every word that came out of a student's mouth." He dreaded his return to Harvard "as a slave whipped to his dungeon." This mechanical accounting further increased the distance between students and faculty to the point where "if a student conversed at all with the tutor, he was suspected of *fishing,* and would be hissed by the class." [78]

Under Quincy, however, students gradually gained a greater degree of choice of courses, particularly in the modern languages. Ticknor and his staff of four instructors flourished; students now had a choice of French, Spanish, German, Italian, and Portuguese. Ticknor was proud that during his fifteen years as a professor he never presented a student's name to the faculty for reproof and that he was never late to a class.

When he resigned in 1835, he was not sorry to leave Harvard. He had found an eminent successor in Henry Wadsworth Longfellow. His attempts to reform Harvard had helped to stimulate similar ventures elsewhere — James Marsh's innovations at the University of Vermont, and his friend Francis Wayland's later reforms at Brown, for example. However, no attempt to create universities in the European sense was successful in the period before the Civil War. Yet Ticknor and his fellow reformers paved the way for the revolution in higher education after the Civil War. As Daniel Coit Gilman testified at Johns Hopkins: "We begin our work . . . after costly ventures of which we reap the lessons, while others bear the loss." [79]

Sooner or later, many of Ticknor's friends also left college teaching. After an experience in Europe that taught them what scholarship could be, Everett, Cogswell, Bancroft, and Longfellow all found academic life in America of slight prestige, poorly paid, boring, and frustrating. All of them found other careers more attractive, whether in politics and diplomacy, in library work, or as independent men of letters. Ticknor found no reason to regret his resignation from Harvard when he received a vivid account of the fate of his successor, Longfellow, as head of the Department of Modern Languages:

Meanwhile I sit here at home, and do the things you wot of; — namely go up the stone-steps of University Hall, darkening the door of No 5 on summer mornings . . . The four-fold team of instructors jogs on its wonted pace; — but during yr absence the harness got very much out of order. The young men treat Surault, as the frogs did King Log: they leap upon him — run over him; and he, fat lord says nought but 'My friend, my friend! — go on — go on!' meaning, with the lesson. — with ancient Sales it is hardly otherwise; except that the language of expostulation is changed to 'My soul! — By George!' As to Bokun (the Portuguese word is Boquim — signifying the mouthpiece of a wind instrument.) I fear matters go still worse with him. He stalks up and down the room, braying, and switching his books with a small black cane, — the students laughing all the while, and trying to persuade him to sing the Ranz des Vaches in *Deutsch* . . . The President frequently honors my lectures with his presence; and as soon as I begin, he gives his spectacles three whirls (you remember the gesture) and then falls into a deep sleep, highly flattering to the lecturer, and highly conductive to decorum among the students.[80]

Academic life in America did not realize the hopes of these evangelists of culture at Harvard. "The force of the new impulse did not last long," James Russell Lowell reminisced of this period. "It was premature, the students were really school boys, and the college was not yet capable of the larger university life. The conditions of American life, too, were such that young men looked upon scholarship neither as an end nor as a means, but simply as an accomplishment." Perhaps the worst side of teaching, Longfellow confided in his journal, "is this having your mind constantly a play-mate for boys — constantly adapting itself to them; instead of stretching out, and grappling with men's minds." [81]

When Ticknor accepted the Smith Professorship in 1817, he intended to make it his life's work. In one sense he fulfilled this intention, for after 1835 his scholarly career ran in grooves originally set by the requirements of his chair. He would probably never have written a history of Spanish literature had he not first gone to Spain to prepare himself to teach at Harvard. People still called him "Professor Ticknor" after his resignation; and for young intellectuals he continued to be a model of the gentleman of letters, "one who had deliberately chosen the pursuit of literature, rather than yield to the allurements of a life of unprofitable leisure, or to those of a more lucrative profession." [82]

In 1818 Kirkland had declared that we "cannot fail to wish that our country may produce fruit of the mind, and besides now and then a rare genius, have authors and books of her own — fine, chaste writers, historians whom all the world should read, sweet poets, and sensible critics." Then might America produce more than an "unsanctified, Carthaginian, perishable prosperity." Many years later, with the benefit of hindsight, Thomas Wentworth Higginson claimed that Ticknor, Everett, and Cogswell had "helped to break up that intellectual sterility which had begun to show itself during the isolation of a merely colonial life; they prepared the way for the vast modern growth of colleges, schools, and libraries in this country, and indirectly helped the birth of a literature which gave us Irving, Cooper, Bryant, and the 'North American Review'; and culminated later in the brilliant Boston circle of authors, almost all of whom were Harvard men, and all of whom felt the Harvard influence." Was it not true that they had in fact helped to produce "historians whom the world should read, sweet poets, and sensible critics"? Despite the failure of his institutional reforms, Ticknor had done his best as a professor to awaken Carthage.[83]

IV

The True Uses of Literature

Literature is plainly among the most powerful methods of exalting the character of a nation, of forming a better race of men, in truth, it may claim first rank among the means of improvement. *William Ellery Channing*[1]

"What have we Americans to do with what is merely curious, or merely critical, in the arts, and sciences, and attainments of Europe?" asked young Josiah Quincy at the Harvard Commencement in 1821. The question posed by Ticknor's brilliant student was one which Ticknor had himself asked and had attempted to answer in his lectures at Harvard. Quincy proved an apt pupil: "We have here, a new world to cultivate, and to elevate . . . When we Americans go forth into the elder world, either in fact, or speculation, let us seek to transplant, not what is merely new, or merely striking, but what is wanting, and what is useful. To us, Europe, and all its arts, and all its accomplishments, are nothing, except by way of example, or stimulus; as they teach us what to seek, and what to shun, in morals or in intellect."[2]

"What to seek, and what to shun, in morals or in intellect" — this was precisely Ticknor's chief concern as professor and author. In 1816 he had decided that "men of letters can work on their contemporaries only in two ways — as publick teachers — or as writers." After his resignation from Harvard in 1835 he continued to serve as interpreter of the Old World to the New, in part through his *History of Spanish Literature,* which was published in 1849. Both in his teaching at Harvard and in his monumental study of Spanish culture Ticknor addressed himself to an issue which fascinated his literary generation: the rise and fall of great literary empires. This was a subject bound to interest Americans eager to establish a cultural identity commensurate with their political achievement and aspirations.

In Ticknor's day there was no clear distinction between civil and literary history, and as literary historian Ticknor never doubted that there was an ineluctable bond between literature and civil welfare. This was the theme of his lectures at Harvard on French and Spanish literature and the leitmotif of his *History*. Although Ticknor discussed French and Spanish writers and their works in great detail, the purpose of his studies was the revelation of the national characters and institutions of the two nations. New England historians who wrote civil history — especially the great quartet William Hickling Prescott, George Bancroft, John Lothrop Motley, and Francis Parkman — regarded themselves as general men of letters. Prescott began his career by writing literary criticism and was about to write a history of Italian literature when his attention was drawn to the reign of Ferdinand and Isabella; Bancroft wrote poetry and reviewed literature; Motley and Parkman wrote novels. After reading Prescott, Thackeray complained to Ticknor that it "is a shame of these historians taking the bread out of the mouths of us *other* romancers. Give me Hallam — he does not degrade history by making her amusing." To these Americans history was itself a major branch of belles lettres. In this sense, Ticknor and these four mid-century New Englanders were all "literary" historians, all men of letters as much as the poet or novelist. But more than this, their basic concern was the course of empire: in their hands history became a mode of ethical discourse.[3]

While in Madrid in 1818, Ticknor wrote Jefferson that his purpose in studying French and Spanish literature was to acquire "general, philosophical notions on the genius and history of each of these literatures." These "notions," which informed his lectures on French and Spanish culture, were a curious mixture of critical, political, and moral principles learned both at home and abroad. Ticknor believed that each nation had a distinct literature which reflected its social, political, and religious condition. To be lastingly significant this literature must embody the character of the people, not a faction or the court. Certain great writers, representative men, expressed the prominent and poetic national traits; they "live more in the solitude of their own fancies and feelings than in the society by which they are surrounded, and go forth from the midst of the popular character, strong in all its prevalent attributes, yet soiled with none of its infirmities." It was the duty of the literary historian, Ticknor believed, to pass moral judgment on authors and the society they represent. The standards by which

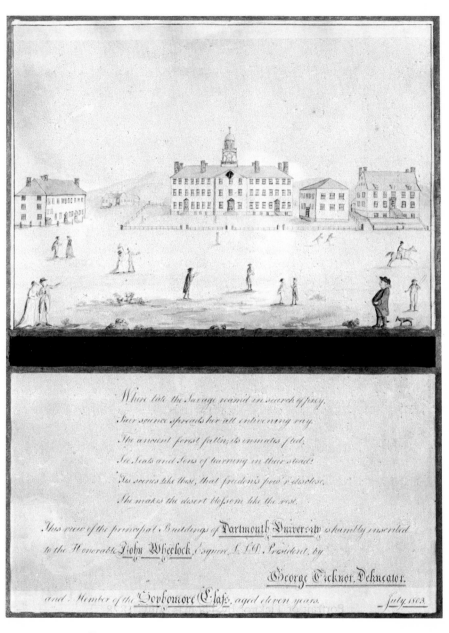

George Ticknor's watercolor of Dartmouth, 1803

Portrait of Ticknor by Thomas Sully, 1828

Portrait of Ticknor by G. P. A. Healy, 1848

Harvard in 1828

Harvard in 1821

Ticknor's library

Park Street in 1858, with Ticknor's house in foreground

Daniel Webster

William Hickling Prescott

George Stillman Hillard

Ticknor's daughter,
Anna Eliot Ticknor

George Ticknor in 1867

they should be appraised were those of a decorous republicanism and a chaste protestantism — the values of a Boston which still regarded itself as a model for mankind.[4]

French and Spanish literature provided Ticknor with apt subjects for literary and political allegory, since in Ticknor's view Spain and France were cultural corpses. The genesis and decay of these great empires revealed grave flaws, despotisms of the right and of the left. Ticknor dealt implicitly with questions which nagged American writers of his generation. They asked what could be the distinctive characteristics of American literature, how could this literature begin, what critical standards should be applied to it. In his lectures and writings Ticknor yoked civil weal or woe with literature and illustrated the downfall of France and Spain. Thus he presented to his countrymen not only the problem of how to create a national culture, but also how to arrest its decay, to achieve a ripeness that was not ominous.

The dream of an American Augustan age persisted. Yet, as in the earlier quarrels in the little literary republic of the Anthology Society, men were by no means agreed on principles of criticism. When Ticknor returned to Boston in 1819, the donnish style and provincial notions of his old mentor John Gardiner were fast becoming outmoded. Ticknor admired Wordsworth and Goethe, Scott and Chateaubriand. His professors at Göttingen had robbed the eighteenth-century English and French writers of much of their luster. Yet Ticknor's tastes still inclined to symmetry, common sense, and decorum in literature as in life. Ticknor was fascinated with Walter Scott's comely daughter Sophia; he summed up her virtues this way: "There is nothing romantic about her, for she is as perfectly right-minded as I ever saw one so young." [5]

This desire to be sensitive to new currents of thought and writing — yet polished and "right-minded" — to be learnedly cosmopolitan yet distinctively American, produced tension in Ticknor's literary world. He and his fellow men of letters — men like Prescott, Longfellow, William Ellery Channing, James Hillhouse, Richard Henry Dana, Sr., Andrews Norton, Edward Channing, Edward Everett, and others — explored for themselves the ambiguities of being an American author speaking English and steeped in European culture. Believing in the interdependence of letters and morality, they were cautious not to introduce literary innovations which might disrupt clear religious and moral conventions or sound political doctrine. Didactic and genteel in manner, they nonetheless imported new ways of thinking, careful to point out to their audience "what to seek and what to shun." They wished to act as an informal American Academy which would set standards of taste and propriety, but they lived to regret some of their handiwork when they saw their unruly pupils, the Transcendentalists. Thus the work of Ticknor and his friends constituted an important transition in the history of American letters: an effort to create a literature which was national but not offensive to an essentially provincial literary taste, and a desire to respond to some of the "romantic" impulses of the times while remaining "right-minded" in approach.

1. *Literary History as Allegory: The Case of France*

By the time Ticknor began his lectures on French and Spanish literature at Harvard, the premises of literary nationalism were widely accepted on both sides of the Atlantic. The quest for a distinctively American literature was fast becoming a cliché in the pages of the *North American Review*. Ticknor was only one of many New England intellectuals — many of whom had never traveled abroad — who were familiar with the nationalistic criticism of Madame de Staël and the Schlegels. His own interest in the relation of national character and literature had ripened before he attended Bouterwek's lectures on literary history at Göttingen. In 1816 he wrote in his commonplace book a list of the dominant traits of each of the major countries of Europe and added that these "characteristics of the six great nations of Modern Europe have never as far as I know been traced with distinctness in any way, and least of all in their influence on literature." In 1817, however, when he heard Bouterwek's lectures on the history of belles lettres, he learned that the German professor had already anticipated ideas slowly taking shape in his own mind, such as the "youthful, fresh" spirit of early national writers, the influence of Christianity and chivalry, and the "perfectly national" tone of the Spanish theater. Like the Schlegels, Bouterwek deplored French neoclassic tragedy as an artificial and derivative literature and exalted writings which spontaneously expressed the feelings of the people — such as ballads.[6]

Having already accepted nationalistic canons of criticism before going to Göttingen, and finding literary nationalism in vogue at home, Ticknor explored the national character of France and Spain through the study of literature. Like Ticknor, Edward Everett was fascinated with the same question: "why tribes of barbarians from the north and east, not known to differ essentially from each other at the time of their settlement in Europe, should have laid the foundation of national characters so dissimilar, as those of the Spanish, French, German, and English nations; these are questions to which a few general answers may be attempted, that will probably be just and safe, only in proportion as they are vague and comprehensive." Everett believed that there were few "exercises of the speculative principle more elevated than this." [7]

Unlike Everett, Ticknor was never one to shilly-shally. Boldly, he announced to his students that the chief characteristic of Greek literature was "an instinctive . . . love for natural rather than conventional beauty"; of Roman, "patriotic pride"; of Spanish "lofty enthusiasm" for chivalry and the Church; of English, "moral greatness . . . tenderness and sensibility"; and of German, "northern mysticism." The central characteristics of French literature, reiterated in his lectures, were courtly artificiality and vice. His political message was not lost on his students. "The great difference between the effects of a patronage of literature by a free government and by a despotic one is this," Quincy remarked in his Harvard Commencement Speech in 1821, "that in the former the virtues of the community purify and sublimate its literature, while in the latter, the vice and intrigue of courts and of courtiers corrupt and degrade it. The history of French literature is a striking exemplification of this remark." [8]

Quincy accurately mirrored Ticknor's distaste — amounting at times to disgust — for French literature. Ticknor's visits to Paris, reinforced by his Federalist inheritance and the hostile criticism of German scholars, convinced him that France was unstable, artificial, irreverent, and immoral. French literature was not a representative national literature at all, since it reflected the taste and character of a despotic court: "a system of careful conventions and strict rules and graceful well adjusted proprieties, could never have been the fair and free result of the national genius working out for itself a national literature suited to its own character; but it might well have been produced by the highest and smallest class of the nation, gathered round the throne, sheltered within its privileges and prevalent with its power, — possessing conventional manners and an artificial refinement — taught to admire antiquity but not to understand it." [9]

This unholy alliance of court and culture explained the absence of religious conviction in French literature, "for it is neither in courts, nor in those connected with them, that we are to seek for the deep feelings of that Religion which has been often and most appropriately called the religion of the oppressed and suffering; — and I need not, I think, tell you that every literature of which we have any knowledge, including the French, has owed its proudest and most imposing monuments to its alliance with Religious Feeling."

Not always had it been so. In the beginning, French literature embodied the natural feelings of the people. The early literature, ballads, chronicles, religious drama, and romances of chivalry, was uncontaminated by foreign or courtly influence. This happy interlude came in the period from 1120 to 1515, when literature went "forth from the rich and abundant soil of the great mass of the People."

But when Ticknor moved to the next stage, the period from 1515 to 1624, the picture darkened. Then the court began to take an interest in literature, and strangled it by "a fanaticism for ancient literature which had well nigh driven all national character out." No longer expressing the pure and fervent feelings of the people, condemned to please a despotic court and to imitate classical models, French writers ceased to be representative. Thus Ticknor treated Rabelais and Montaigne as anomalies because they did not fit his scheme, men who "neither received much from . . . their age nor gave much to it." [10]

The bleakest days for authors came in the third and fourth epochs, from the age of Louis XIV to the Revolution and Napoleon. The third period from Richelieu's ministry to the death of Voltaire comprehended "whatever has obtained an authentic classical authority in France." Corneille's capitulation to the arbitrary rules of the Academy symbolized the degradation of French literature, an "unnatural state of things" which had been "entailed on the community forever." Literary courtiers then produced only "a literature of elegant society . . . bearing everywhere the seal of their conventional manners and feelings and their disciplined taste." In cutting off literature from "the generous nourishment it would have received from the abundant soil of the mass of the People, . . . [the Academy] made the real Judges . . . so few, that an author who came before them found himself subjected to a courtly and capricious despotism rather than to an enlarged and liberal publick opinion." Ticknor pictured the courtly artist's fate in a translation of a Spanish poem:

> The nightingale loved better far
> His nest of straw and simplest food,
> Tho' all his heart he pours unheard,
> Hid in some sheltering wood,
> Than still to sing his gayest notes,
> To please some prince's dainty ear,
> While prisoned in by golden wires,
> He lives in luxury and fear.[11]

The last stage of French literary empire was even worse than the age of Louis XIV, for the Jacobins and Napoleon betrayed republican principles. In "intoxicated self-complacency in what they imagined to be their progress" toward perfection, the *philosophes* had spread a "diseased excitement" among the mob and had themselves been among the first victims of Jacobin fanaticism. Then "for the first time in the records of the world, the history of letters is deliberately and continually stained with blood . . . these fifteen months have left traces such as can be found in no other passage of the world's history, however dark and Barbarous." Condorcet poisoned himself to avoid a worse fate; some went insane at the sound of the falling blade of the guillotine; and many were jailed or beheaded.[12]

Under Napoleon writers were chained to their pens to serve the dictator. Since all literature had become political, mistakes became fatal. No longer did men of letters enjoy "that ease and leisure which elegant literature in some form always requires," but instead were harried by poverty, political persecution, and social unrest. Slowly, writers introduced into French literature an English or German tone which blended poorly with "the original colouring of the literature."

The moral tone of French letters had never been high, but in Ticknor's opinion the French literature of his day became more and more a lost cause. "Victor Hugo, Balzac, the shameless woman who dresses like a man and calls herself George Sand, Paul de Kock, and I know not how many more . . . are daily working mischief throughout those portions of society to whom they address themselves." Was it not possible that the last stage of decline had begun, and that literature was completing the ruin of France? The Smith Professor of French and Spanish Literature had spoken, and his students had dutifully listened. On May 2, 1821, Emerson made the following entry in his journal:

Mr. Ticknor has finished his course of lectures. French literature is a confined literature of elegant society, therein distinguished from all others which have appeared, for all others are national; the results of the feelings, situation, circumstances, & character of the whole people which produced it. But in France, from the Court of Louis XIV went out the rules & spirit to which all its classics conform, & must continue to do so.

Professor Ticknor named six characteristics of the Body of French Literature.

1. Such a conventional regularity
2. So little religious feeling
3. Such a false character in the expression of love
4. So little deep sensibility
5. Such an ambition of producing a brilliant effect
6. So remarkable a restriction of success to those departments which will give some kind of entertainment.[13]

Later a Boston *grande dame* would put the matter more bluntly: "The French are a low lot. Give them two more legs and a tail and there you are! I think they have an original nastiness that beats original sin." Ticknor's story of French degradation was history teaching by horrible example. His desire to interpret France and French literature allegorically clouded his literary perception. His moral pronouncements and his desire to fit all to his "philosophical notions" had quite obscured the writers themselves. The rigidity with which he distorted French literature betrayed his distaste and his anxiety. The quicker done with France the better. Spain was a more alluring subject.[14]

2. *A Broken Column*

After reading Ticknor's *History of Spanish Literature,* Ticknor's friend and biographer George Hillard announced that the book would appeal to readers with "an enlightened curiosity as to the causes which have raised Spain so high and brought her so low." Enlightened or not, Americans of the day were fascinated by catastrophe. They flocked to see Thomas Cole's panoramic canvases depicting "The Course of

Empire," a progression from primitive society through a pastoral scene, to a state of sybaritic and ominous civilization, and finally to a barbarian invasion which destroyed the city and left it in silent ruin. America was still a land without ruins, but the ruins of the Old World evoked nostalgia and uneasy foreboding in many Americans. Through much of the popular and serious writing of the day there ran a grim theme of apocalypse.[15]

To Ticknor Spanish literature, like the nation itself, was "a broken column — a ruin before the building was completed." From his first acquaintance with Spanish culture Ticknor had been more interested in Spanish literature than in French. The history of French literature, Ticknor believed, had "been so often examined, that most of the possible results of its combinations [of interpretations and facts] have been already discovered." For the critic and bibliographer Spain was newer ground.[16] Thus when Ticknor resigned from Harvard at the age of forty-four, he decided to devote his scholarly career to exploring the meaning of Spain. His Harvard lectures filled three large manuscript volumes; for the next fourteen years he continued to develop the themes and outline of his lectures into the three volumes of his *History of Spanish Literature*.[17]

Like his fellow historians and scholar-princes of Boston, Ticknor assembled a superb library to support his research. He had a genuine passion for books and displayed the shrewd instincts of a Yankee trader in ferreting them out. During a second voyage to Europe in 1835–1838 with his family he combed the bookstores and libraries of Europe for rare Spanish books. His Spanish library was probably the best private collection in the world, and perhaps as valuable as any public one.[18]

Ticknor housed his books, eventually numbering over fourteen thousand, in a spacious and bright room in his house at Nine Park Street, which he had bought in 1829. In this library he sat at his writing desk as the morning sun began to stream in the large windows, or talked with Prescott as the sun set behind the Brookline hills. The house was at the corner of Park and Beacon Streets, opposite the State House, high on Beacon Hill where the Ticknors could see Boston Harbor and smell the east wind coming in with the tide in the summer or, in the winter, watch the snow falling on the elms lining the mall of the Boston Common. Books in rich leather bindings crowded the mahogany shelves, statuettes and mementos of Europe filled every table and cornice, and a portrait of Sir Walter Scott occupied the place of honor over the white marble mantel.[19] From this vantage point Ticknor looked out on Spain, never doubting that the perspective from Nine Park Street had the proper moral elevation. Though he twice revisted Europe for long periods, he never saw Spain again. His mind was set.

Ticknor wrote his *History of Spanish Literature* not only for scholars — who alone could appreciate the extraordinary thoroughness and bibliographical skill it demonstrated — but also "for *general* readers." In a letter to Sir Charles Lyell shortly after the publication of the *History* Ticknor wrote that "for a great many years I have been persuaded that literary history . . . should be made, like civil history, to give a knowledge of the *character of the people* to which it relates." Prescott approved the way in which Ticknor linked "the intellectual movement of the nation with the political and moral changes that have exercised an influence over it." [20] Ticknor was determined to make the object lesson clear to every reader.

While at Göttingen Ticknor had concluded that the Spaniards were peculiarly religious and loyal. His visit to Spain confirmed him in this belief and fed his curiosity about that seductive yet anachronistic and benighted land. In his inaugural address at Harvard in 1819 he declared that from the beginning Spanish literature "has never had but one tone; and that tone has been purely and exclusively Spanish, nourished by a high moral feeling, and a proud and prevalent sense of honor, loyalty, and religion . . . the poetry of Spain seems to identify itself with achievements that belong rather to its history; and, as it comes down to us through the lapse of ages, almost realizes to our fancy the gorgeous fables and traditions of the elder times." [21]

In France the court had uprooted literature from the "abundant soil of the People," but in Spain literature continued to express the popular traits of religious devotion and chivalric loyalty. Why, then, did Spanish culture decline? Ticknor's answer was that loyalty degenerated into blind obedience to despotism and religious fervor into the horrors of the Inquisition. These were the cardinal sins, Ticknor reiterated, but the Spanish writers committed venial sins as well. They stimulated the popular taste for violence and revenge, coarse humor and libertine thought and language.

In Spain, as in France, the earliest writers "rested on the deep foundations of the national character, and, therefore, by their very nature were opposed to the Provencal, the Italian, and the courtly schools." The bold simplicity of *El Cid,* the ballads, and early religious drama expressed the life and feelings of the people. In a note written while he was at Göttingen Ticknor reminded himself to "consider the influence of the gradual formation of the Governments of Modern Europe on Modern literature, the total change of character by the increasing influence of the Princes, the overthrow of Chivalry and its institutions etc and the formation of systematick politicks. — This nobody has done or thought of, as far as I know." Primitive Spanish literature illustrated the state of manners before nations had emerged "from the chaos in which they had long struggled, and out of which . . . they have been gradually wrought into those forms of policy which now give stability to governments." [22]

Tragically, as Spain consolidated its government and power, it shackled itself; "one institution, destined soon to discourage and check that intellectual freedom without which there can be no wise and generous advancement in any people, was already beginning to give token of its great and blighting power." This institution was the Inquisition. It was the more dangerous and shameful because it distorted the two salient traits of the national character, faith and loyalty. "The Spanish nation, and the men of genius who illustrated its best days, might be light-hearted because they did not perceive the limits within which they were confined . . . but it is not at all the less true that the hard limits were there, and that great sacrifices of the best elements of the national character must follow. Of this time gave abundant proof. Only a little more than a century elapsed before the government that had threatened the world with a universal empire was hardly able to repel invasion from abroad, or maintain the allegiance of its own subjects at home." The fact that Lope de Vega and Cervantes were as active as the Church in "joining in the general jubilee" underscored the tragedy, for in Ticknor's view these writers represented the popular will.[23]

Spanish writers expressed not only the bigotry but also the lesser vices of the national character. Restraint in some realms produced lawlessness in others. Lope and Calderón fed the popular appetite for plays teeming with violence, revenge, and coarse humor, sacrificing "a decent morality" for popularity. Lope's religious plays were "almost wholly gross and irreverent." Calderón's code of honor could be observed only by "shaking all the foundations of society and poisoning the best and dearest relations of life." Hierónimo's chivalric allegory of Christ's life shocked Ticknor. Cota's *Celestina* he found "foul with a shameless libertinism of thought and language." [24] Instead of pandering to vulgar tastes the writer must ennoble his audience. Calderón was at his best in writing "glowing impossibilities" which uplifted the people, "idealized drama, resting on the purest and noblest elements of the Spanish national character." Tirso de Molino's play *Bashful Man at Court* appealed to Ticknor, for it was a rags-to-riches tale of "lofty and beautiful ideals." The hero of the piece, a nobleman raised secretly as a shepherd, persuaded the court of his ability, and "with noble pride, struggling against the humble circumstances" of his birth, he won a noble lady in the end. A Bostonian could appreciate such a story.

Ticknor liked clear-cut, common-sense interpretations, not "the ingenuity of a refined criticism." Disagreeing with "metaphysical" interpretations of *Don Quixote,* he said that the book was, as Cervantes claimed, a satire on the romances of chivalry, no more and no less. The view that the satiric episodes should be read symbolically as a study of "the endless contrast between the poetical and the prosaic in our natures" Ticknor rejected out of hand as a "conclusion contrary to the spirit of the age," and a contradiction of his thesis that Cervantes expressed the traits peculiar to the Spanish character.[25]

As the Inquisition and the despotic monarchs grew in influence, Spanish power and culture declined apace. To Ticknor, this deterioration was the inevitable result of the moral laws of Providence. Even so, Ticknor found it difficult to accept the implications of his own description of the rise and fall of Spanish literature. His trip to Spain as a young man had perplexed him: here was an Arcadian, poetic, pious, magnanimous, colorful, brave people, "less changed, and in many respects less corrupted, by the revolutions of the last century" than any other European group. Yet with all its "vast and showy apparatus of despotism and superstition" the nation was dead to republican and Protestant values. By a corruption of its virtues, Spain and its culture had become "a broken column." [26]

Ticknor's bleak verdict cast doubt upon the ability of Spaniards to redirect their destiny. "The law of progress is on Spain for good or evil, as it is on the other nations of the earth, and her destiny, like theirs, is in the hand of God, and will be fulfilled." Only the intervention of Providence could break the evil bond between the intolerance of the Spanish character and the institutions of church and state which reflected this intolerance. But the Spanish people, because of their actions, did not merit such an intervention. Thus it seemed only a ritualistic gesture when Ticknor added that if the Spaniards abandoned their "loyalty to mere rank and place" and their "blind submission to priestly authority," they might still enjoy "a future before them not unworthy of their ancient fortunes and fame." His real judgment, coming as it were from a minister in the privy council of Providence, was this: "if they have failed to learn this solemn lesson, inscribed everywhere as if by the hand of heaven, on the crumbling walls of their ancient institutions, then is their honorable history, both in civilization and letters, closed forever." On the fourth of July, 1869, Ticknor wrote his friend King John of Saxony that he never believed Spain would rise again: "Above half a century ago, just after they had driven out Buonaparte I spent some months in Spain, and thought I could foresee fifty years of revolution and only darkness beyond. The same has been the case with every successive year since." [27]

The very statement that "progress" might be "for good or evil" in all nations betrayed an ambiguity in Ticknor's mind which also perplexed his readers. One Bostonian wrote of the *History* that "the general lesson it teaches is eminently favorable to that law of progress which it is the pride of the nineteenth century to recognize." But another reflected that the narrative disclosed that "few nations have paused for any length of time at that point in their progress in which the vertical sun of power and prosperity casts no shadow. That inevitable law of the natural body, by which the principle of decay begins its corroding work so soon as the full maturity of its development has been reached, prevails also in political societies."

Unlike his more optimistic fellow historians, Ticknor had portrayed no party of the present to vanquish the party of the past in Spain. Although Ticknor agreed with Bancroft that "tyranny and wrong lead inevitably to decay," as time passed he became less and less sure that "freedom and right, however hard may be the struggle, always prove

resistless." Was it true, he wondered, that "ancient nations learn to renew their youth."? And how did his apocalyptic narratives of France
and Spain relate to America? [28]

3. *Literary Nationalism*

A Bostonian told Francis Grund in the 1830's that "literary reputa-
tions are in this city not acquired, as in other places, through the medium
of public opinion; but by the aid of a small coterie, composed of a few
'leading citizens,' who have the power of setting a man up, or putting
him down, just as they please." The system was simple: "Mr. A. or
Mr. B., wealthy gentlemen in Beacon-street, declare Mr. Smith a fine
scholar; and immediately half a dozen of their clique will repeat the
same assertion. The individual in question is thus made fashionable, so
that any one speaking against him is considered unacquainted with the
usages of society." [29] Ticknor was assuredly a member of this Brahmin
academy. As in the days when the members of the Anthology Society
set themselves up as arbiters of literary taste and propriety, Ticknor and
his circle continued to be critical judges in the republic of letters. In
culturally provincial Boston, however, Ticknor's nationalistic canons of
criticism introduced some questions difficult to answer. Who constituted
the audience of the American writer? By what standards of style and
diction was he to be judged? What subjects and themes might he illustrate as an American? Might he work within older traditions or did he
need to create a new national voice?

Ticknor confronted these questions both directly, in his own work as
American man of letters, and indirectly, as judge of the work of other
American writers. Ticknor believed that his *History* should be a book
of interest and moral utility to the general reader, not merely to an international group of scholars. Yet his study was so learned, as one reviewer
commented, that not more than six men in the world were qualified to
appraise it. Meanwhile his book became known in Boston, Thackeray
said, as the book which everyone has and nobody reads. Ticknor had
spared no pains to demonstrate that the effect of the court on literature
was uniformly bad, but his *History* was the book recommended by
Macaulay to Queen Victoria when she inquired "what new book he
could recommend for her reading." Although Ticknor tried to prove that

all good literature was peculiarly national, Henry Hallam found in his writing "nothing in the turn of sentiment or taste which a reader can recognize as not English." J. Lothrop Motley complimented Ticknor for writing a book which was "an honor to yourself and to *American* literature." Motley's fellow historian Prescott assured Ticknor that his work would occupy "an important and permanent place in *European* literature." [30]

The British critic Richard Ford helped to explain these incongruities when he wrote that Ticknor's book was "framed more on the Addisonian models in the Spectator than after the sifting, searching criticism of the present age." Americans were "young in the literary race," said Ford, "and timid, perhaps from fancied insecurity of position, they scarcely venture to descend from the dignified propriety of the chair." "Fancied insecurity of position" — Ford had put his finger on a sore point. Ticknor never abandoned the judicial view of criticism which had dominated deliberations in the Anthology Society. In questions of usage and style, the supreme court still sat in London. Ticknor anxiously awaited the transatlantic verdict on his *History,* and was delighted to hear from Abbott Lawrence, American Minister to England, that his work had been well received there. "How delightful to have and hear justice meted out without reserve," Lawrence wrote to him, "to those of my countrymen who have devoted their lives to letters and thereby to the elevation of the literary character of the American people." Prescott obeyed the dictates of British critics less meekly than Ticknor, but he reluctantly conceded that "one and the same language cannot have two standards of purity." Weary of English sniping at "Americanisms," Prescott complained that "one would be glad to avoid *isms* of any kind. — But I shall be glad if the time should ever come when we can assert our independence of these island pedagogues. We are obliged to write a language, which is not spoken around us, are brought before foreign tribunals, tried by foreign laws, while even the venerable authority of ancient British precedent is over-ruled. We have achieved only half our independence." Still, Prescott suppressed his love of colloquialisms in his formal writing and took British literary usage as the law; he admitted to Ticknor that what mattered to him was "the approbation of my friends here and abroad — and of the few." [31]

Although Ticknor and his friends admired Wordsworth and Scott and Goethe, although they sometimes slipped into the rhetoric of ro-

mantic and nationalistic literary criticism, they still reflected in large part
the standards of literary judgment of the London of Johnson and the
Boston of the Anthology Society. Novelty would not seduce them from
their love of balanced periods and formal diction, their abhorrence of
grotesque imagery, their preference for common sense and unmistakable
morality. Provincial by habit, didactic by conviction, they were nationalists mostly by accident of time and place.

The caustic Federalist Fisher Ames had ridiculed the swagger and
puffery of the literary nationalists of his day in his article, "American
Literature." "It might indeed occur to our discretion, that as the only
admissible proof of literary excellence is the measure of its effects, our
national claims ought to be abandoned as worthless the moment they
are found to need asserting." Vanity was only a "sign of mediocrity, if
not of barbarism." Bluntly Ames declared that with the exception of
"the works of two able writers on our politics, we have no authors . . .
Shall we match Joel Barlow against Homer or Hesiod? Can Thomas
Paine contend against Plato?" In 1820, in the famous article in the
Edinburgh Review which provoked a spate of injured replies, Sydney
Smith echoed Ames. The effect of inflated American claims, he said, "is
unspeakably ludicrous on this side of the Atlantic — and, even on the
other, we should imagine, must be rather humiliating to the reasonable
part of the population. The Americans . . . should make it their chief
boast . . . that they are sprung from the same race with Bacon and
Shakespeare and Newton." [32]

Ticknor had stated in his lectures on French and Spanish culture that
these national literatures had begun with primitive ballads, epics,
chronicles, and plays. Was this the appropriate way for Americans to
start? Impossible, said Richard Ford: "Mr. Ticknor evinces a delightful
feeling for these racy relics of old Spain [ballads] of which his new
country can never boast. North America was 'raised' when unimagina-
tive calculators and political economists — poetry's worst foes — were
in the ascendant . . . her matter-of-fact Franklin, with a bar of prosaic
iron, struck the poetic thunderbolt from the hand of Homer's Jove."
Joseph Cogswell agreed: "the United States has gone through no period
of infancy; no pastoral state in which poetry grows out of the simplicity
of language." Ticknor decided that American literature must be a con-
tinuation of English, which "is our own." "Scott belongs to us as he does
to you," Ticknor wrote the British novelist Maria Edgeworth; "thank

God that Milton's language is our mother-tongue, and Shakespeare's name compatriot with our own." [33] No, it was ridiculous to think that the United States would have to recapitulate the entire literary development of other nations. Since American literature stemmed from English, American writers could draw for inspiration from this common tradition. Ticknor's friend Judge Parsons believed that American authors should study early English writers: "in the first place immediate contact with a superior mind . . . gives an elevated tone . . . But the principal advantage is that by following, or rather accompanying the march of powerful minds, we get something of their speed and impetus, which continues when we are left to ourselves." Ticknor praised the New Haven poet James Hillhouse for drinking from "those wells of English undefiled, the old Ballads, and Drama, and the Poetry of Elizabeth's time generally — the healthiest nourishment, I have heard of for a poetical spirit." [34]

Although American writers shared with the English a rich literary tradition and common standards of style, should not Americans write about distinctively national subjects? Edward Channing and many other New Englanders insisted that Americans should write of the scenery and history of their own nation: "All these things are for the native. They help to give a character to his country and her literature, and he loves them too well, to be concerned at the world's admiration or contempt." [35]

The aesthetic theory most prevalent among the intellectuals of Ticknor's circle, associational psychology, held that objects acquire aesthetic significance only if associated with a pre-existing train of ideas or images. Thus when a person looked at a landscape, it was not so much the scene itself as its associations which aroused emotions of beauty or sublimity. There were two broad types of associations, national and private. The author who wrote of subjects with national associations could expect a stronger aesthetic response than if he wrote about topics with merely private associations.[36] More than any other writer of the day, Sir Walter Scott taught Americans how to use traditions and landscapes rich in association. Stimulated by his example, authors searched for American legends, historical episodes, and scenery for American romances. Rufus Choate, a scholarly lawyer, wrote a tract entitled *The Importance of Illustrating New England History by a Series of Novels like the Waverly Novels*. Ticknor had unbounded admiration for Scott, who "began, upon the foundation of the old ballads, traditions, and histories of [Scotland]

. . . to renew its literature." [37] But where could Americans find such a rich mine of legend for their own use?

To Ticknor Plymouth Rock was a sublime symbol of American destiny: "I have seldom had more lively feelings from the associations of place than I had when I stood on this blessed rock; and I doubt whether there should be a place in the world where a New England man should feel more gratitude, pride, and veneration than when he stands where the first man stood who began the population and glory of his country. The Colosseum, the Alps, and Westminster Abbey have nothing more truly classical, to one who feels as he ought to feel, than this rude and bare rock." [38] "Should feel" — "ought to feel" — it took Ticknor some effort to kindle enthusiasm for a meager tradition only two hundred years old. "There is nothing to awaken fancy in that land of dull realities," wrote Cogswell about America; "it contains no objects that carry back the mind to the contemplation of early antiquity; no mouldering ruins to excite curiosity in the history of past ages . . . no traditions and legends and fables to afford materials for romance and poetry." Even the nationalist Edward Channing was forced to admit that the American author faced "a want in his readers of romantic associations." Other friends of Ticknor, notably Sparks and Bancroft, despaired of Americans' finding adequate poetric subjects at home.[39] Despite his patriotic tribute to Plymouth Rock, Ticknor believed that it was false to suppose American writers must deal only with American subjects. Longfellow clearly expresed Ticknor's view when he wrote that a "national literature is the expression of national character and modes of thought; and as our character and modes of thought do not differ essentially from those of England, our literature cannot. Vast forests, lakes, and prairies cannot make great poets. They are but the scenery of the play; and have much less to do with the poetic character, than has been imagined." [40]

Ticknor's friend James Hillhouse agreed. "Let our countryment pause, ere they adopt an opinion sometimes gravely urged — that an American must illustrate an American theme, or never hope to be engrafted on the affections of his country." Spenser, Shakespeare, and Milton observed no such canon; why should Americans circumscribe their imagination "within a couple of centuries, and the transactions of a few thinly-peopled colonies?" A young student of the nationalist controversy who admired Hillhouse concluded that "there is an unexhausted treasury accumulated in other ages and other climes" to serve as subjects for American poets. This student was Ralph Waldo Emerson, who would sound a quite different note later in his declaration of cultural independence, "The American Scholar." [41]

The staunch defender of bold writers of an earlier age, Ticknor seemed to be either unaware or scornful of most of the great writers of the American renaissance. One looks in vain in his writings for any appraisal of Emerson, Thoreau, or Hawthorne, much less Melville, Poe or Whitman. In this blindess he was, of course, not alone. Most of these authors came to maturity when Ticknor was an old man, and with the exception of Hawthorne they spoke a language which sounded abrupt and bizarre to his decorous ear. Many of the literate men of the younger generation who might have been expected to read these writers with a more charitable eye were equally obtuse. Richard Henry Dana, Jr., the aristocratic author and lawyer who had circled the Horn and carried hides in Monterey, thought Thoreau a "solitary idler." He failed to recognize Melville's genius even though he had met Melville and shared his passion for the sea. For Dana as for Ticknor, Daniel Webster was "the great man of the age" in letters as in politics. Ticknor cared little for James Fenimore Cooper and was surprised to find his novels so well received in England and on the continent; "my limited admiration of them seemed almost to offend people," Mrs. Ticknor remarked. Ticknor never applied to the writers of his day, who have since become classic, his own dictum that "criticks certainly ought to give place to those who without or even in defiance of art and rules, perform wonders in literature." [42]

With few exceptions, the American writers Ticknor did admire have vanished from memory as surely as the snows of yesteryear. Some of those he approved — Washington Irving, William Ellery Channing, Longfellow, Webster, Prescott — have enjoyed a lasting though minor reputation. But few today recall his good friend James Hillhouse, the author of tiresome poetic dramas on medieval themes. Or James Percival, the tormented recluse of New Haven, who knew thirteen languages and wrote anemic and allusive poems. Or Richard Henry Dana, Sr., an alienated and ineffectual man of letters who wrote Addisonian essays and Wordsworthian poetry. These authors turned to Ticknor for advice and support, for he could promote their work at home and abroad.[43] He, in turn, hoped that they might enrich American literature. Yet as the brutally frank John Quincy Adams said of their ilk, "It would take nine such poets to make a Tate." So burdened were the writers of the time with didactic purpose, so intimidated by the demand of the critics for a majestic literature, that courageous was the author who dared put pen to paper at all. James Russell Lowell satirized the extravagant hopes and critical blindness of the early literary establishment: "Meanwhile, we were busy growing a literature. We watered so freely, and sheltered so carefully, as to make a soil too damp for anything but mushrooms; wondered a little why no oaks came up, and ended by voting the mushroom an oak, an American variety." [44]

Yet some Europeans shared Ticknor's appraisal of his contemporaries. Lord Holland considered Channing the best living English writer, and he was delighted to find that Queen Victoria was already familiar with Channing's work when he placed one of his volumes in her hands. Samuel Rogers, a British poet and arbiter of taste, sensed in Hillhouse a kindred spirit: he wrote Ticknor about Hillhouse that "nightingales in the West sing delightfully; and may such music be heard along your shores, when old England in her turn has given way, and her groves have become as silent as those of Greece and Rome." [45] Rogers' metaphor appropriately described the derivative tone of the American writers Ticknor admired; as literary nationalists were fond of pointing out, nightingales were not indigenous to America.

To Ticknor a writer need not speak in a distinctively American voice, need not treat American subjects, need not create a new literary tradition in order to be national. Did this reduce literary nationalism to absurdity? Not at all, as his friend Hillhouse explained. Although we as Americans could not boast of "a history abounding in poetical incidents, we possess the only one which discloses the true rules of civil liberty. Half mankind are searching in our annals for the mighty incantation, by whose agency a government may be puissant, yet the rulers powerless, — the law despotic, yet the people free, — the poor replenished with knowledge, yet the rich fearless of evil." Should not "the teachers of such secrets . . . borrow, without overwhelming obligations, from the historical record of other nations, those topics for entertainment and instruction, which the poetic art requires?" Their audience was the world, not simply their nation, their message the means of civil salvation.[46]

It was a moral and political attitude, then, which made a writer American: not his style, his subject, his literary tradition. The critic Edwin Whipple observed that Ticknor's *History* lacked "imaginative sympathy and insight; he never thoroughly put himself in the place of Lope de Vega, Cervantes and Calderón." But Ticknor had little desire to project himself imaginatively into their world; his main duty was to pass judgment on their world. Through keeping uppermost the didactic purpose — to teach "the true rules of civil liberty" and moral purity — the American man of letters might safely blend the cosmopolitan and the national, the scholarly and the popular. Henry James was fascinated by the easy way in which Longfellow's " 'European' culture and his native kept house together." Ticknor was in similar fashion untroubled by any clash between his provincial tastes and his nationalistic theories, so sure was he of the moral convictions which guided the Brahmin academy.[47]

4. *The Writer as Moralist*

"The apprehension of the approach of cholera excites very little sensation here," Ticknor wrote George Bancroft in 1832. "We are such a moral, cleanly population, that, if we have it at all, we must have it very lightly." [48] But even Bostonians were not absolutely certain that cholera, the scourge of Europe, would not strike. Ticknor's study of the rise and fall of the literary empires of France and Spain made him vigilant for any signs of moral contagion in his native city. His friends joined him in this watch and ward. While Ticknor was lecturing on Shakespeare in Boston, his minister, William Ellery Channing, urged him to "speak in the character which I always wish you to sustain, of a true friend of the moral as well as the intellectual progress of your fellow creatures." He warned him against making Iago too interesting or creating sympathy for Romeo and Juliet, "who are greatly criminal when abandoning themselves to one passion." The warning was hardly necessary. Ticknor agreed with Hillhouse that the poet should "delight, purify, and exalt our nature, by alluring exhibitions of the beauty and grandeur of virtue, and . . . fortify us against the evil passions by impressive delineations of their insidious disguises, their terrible energy, and their fatal consequences." [49]

"The writer must present no deceptive portrait of our moral nature," warned the Unitarian pope, Andrews Norton. "He must show what is good as good, and what is evil as evil." Norton believed that "a correct and refined moral taste is the most important constituent of a correct and refined taste in literature." The writer must be constantly on his guard lest he corrupt the public. "The obscene jests, the low ribaldry, the coarse allusions which shed a disastrous light on so many pages of misguided genius in former times find no sympathy in ours," Judge Story told Harvard students in 1826. "He who would now command respect, must write with pure sentiments and elevated feelings; he, who would now please, must be chaste as well as witty, moral as well as brilliant." James Russell Lowell put the matter succinctly when he said, "Let no man write a line that he would not have his daughter read." [50]

These precepts narrowed the scope of acceptable literature, past and present. This was the age when Thomas Bowdler issued an expurgated edition of Shakespeare. Falstaff would hardly have been at home in a Beacon Hill drawing room. Even George Washington's prose needed to be cleaned up a bit for the public. When Jared Sparks edited Washington's manuscripts he bowdlerized "old Put" to "General Putnam" and "flea-bite" to a sum "totally inadequate to our demands." The criterion that an author must write for his daughter's eye, in an age when pianos as well as people had "limbs," not legs, led to a feminization of taste. The rule of the "iron madonnas," patronesses of the arts whose sensibilities could not be offended, circumscribed both the matter and the manner available to the writer. Ticknor and his fellow Brahmins helped to give these madonnas their scepters and to formulate the canons of genteel literature. George Hillard, Ticknor's sickly and slightly precious friend who longed to be a gentleman essayist or poet but had to make his living as a lawyer, perfectly expressed the genteel temper: in times when sensitive people were "constantly repelled by some iron reality," the poet's task was "to idealize life; to connect the objects of thought with those associations which embellish, dignify and exalt, and to keep out of sight, those which debase and deform." [51] But the exacting morality of the Brahmins was not merely the result of squeamishness or priggishness; it also stemmed from anxiety. They attributed such power to literature that they believed that an author could undermine the moral foundations of the family and even shake the state.

Authors should take care, said Judge Story, to idealize "feelings belonging to ordinary life," not "the peculiarities and morbid visions of eccentric minds." If a critic felt kinship with "eccentric minds" — as Ticknor did with the fate of young Werther — he had best confine his sympathy to the study and not proclaim it publicly. It was the duty of the Brahmin guardian to protect the public. Prescott realized that the poetry of Byron should be dismissed as "lawless . . . affected, violent, morbid" and full of "extravagances which outrage the reader, offend the taste, and lead many persons of excellent principles and critical discernment to condemn him, both on the ground of moral and literary pretensions." But privately he admitted that "there is, with all this smoke and fustian, a deep sensibility to the sublime and beautiful in nature, a wonderful melody, or rather harmony, of language . . . He has great attractions, and, pouring out his soul unreservedly, turns up the depths of feeling which even those who acknowledge the truth of it would shrink from expressing themselves." [52]

Emerson and the Transcendentalists alarmed Ticknor and his friends. Ticknor's brother-in-law Andrews Norton led proper Bostonians in their onslaught on these ungrateful pupils. Norton had cut the cable to the once secure Calvinist moorings and was appalled to see his students sailing into the uncharted waters of Transcendentalism. Ticknor had helped to introduce his Harvard students to modern European thought, but as one who believed that literature should be a handmaiden of religion, he, too, joined in the battle against the new infidelity. Longfellow noted in his journal one evening after having tea with the Nortons and the Ticknors at Shady Hill that they "all hold in great contempt apparently, all peepings and movings of the wing among the young and sometimes extravagant young writers of the day." Two years later, in 1840, Ticknor wrote in disgust to Maria Edgeworth of a "tendency in a few persons among us to a wild sort of metaphysics, if their publications deserve so dignified a name." This school, Ticknor continued, borrowed German notions which they "rendered grotesque by a free infusion from the style of Carlyle, whose follies of form and style they have adopted, without finding any of his power." [53]

Carlyle — and, by association, Emerson — became a whipping boy for proper Boston. Prescott wrote to Bancroft about *The French Revolution: A History* that Carlyle's coloring "produces a grotesque and ludicrous effect . . . such ridiculous affectations of new-fangled word . . . in short, the whole thing, in my humble opinion, both as to *forme* and to *fond,* is perfectly contemptible." The elder Dana spoke of *Sartor Resartus* as "Botcher-Botched." Edward Everett, rising to the occasion at a Brahmin gathering, "compared Carlyle's style to the composite of the thunderbolt which consisted of twelve parts: — three with a twisted hail storm and three with glittering fire, — three watery clouds and three empty winds." He admitted privately, though, that he had "read nothing of Carlyle." [54]

Everett reported that talk at the dinner table at his father-in-law's house dealt "little favor" to Emerson, either; the consensus was that he expressed "brilliant thoughts, mingled with much unintelligible nonsense." When someone asked Ticknor's acid friend Jeremiah Mason if he could understand Emerson, Mason snorted, "No, *I* can't; but my daughter can." This was the ultimate affront: if one of Boston's best lawyers couldn't understand the philosopher, he wasn't worth understanding. Everett charged that Emerson "destroys all the principles of thinking, judging, and acting — all evidence — all experience — all moral laws formed upon the observed relations of things." [55]

For Ticknor, Norton's *Evidences of Christianity* had settled theological matters. The right of private judgment of the Scriptures was one thing; the tendency of the Transcendentalists to "go aballooning thro' infinite space" — as Dana scornfully expressed it — was something else again. Ticknor fully approved of Norton's attacks on the Transcendentalists, believing in general that within a "society where public opinion governs, unsound opinions must be rebuked, and you can no more do that, while you treat their apostles with favor, than you can discourage bad books at the moment you are buying and circulating them." Bad ideas must be suppressed and their advocates ostracized. Ticknor took a certain pride in his rigidity; when the intellectual peace of society was at stake, why venture on the unknown? Edwin Whipple recalled that once a young man visited Ticknor — "for the first and last time" — and suggested that the extraordinary success of Samuel Gridley Howe in teaching the blind and deaf Laura Bridgman had "introduced some new problems in the philosophy of perception as expounded by recent metaphysicians; but who was stunned into silence by Mr. Ticknor's decisive answer, that, 'Mr. Locke's opinions had satisfied him on all matters of that kind' . . . his judgments ever had something of this positiveness; his intellect was not open to new ideas; he excluded from his toleration what he had not included in his studies and experience; and he sometimes weighed heavily on the Boston mind during the period he was supposed to have undertaken its direction." [56]

From the days of the Anthology Society onward, Ticknor believed that the American republic of letters should buttress a conservative political, moral, and religious establishment. Schooled in the rise and fall of empires, Ticknor never lost the conviction that the writer should be a guardian of the commonwealth. With Daniel Webster he held that "truth in taste is allied with truth in morality." Literature was potent not only in "exalting the character of a nation" but also in deflecting it from righteousness. Together with the statesman, the man of letters must preserve the moral order and prove that "mankind can be trusted with a purely popular government . . . the last solemn experiment of humanity." [57]

To Ticknor's dismay as he grew older, the republic of letters, his elite corps of guardians, would splinter into factions. A new generation of writers, the authors of the American renaissance, would largely reject the critical canons and social views of Ticknor and his friends. Anglophile and eclectically genteel, the Brahmins of Ticknor's circle were unprepared for the barbaric yawp of strident nationalists; rationally Christian, they feared that Transcendentalism would dissolve sound religion. Their hope for a united voice in statesmanship would be ominously drowned out in the cacophony of egalitarianism, sectionalism, and partisanism. And soon the slavery issue would split even the Brahmin establishment.

V

Gentleman of Letters

Blindness to the real value of intellectual accomplishment lies
at the root of common opinion; and must first be cured. The
possessors of wealth may, then, be disenchanted of the notion,
that their sons, if not installed in the counting-room, or distributed among the professions, must be blotted from the roll
of useful citizens . . . We should have a class performing the
functions of an Aristocracy, without its intolerable appendages.
James Hillhouse[1]

"I am patriotic and provincial to my fingers' ends," Oliver
Wendell Holmes, Sr., wrote to Lothrop Motley, "but I do sometimes feel
that, aesthetically speaking, America is a penal colony."[2] Mediators
between the culture of the Old and New Worlds who were both "patriotic and provincial" often shared Holmes' discomfort. Who could deny
the contrast between America and Europe in wealth of tradition, art,
libraries, literary society, in all that meant most to gentlemen of letters?
The grosser seductions of Europe — the moral traps which American
parents feared — Ticknor could easily resist; but its subtler temptations
— its aristocratic way of life, its ancient traditions, its aesthetic richness
— were more insistent and aroused envy, nostalgia, malaise at the temper
of life in "a penal colony." Yet Ticknor was no expatriate. Throughout
his life he sought ways to make his peace with both worlds.

Jefferson had feared that Americans abroad would be "fascinated
with the privileges of the European aristocrats" and would abhor "the
lovely equality which the poor enjoys with the rich" in America. A convinced Tory in sentiment, yet a loyal republican, Ticknor admired the
aristocrats of Europe, even though he did not hesitate to criticize their
moral lapses or abuses of power. "No other American has had such an
entree into the closed circles of the Old World," Charles Eliot Norton
wrote to Thomas Carlyle about his Uncle George. "Mr. Ticknor deserved
all his success; he was a 'scholar and a gentleman' and had an attractive,

if not very deep, nature. His very defects — the worst of which were lack of imagination and lack of humor — served him in conventional society. He could take it all as much in earnest as if he had been born with a title and an entail." [3] Still, Ticknor knew full well that the tenor of American society and institutions was antiaristocratic. He realized that the United States lacked the long tradition, stemming from feudal times, which gave European aristocracy its distinctive coloring.

A patrician in a democratic age, he helped to shape one of the most exclusive social groups in mid-century America, the Brahmin caste of New England. Wealth, family, occupation, education, social connections, political and religious views, morality, and cultivation merged to define the "gentleman," though uniformity in these respects was not requisite to the Brahmin life-style. Ticknor the latter-day Federalist agreed with James Hillhouse that America "should have a class performing the functions of an Aristocracy, without its intolerable appendages." *"Politics* and the *Love of Money* control our hearts, and direct our energies with an exclusiveness not elsewhere found," Hillhouse warned. American society "must and *can* be convinced that our greatest want is the want of an order combining superior means with illuminated minds; and that the two especial testimonies, required by their country, at the hands of the opulent, are, — building towers of light to preserve rational liberty amidst the fogs and shallows of democratical fanaticism; and bequeathing to . . . [America] sons equipped, either for public or private life, by a consummate education." [4]

As time went on, Ticknor became increasingly aware of the consequences of his decision to become a man of letters. As a professor, he found it simple to justify his career, for college teaching was a recognized profession (though often considered second-rate), and Harvard was a revered Boston institution. After he resigned his professorship, he came to realize that the scholar in America was usually a solitary figure, one like the senior Dana or Hillhouse; he came to understand why the first New Englander who attempted to be a professional writer — Dana —sardonically entitled his journal *The Idle Man*. Without an established profession of letters, with few colleagues to encourage and criticize him, without the vast resources of European cultural centers, the American man of letters often felt isolated. Even the popular Prescott once exclaimed that Ticknor was "the only friend I know in this bustling, money-getting world, who takes an interest in my peculiar pursuits, as well as in myself." [5]

When Ticknor first turned to a literary career, every Bostonian was expected to have some useful occupation. Justifying a literary career continued to be perplexing, for the scholar was expected to prove to merchants his industry, to ministers his piety and morality, and to statesmen his sound political influence. If the gentleman of letters cared at all about the opinion of those outside the professions, he had somehow to show that he was not a drone. Perhaps the best defense for the literary man was offense: "in this bustling, money-getting world" the gentleman of letters could stand at the door of the social inner sanctum, certifying the culture of those who passed within. Such a high priest of the Brahmin caste was George Ticknor.

1. *The Autocrat of Nine Park Street*

Charles William Eliot, president of Harvard, once recalled that Ticknor, his uncle, thought it "unseemly for Samuel A. Eliot [Charles's father] to sing in the little King's Chapel choir and to invite its humbler members to practice in his own house." [6] Times had changed since Ticknor relished his rough trip with contrabandists in Spain, sharing their food and talking late in the evening under the cork trees. Boston was changing, and Ticknor with it.

Ever since Ticknor's return from Europe in 1819 his fellow citizens had found him a force to be reckoned with socially as well as intellectually. When famous persons came to Boston, Ticknor was one of the attractions of the city to be displayed along with the State House and the Common. On Lafayette's triumphal tour in 1824, "Ticknor gave . . . a supper party which had quite a foreign grace about it," Josiah Quincy recalled. "A likeness of Lafayette, engraved upon a bright red paper, was found under the glass by the side of each plate. As the guests seated themselves at the table, everyone, except the General, took up the picture and pinned it upon some part of the dress, where it looked like the decoration of some noble order." Naturally when the Prince of Wales came to Boston, it was Ticknor who escorted him to Harvard.[7]

The city was growing rapidly and becoming conscious of its power and position. We Bostonians "all carry the Common in our heads as the unit of space," Holmes wrote, "the State House as the standard of architecture, and measure off men in Edward Everetts as with a yardstick." The population had jumped from 43,000 in 1820 to 61,000 during the next decade, and by 1842 it had passed 100,000. The huge wharves of the waterfront were jammed with ships whose spars and rigging made a vast spiderweb. The 1830's was the great decade of sailing ships, when almost 1500 vessels a year tied up to Boston docks. Soon Donald McKay would build his beautiful clipper ships across the harbor in East Boston. Men from Cape Cod, from the interior towns of Massachusetts, from New Hampshire, from seaport villages north of Boston flocked to the city to make their fortunes in commerce, banking, insurance, real estate, and other Yankee ventures. Gradually, investments shifted from shipping and foreign trade to manufacturing, and spindles began humming in the towns along the Merrimac River. By 1850 the "Boston Associates" were consolidating an empire of finance, manufacturing, and transport which included the new railroads fanning out from the cities. The Lawrences, Sears, Lowells, Appletons, Cabots, Eliots and others grasped the levers of economic power.[8]

Merchants rose early and went to their countinghouses and offices on Central Wharf or India Wharf or on State Street. They continued the eighteenth-century custom of gathering about one o'clock near the Old State House to discuss the affairs of the day before going home to the "formidable rite" of the mid-afternoon dinner. Although they might have a puritan distrust of the other pleasures of the flesh, the Boston elite did not stint on food and drink. A fashionable young lady exclaimed in exalted tones that "we *admire* roast beef and *dote* on oysters." Tocqueville found that Bostonians "have but a single fault, which is that of drinking too much," and admitted that he had trouble keeping pace with their toasts. The ruddy portraits of proper Bostonians of the day reveal the rich tones of claret and burgundy more than the blueness of their blood. For years a favorite topic of conversation was the quality and price of Madeira; penurious old Ward Boylston used to say to his dinner guests that "this wine, adding compound interest to its cost, is worth a crown a glass." [9]

Although Boston was rapidly becoming a large city, it still retained some of the atmosphere of the overgrown town Ticknor had known in his youth. West Boston and some other sections were run-down, but as a whole the city struck visitors as unusually prosperous and attractive. It was not until the heavy immigration of the Irish in mid-century that extensive slums and wide-spread poverty appeared. In 1829 all Boston had only twenty-four policemen. A visitor to Boston was surprised to note that at a large public gathering on the Common no police were present, and when the crowd dispersed, no litter had been left behind. One reason for the small police force was the persistent spirit of watch and ward which Timothy Dwight had applauded. Francis Grund, a witty Viennese immigrant who came to Boston in 1827, reported that "I have heard it seriously asserted . . . that there are no better policemen than the ordinary run of Bostonians; and that, as long as their natural inquisitiveness remained, there was no need of a secret tribunal; every citizen taking on himself the several offices of spy, juryman, justice, and — *vide* Lynch law — executioner. This is by some called the wholesome restraint of public opinion." [10]

All over town new wealth produced new buildings: square business blocks of Quincy granite, the Tremont House — a hotel that was "the crack house of the place" — the massive Quincy Market, and the new brick mansions that rose on the quiet old pastures on Beacon Hill. In 1829 Ticknor bought the southeast portion of one of the first houses built on the Hill, the enormous and handsome four-story Federal mansion built by Thomas Amory in 1804, then called "Amory's folly" because of its size. He had previously lived in rented rooms, but this house at Nine Park Street was to be his home for the rest of his life.

The entrance to Nine Park Street was a fine curved staircase with wrought iron railings; a small tree on the right of the door and thick wisteria vines climbing on the left blended with the soft patina of the bricks. The large door, flanked by sidelights and a fanlight, opened into a marble hall and a broad staircase which led to the inner sanctum, the library on the second floor. The decor of the library mixed chaste classicism — white marble statuettes, a frieze under the mantel, pilasters on the bright mahogany bookcases — and overstuffed Victorian —a clutter on the mantel, ugly bulbous hanging lamps, tablecloths with ornate fringes. It was an eclectic period in taste in interior decoration as in literature. Presiding over the scene was a portrait of Sir Walter Scott, who, Anna Ticknor wrote George Bancroft, sits "in his own oaken chair, in a green coat, buff waistcoat, and black cravat, and looks very much as, if you waited a moment, he would nod his head, and begin one of his best stories." The big room, with its easy chairs and couches, was made quite as much for society as for study, and here for decades George and Anna Ticknor held court.[11]

Hawthorne described an interview with Ticknor in this library. He found Ticknor in his slippers, sitting at his writing desk; Ticknor rose to receive Hawthorne "with great distinction, but without any ostentatious flourish of courtesy."

Mr. Ticknor has a great head and a queer face, with a nose the reverse of aquiline, though not exactly a pug or snub; his hair is gray or grizzly; he has a comfortable roundness of person. You recognize in him at once the man who knows the world; the scholar, too, which is probably his more distinctive character, though a little more under the surface . . . He is not, I apprehend, one of the highest or profoundest of men, but a man of great cultivation and refinement, and with quite substance enough to be polished and refined, without being worn too thin in the process. Fond of good dinners; appreciative of the quality of wine; a man of society. There is something peculiar in his manner, and odd and humorsome in his voice; as one who knows his own advantages and eminent social position, and so superimposes a little oddity upon the manners of a gentleman.[12]

In a less than reverent tone, Theodore Parker, a Unitarian minister whom Beacon Hill thought radical, commented that "no man could consider himself of any account in the world, if he was not admitted to Mr. Ticknor's study." As in his days at Harvard, Ticknor continued to serve as counselor to scholars, book lender to the American republic of letters, patron and friend of artists and writers, and genial host to his fellow gentlemen and scholars.

To those outside the magic circle he often appeared cold and haughty. William Cullen Bryant believed that Ticknor "had his own set of people and seems to have looked down on everyone else." Ticknor's minister, Ezra Gannett, admitted that Ticknor was abrupt with anyone coarse in speech or conduct, and that he "might be misunderstood by those who confound a quiet self-respect with an indulgence of aristocratic temper." Even Ticknor's closest friend, Prescott, in composing a letter introducing Ticknor as a man distinguished by "social position," "cultivation," and "warmth of heart," changed his mind and crossed out the "warmth of heart." In 1823 when Ticknor was only thirty-two, Emerson thought it a formidable undertaking to ask Ticknor for letters of introduction for his brother, writing to William Emerson that "as to Mr. Ticknor, I have not yet been, counting on some future day to possess my senses and

cravat in more composedness than amid this vulgar din of affairs."
Many years after Ticknor's death, when the scholar was a legend —
instead of the institution he had been during his lifetime — Oliver Allston
wrote thus of an encounter with an old gentleman: "As he addressed
me in his affable manner, his eye descended over my person, taking in
the cut of my clothes, the quality of my handkerchief and necktie, even
the polish on my shoes — twice, the while he maintained his well-bred
conversation, discreet in every gesture and accent, but as if to assure
himself that I was 'all right.' So might George Ticknor have surveyed a
stranger in Boston, ninety years ago." [13] In his youth Ticknor had de-
ferred to his elders and had been the earnest inquirer and listener; as he
grew older he became more and more dogmatic.

To the world Ticknor seemed as foursquare as his mansion. "No man,
we imagine, was ever less troubled with self-dissatisfaction," commented
one of his contemporaries. "He felt the limits of his faculties and qualities, if he felt them at all, only as useful and secure defenses." Throughout his life Ticknor conformed to a rigid morality, a strict code of
manners, and stern standards of taste. His strong will condemned any
laxness in himself or others; his severity of judgment bred anxiety. He
was impatient with weakness or vacillation. "His love of truth and right
being so often shocked, his hatred of baseness or corruption, and distrust of fanatics and demagogues, so often roused," commented his
daughter Anna, "— these very virtues sometimes gave him the appearance of intolerance or loftiness." His earnestness and resolution seemed
to blind him to the fact that others, of equal zeal and high intentions,
could disagree with him in good conscience. For him life was a set of
self-evident duties, not a calculus of pain and pleasure.[14]

Despite an outwardly successful and privileged life, Ticknor suffered
from an increasing sense of alienation as he grew older. His work at
Harvard failed to realize his hopes. His *History of Spanish Literature*
was an authoritative work, but his published writings stopped far short
of his ambitions. Above all, he became increasingly despondent about
the destiny of the nation. On first acquaintance the perceptive Longfellow
thought Ticknor an "exceedingly . . . affable" man, but in time concluded that "he is disappointed in many things." Ticknor's daughter
Anna admitted that he was "often disposed to be anxious," but added
that he deemed it a duty to cultivate cheerfulness "as part of the requirements of manliness and kindness, as well as of religion." [15]

Hawthorne, a student of character through portraits, might have seen a grim transformation in the interpretation of Ticknor by G. P. A. Healy in 1848, a year of revolutions that profoundly depressed Ticknor. In an earlier portrait painted by Sully Ticknor sits in a relaxed pose, his eyes large and expressive, with a sunlit landscape in the background. Light predominates in Sully's portrait; it conveys an airy, somewhat dreamlike image. In Healy's painting all this has changed: now one looks at Ticknor from below, whereas in Sully's portrait he was on the same level as the viewer; instead of looking face on, he now sits stiffly and looks from the side, with half his face in shadow; his jaw and mouth are hard-set, and his eyes are frosty and penetrating. The sunlit landscape of Sully's painting has given way to a dark background which blends so indistinctly with Ticknor's dark suit and black curly hair that one can hardly tell where Ticknor leaves off and the darkness beyond begins. Although the features, the dark, ruddy skin, are the same, the public image of the man, the conception of the artist, perhaps the man himself, are now different. A harshly realistic bust of Ticknor as an old man, executed by Martin Millmore in 1867, carries still further Healy's somber interpretation.[16]

Ticknor found refuge from his anxieties in his family life. He was a model Victorian husband and father. He encouraged his wife's intellectual and artistic pursuits. He was devoted to his four children: Anna Eliot, the oldest daughter; Susan Perkins, who died in 1825 when only a few weeks old; George Haven, born in 1829; and Eliza Sullivan, who later married William Dexter. In that age when women were becoming better educated and were entering more actively into social and intellectual life, Ticknor often gathered around the fireplace with his daughters and their friends to study literary classics. The salons of the Ticknors were models of the changing pattern of Victorian social life described by John Stuart Mill:

The association of men with women in daily life is much closer and more complete than it ever was before. Men's life is more domestic. Formerly, their pleasures and chosen occupations were among men, and in men's company: their wives had but a fragment of their lives. At the present time, the progress of civilization, and the turn of opinion against the rough amusements and convivial excesses which formerly occupied most men in their hours of relaxation — together with (it must be said) the improved tone of modern feeling as to the reciprocity of duty which binds the husband towards the wife — have thrown the man very much more upon home and its inmates, for his personal and social pleasures; while the kind and degree of improvement which has been made in women's education, has made them in some degree capable of being his companion in ideas and mental tastes.[17]

Agreeing with Thomas Arnold that "the very idea of family life" demanded a "peculiar sense of solemnity," Ticknor regarded his home as a haven from the turmoil of business and politics around him.

Ticknor's maiden daughter Anna — plump and plain with frizzled black hair, cultivated and earnest — carried on her father's pioneer efforts to educate women. From headquarters in the library at Nine Park Street she marshalled an army of over two hundred Boston ladies, including such talented people as Elizabeth Cary Agassiz, to liquidate ignorance and promote taste among her countrywomen. With fellow Brahmins as teaching staff she organized the Society to Encourage Studies at Home, an adult education project which taught, by correspondence, history, English literature, science, art, and foreign languages. In the cause of culture, Anna proved to be as well-organized and public-spirited as her father. Through her letters she became "a friend of many a lonely and baffled life," giving advice to Negro schoolteachers in the south, telling women how to decorate their houses, and dispensing Victorian morality.[18]

In a children's book called *An American Family in Paris,* published anonymously in 1869, Anna painted a delightful vignette of life with father. The kindly autocrat of this family, Mr. Lewis — a thinly disguised portrait of George Ticknor — is a pedantic parent, a walking guidebook who gives his children lectures on manners, history, art, and literature. The family at times gently ridicules his Olympian manner. Once when his wife asked a simple question, Mr. Lewis retorted in offended omniscience:

"I did not know that *you* needed lessons in history! Allow me to remark that Francois I. followed his cousin Louis XII.; then Francois I.'s son and three of his grandsons tried their hands at being kings, but all had a very short chance at it. Their cousin Henri IV. came in, his son Louis XIII. followed, and Louis XIV. was his son."

"There, there, that is enough," said Mrs. Lewis, laughing; "goodness, what a long lecture! I am quite out of breath. If I had not known it all before (except of course I forgot the last little bit), do you suppose I should have learned much by your rattling off such a list? Fanny, did you hear your father teaching me history?"

"Yes, mamma; I am glad you did not know it all." [19]

Fanny learned "how charming really high-bred people are." When Fanny asked her mother what it meant to be "well-bred," Mrs. Lewis replied that a person with "high-bred" manners was "desirous to please without being obsequious," one who didn't loll in a chair, or talk loudly, or laugh too heartily. Just like the Parisian aristocrats we are living with, said her mother: " 'They're not a bit stiff; do you think they are?' 'Oh, no, not a bit,' answered Fanny, 'they don't frighten me half so much as old Mrs. Jones does at home; and she's polite half the time and not polite the other half.' "[20]

In 1834 Ticknor experienced the greatest personal sorrow of his life. His five-year-old son, George Haven, died. To a man who tried to force himself to be cheerful as a religious duty, the anguish and mystery of death was especially bitter and perplexing. In words resembling those of Emerson, who also lost a beloved son and found little explanation or compensation in his religious beliefs, Ticknor wrote to a friend, "I am sad, very sad . . . because I can no longer see his bright smile or hear his glad voice; because I turn my head suddenly at some familiar sound, and he is not there; because I listen and it is not his light step." For his wife, already ill, this loss was crushing. "The human frame cannot always be braced to bear what the will demands of it," she later wrote.

Ever since Ticknor's decision to resign from Harvard they had contemplated a European trip. Now, burdened with grief and eager to leave the scene of their sorrow, they left for the Old World to allow Anna to regain her health and "to go through as vigorous a course of improvement as we can, by an industrious use of the advantages we may be able to enjoy."[21] In Brahmin Boston a European trip provided many a pilgrim with a pedigree by association. Ticknor's second tour would fortify the social and scholarly position he had already won and would make him more than ever a mediator between the elite society of the Old and New Worlds.

2. *The Grand Tour*

As Ticknor was beginning his second trip to Europe, William Ellery Channing wrote him a warning letter echoing Elisha Ticknor: "There are some moral dangers in travelling of which it is well to be aware. It often deprives us of the arm of religion, breaks in on our good habits, and keeps the mind fixed too exclusively on the outward." Two years later he cautioned Ticknor again not to "look upon yourself as authorized to spend years of your life in literary and elegant leisure." Ticknor's daughter felt compelled to say that her father "always, to the end of his life, regarded the years he passed in Europe as being in some degree sacrificed." [22] Bostonians still needed to prove that pleasures — like the grand tour — were really duties, just as they tried to convince themselves that duties — like hot oatmeal in the morning — were pleasures.

The sacrifice this time was considerably less Spartan. Ticknor's family accompanied him. Never did he experience the despondency and homesickness that had beset him previously in Europe. He also had a large acquaintance in England and on the continent, and now could travel in elegant style rather than "in the manner of a clergyman." Indeed, this trip resembled a triumphal return more than a pilgrimage. Now he rode over Europe in a luxurious private coach pulled by four horses called a berlin, and had three servants, a postillion, a courier, and a maid. Ticknor's young American friend, Samuel Ward, who accompanied them on the continent, was delighted with such regal transport: "Naturally with this train and with the interested help of Peter the courier, when we arrived at night we were led to the princes' apartments, the princes being mostly absent, and fared sumptuously. All day we could be poets and artists, and aristocrats all night." [23]

By the middle 1830's, as Ticknor was shrewd enough to recognize, American tourists were no longer so exceptional as in 1816, and could no longer capitalize so easily on the newness of their symbolic value. Thus the outward signs of status — the traveling coach, the sword and gold-buckled shoes, fastidiousness in obtaining and presenting letters of introduction, observance of courtly formality — were becoming important keys to unlock the inner chambers of European society. As one disenchanted observer said, Americans abroad were trying now to "impress all with whom they came in contact with the belief that, although the spirit of the American constitution recognizes no nobility, such an order of society nevertheless exists *de facto;* and that they themselves belong to the 'few select' of that 'large Augean stable.' " [24]

Through the pages of Ticknor's journals of his second trip marched, like puppets, a succession of kings, princes, dukes, counts, viscounts, marquesses, and barons. His diction became more lordly, full of words like *"recherché,"* "ultra," "noble," and "vulgar." Ticknor seemed to be more impressed than previously by aristocratic rank and trappings, but he was not a hypocrite or toady. Still he was mainly interested in people who were culturally as well as socially distinguished. Again he won the esteem of many eminent people by his broad knowledge, his earnestness, his refined manners, and his zeal for exportable culture. Count Circourt, one of Ticknor's erudite Parisian friends, told Prescott in 1844 that Ticknor had left an indelible impression of respect upon him "and upon the mind of every distinguished person who has been happy enough to be acquainted with him in France. Indeed, no American traveller since Franklin and Livingston, has left among the highest intellectual circles of the old world a stronger conviction of the sound and brilliant development of intellect in the new one." [25]

The European pilgrimage almost began in disaster. As the Ticknors' ship approached Liverpool, a fierce gale arose in the Irish channel. Deciding to chance a run downwind along the Mersey River rather than to tack northward, the pilot steered the ship over the bar and through the mountainous yellow waves, the wind and tide together carrying the vessel under bare poles at eighteen knots. Along the riverbank people on housetops watched the ship wend its way among the treacherous sandbanks. When they finally set foot on solid earth again, they learned that four ships had been lost in the storm, including a large brig.[26]

Once ashore, the Ticknors set out for London, "the condensation of existence." Ticknor's conquests were even more dazzling than in the previous trip. Everyone wanted to see him. He and his family had more invitations than they could accept to London breakfasts and literary dinners, to noble country houses, to scholarly meetings. He talked at length with Samuel Rogers, Robert Southey, William Wordsworth, Joanna Baillie, Maria Edgeworth, Francis Jeffrey, and Sidney Smith. At Holland House he dined with the Prime Minister, Lord Melbourne, and with Earl Grey; at Wentworth House and other mansions the Ticknors tasted the country life of the nobility. "Nothing . . . has gratified us more," he wrote to a friend, "than the visits we have made in the comfortable houses to which we have been invited in England and Ireland."

He noted proudly that the intellectuals at Holland House gave high praise to Prescott's *Ferdinand and Isabella* — John Allen saying that parts of it were better than Henry Hallam's discussion of the middle ages — and that Lord Holland himself thought Channing "the best writer of English alive." Happily, he remarked that "we are getting on in the world. Such things could not have been heard in such salons when I was here twenty years ago." Sydney Smith, who a generation before had asked the dread question, "Who reads an American book?" was cordial to Ticknor. Mrs. Ticknor, not so reverential as her husband, spoke of seeing at Oxford "the Palaces, where I *suppose* wisdom resides," and she tired of the competitive wit of London literary circles, "these gilt-edged, wire-woven, and hot-pressed beaux-esprits." [27]

After a tour of England, Wales, and Ireland during the summer of 1835, the Ticknors went to Dresden to spend the winter. There they stayed for nearly six months, pleased with the libraries, art, and literary society of the Saxon capital. In full regalia the Ticknors were presented at court. Ticknor struck up a friendship with Prince John. John, who became king of Saxony in 1854, was a scholar who had published a German translation of Dante in 1833. Frequently they met in the palace to talk about literature, and for more than thirty years they maintained a correspondence about comparative politics and comparative literature.

As a loyal republican, Ticknor found Saxony a perplexing anomaly. He believed that in this nation where "the Government is and does everything . . . half of what constitutes a man's business life and awakens, stimulates, and sustains his activity in our country is never felt or expected." Yet under benevolent sovereigns all was orderly, quiet, and regular in Saxony, and the people happy. "A real Yankee would make quite a stir, I assure you in a Saxon village," he wrote a Boston merchant; "a free constitution which should call into action the faculties and resources of the whole population and make each individual more truly a man by extending his relations, interests, and duties, would no doubt . . . create a great advancement of its condition." But Ticknor was not sure that this would really improve the nation: "it would seem almost a pity to put at hazard by political excitement and change, not only the comfort and contentment, but the quiet fidelity and loyalty of the great mass of the people. What should be done in such a case is a much more difficult moral question than what should be done in a country like England where the movement is already begun, and many, or nearly all, of its inevitable mischiefs are already realized." [28]

This Yankee at the Saxon court soon had an opportunity to look further into this question. When the Ticknors stopped at Vienna in June of 1836, Ticknor conversed privately with that "Phoenix of Tories,"

Metternich. Armed with a letter of introduction from Alexander von Humboldt, Ticknor saw the prince repeatedly at public occasions. One afternoon Metternich invited him to come for a private conversation in his chambers which lasted for more than an hour and a half. Dismissing a Hungarian count in a splendid Hussar's uniform, Metternich walked with great dignity with Ticknor into his cabinet, sat Ticknor in an easy chair, and proceeded to talk as if he thought Ticknor the judgment of posterity. Sixty-three years old, with penetrating blue eyes and Roman nose, of courtly manner and an imperial temperament, Metternich impressed Ticknor as a consummate statesman of the old school. Ticknor could not avoid admiring the autocratic prince and he felt privileged to be privy to his thoughts.[29]

The prime virtue of a leader, Metternich said, is to be "reasonable . . . in his expectations . . . I am myself moderate in everything . . . I am thought to be a great absolutist in my policy. But I am not. It is true I do not like democracies; democracy is everywhere and always . . . a dissolving, decomposing principle . . . This does not suit my character." For a man of constructive temperament, he went on, monarchy is the only proper government, for "monarchy alone tends to bring men together, to unite them into compact and effective mass . . . to render them capable . . . of the highest degrees of culture and civilization." Ticknor, the republican, objected: only in a republic can individuals be of real consequence, for there they "are more truly *men,* have wider views and a more active intelligence," than in a monarchy, which stifles initiative.

Politely, Metternich heard Ticknor speak his piece. Then he replied that in a democracy, where man is set against man in rivalry, the mass will not be efficient. In America democracy can be a reality, but in Europe it can only be a lie. "I have always . . . been of the opinion expressed by Tocqueville," Metternich declared, "that democracy, so far from being the oldest and simplest form of government . . . is the latest invented form of all, and the most complicated. With you in America it seems to be *un tour de force perpétuel.* You are, therefore, often in dangerous positions, and your system is one that wears out fast." To Ticknor's reply that the "young constitution easily throws off diseases that would destroy life in an old one," Metternich countered that the United States would inevitably become more democratic" and argued that a democracy could never "end in a quiet, ripe old age." The great difference between a monarchy and a democracy is that a democracy cannot *"prevent* evil."* With conviction he declared that "it is with *tomorrow* that my spirit wrestles." [30]

"I do not like my business," Metternich confessed. "When I was five-and-twenty years old, I foresaw nothing but change and trouble in my time; and I sometimes thought that I would leave Europe and go to America." Several times he repeated: "The present state of Europe is disgusting to me." Attentively, Ticknor listened; he would ponder the prince's remarks for the rest of his life. Alexander von Humboldt soon wrote to Ticknor that "Prince Metternich . . . was delighted with the conversation he had with you. Born in a republic, you nevertheless appeared more reasonable in his eyes, than what he calls my liberalism." The very fact that Ticknor was a citizen of a republic which had no feudal tradition made his political opinions respectable to Europeans who despised any but the most conservative views in their own lands. Perhaps the prince believed that Ticknor would have been a loyal monarchist in Europe. Princess Metternich told Ticknor that "she did not like liberals in Europe, but that it was another thing in America, where the government was democratick, and it was a man's duty to be liberal." [31]

Europe fortified Ticknor's patriotism. After spending about half a year abroad, Ticknor wrote Prescott that "it is still very comfortable to be an American . . . I would not change my passport — signed by some little scamp of an under-secretary at Washington, whose name I have forgotten — for any one of the fifteen hundred that are lying with it at the Police in Dresden, from Russia, France, and England." Ticknor's old friend Richard Henry Dana, Sr., nostalgic for Europe although he had never seen it, wrote asking for "something to comfort an old Tory." Ticknor could only repeat Metternich's comment, which he said was "eminently true" to his own feelings, that "the present state of Europe is disgusting to me." Ticknor found "a principle of decay at work" which the fumbling governments of Europe were fostering rather than arresting. The upper classes were weak, presumptuous, and morally degraded. Governments were "anxious about the future, temporizing, and alternately using an ill-timed spirit of concession and an ill-timed severity." True power rested with the bourgeoisie, since everywhere governments "were trying to associate to their interests the wealth of the middling class and to base themselves on property. But this is revolution. Personal

interest will not work like the principle of respect to superiors and submission to authority as such." By contrast, Americans enjoyed "the great
basis of purity in . . . domestic life and relations, which is so broadly
wanting here. We have men, in the less favored portions of society, who
have so much more intellect, will, and knowledge, that, compared with
similar classes here, those I am now among seem of an inferior order in
creation." Ticknor concluded that "notwithstanding the faults that freedom brings out . . . it is much more gratifying and satisfying to the
mind, to the affections, to the *soul* to live in our state of society than in
any I know of on this side of the Atlantick." [32]

Ticknor believed that while the European upper class was "broken
by extravagance and degraded by luxury," the middle class was "as
purely money-getting as is our people with less acuteness, cleverness, and
generosity of feeling." Worse still, the family was disintegrating in Europe, the code of sexual morality ruinous. Essentially, then, Ticknor believed that Yankees could extract the greatest good from the sordid
spirit of the age. American acquisitiveness was more humane, American
popular rule more disciplined, American morals more pure. One might
lament the decline of reverence, hierarchy, and tradition, but in an age
of steam, railroads, and bourgeois ascendency it was best to live in
Boston. [33]

After visiting Vienna the Ticknors traveled in a leisurely fashion to
Rome, where they spent the winter. Ticknor admired the relics of antiquity and the Italian climate, but he found the papal government ruth-
less and ineffectual, much of the city sordid, and the fashionable society
of Rome immoral and insipid. Killings and robberies were so frequent
that bakers would not deliver bread unless accompanied by a policeman.
Nobles rushed to bar the doors of their *palazzi* when the mob grew
restless.

Only because the Church had enmeshed the people in fear and superstition had a rebellion not broken out already. For the Catholic Church
Ticknor had little but scorn — much to the dismay of several Europeans
who tried to convert him. Referring to the prevalent taste for miraculous
relics, he asked, "Is Catholicism essentially a religion of follies — or
rather are such follies essential to Catholicism?" Once he stopped to visit
Prince Massimo: I "found Cardinal Gregorio, in the midst of a little
circle of Monsignors, putting himself in attitudes and showing off the
gestures and movements of an English boxer. Considering his age and

profession, and that he has more than once been a prominent candidate for Pope, I thought he might have been better employed." [34]

Ticknor was appalled that Princess Gabrielli, daughter of Lucien Buonaparte, had to send her daughter to a convent to protect her from Roman society; to him such a move was "a distinct proof that society here is in a false and ruinous state, and that domestick character and happiness have no foundations, whereon to be built or to rest." Witness the fate of her family, Ticknor said: her sister married "Count Posse who blew his brains out in Texas"; Prince Musignano was suing his parents for his wife's dowry; Queen Caroline was quarreling with Joseph and Jerome for the family inheritance; the Princess Canino was jealous of her husband and wouldn't join him in Italy; one of Princess Canino's daughters tried to drown herself; another was "married secretly to a vulgar tradesman"; one son was exiled to America for taking part in a murder; and another son was awaiting trial for the same murder in the Castel St. Angelo. Of the whole Buonaparte family, Ticknor claimed, only the Princess Gabrielli was happy and respectable. One black sheep might be allowed in a family — after all everyone knew that one of John Adams's sons was a renegade — but the Buonapartes carried things too far.[35]

Needless to say, Mrs. Ticknor's opinion of Roman society did not improve when she saw the princess breast-feeding her baby in public. The princess' husband said of those who objected to the practice, "c'est la pruderie." Anna confided that night in her journal, that "such being the state of opinion of my host and hostess, I did not enlarge on my own or my country women's notions upon the subject." She found Roman aristocracy more to be pitied than copied: "The more I see of Roman society, the less real attraction do I find in it, and so few materials for happiness, as to make it quite a sad picture." [36]

There were some brighter moments in Rome, however. At one of Princess Gabrielli's soirees Ticknor met a Monsignor Piccolomini, "a great name that has come down from the time of Wallenstein — says his mother was named Jackson and that her family is connected with that of our President General — a droll story if it be true." Ticknor found Piccolomini's stories "better than his genealogy." And one could escape the Roman present by fleeing into the Roman past. After seeing the Forum, the Baths of Caracalla, and Saint Peter's, Ticknor visited tombs of solid Roman citizens "who died nearly two thousand years ago . . .

all just as it was left the last time Roman hands and Roman piety sealed it up, little thinking who would open it up, or how it would be visited. It is one of those spots, in which you are entirely satisfied." [37]

The Ticknors spent the winter of 1837–38 in Paris. Again Ticknor attended the salons and met the respectable literary men of the day, among them the historians Guizot and Thierry, talked with Lamartine, and once more saw Chateaubriand. But "popular" writers, like Hugo, Balzac, and George Sand, were beneath notice. The character of the theater was even more reprehensible than twenty years before; contemporary French drama "contains hardly any indecorous phrases or allusion," Ticknor observed, "but its whole tone is highly immoral." "I know nothing that more truly deserves the reproach of being immoral and demoralizing," said Ticknor, "than the theatres of Paris and the popular literature of the day."

Society had become even more political in temper, but now Parisians were less hopeful about republicanism. Even though Thierry still considered himself liberal, he thought that the people would not "choose the most elevated minds for the most important places." How could Ticknor gainsay him when America had just elected Van Buren? Guizot, worried about American mobs and slavery, told Ticknor that he had "ceased to believe in the stability of our popular institutions." [38]

Ticknor took seriously his duty of instructing his countrymen in the ways of the Old World. Whatever its moral or political limitations, Europe was still a good place to round off social angularities, as Ticknor's daughter showed in her book, *An American Family in Paris*. Ticknor knew to perfection the proper social forms; "no one has been more successful in creating among foreigners a just appreciation of the intelligence and refinement that may be found in the best social circles of America," commented a fellow Brahmin. Charles Sumner, who had been one of Ticknor's best students at Harvard College, plied him for advice and letters of introduction to use on his European pilgrimage. "Like the continent"—Ticknor wrote him, "love Italy,—trust Germany. All is unlike England." With or without Ticknor's help, Sumner concluded that Paris "is a perfect Sodom without religion and without any morality between the sexes." When the Duc de Broglie failed to acknowledge the letter of introduction Ticknor had written for Sumner, Ticknor advised the American to visit the duc at his home and told him what to talk about, assuring him that Broglie "is a person to be dealt plainly with because he means sincerely." But Americans should not seem too forward: *"laissez-aller* is eminently the rule in London. It is rarely safe for a stranger to make any advance to an Englishman." The most important advice he gave Sumner was to stay in Europe until he had seen and done all, "for otherwise you will want to go back again, and *that* is a most disagreeable disease. I never had it and have no fear of it, — but I have witnessed it more than once, and it is, like a relapse — much worse than the original complaint." [39]

Alienation and nostalgia were chronic diseases of the traveler. When Ticknor returned to Boston in June of 1838, after a last tour of England and Scotland, he found it hard to settle down. He confessed to Sumner that it was hard to move back to Nine Park Street, "for, having lived eight years in Hotels, I prefer the vagabond life, and eschew the responsibilities and weariness of housekeeping. Mrs. Ticknor contra-abuses me for such unsuitable tastes." But no more than George Apley could Ticknor be a vagabond; Boston would not allow it. His daughter wrote, apropos of his return in 1838, that "his love of home, his pride in his country, and his preference for a regular, domestic life, always . . . made him regard his absences as periods taken out of his legitimate life." [40]

Poised between two worlds, Ticknor was neither expatriate nor chauvinist. To the end he remained provincial in outlook but patriotic by conviction, a mediator between the ominous ripeness of the Old World and the happy but raw estate of the New.

3. *The Brahmin Caste of New England*

Macaulay was astonished that Prescott, after the "most brilliant visit ever made to England by an American citizen not clothed with the *prestige* of official station," should have returned to Boston of his own free will. Prescott appreciated his reception in England, but after describing the Ascot races, a dinner at Sir Robert Peal's, and a conversation with the Duke of Wellington, he asked his wife, "Is this not a fine life? I am most sincerely tired of it . . . and would not exchange my regular domestic and literary occupations in the good old Puritan town for this round of heedless, headless gayety, — not if I had the fortune of the Marquis of Westminster, the richest peer in England."

He wrote Ticknor from London that "I am quite sure, having once had this experience, nothing would ever induce me to repeat it. As I have heard you say, it would not pay." [41]

Why did the Boston elite prove to be so attractive to Ticknor and Prescott? What were the qualifications and aspirations of Ticknor and his fellow patricians? In her novel of manners, *The Barclays of Boston*, Mrs. Harrison Gray Otis, Jr., told how difficult it was to speak of stratification: "Now how shall it be written? That the Bartons were not of the same rank as the Barclays, — no such word as rank in democratic America. Not of the same class, — that will never do . . . The fact is, and the truth must be told, it is very hard, indeed, to describe certain things in America." The rollicking "widow Otis," — a plump and plain woman who later contributed to the Civil War effort by selling kisses at five dollars apiece — had been generous in her definition of the elite. She once had a party which included "President Fillmore, Lord Elgin, and an Indian chief." Boston thought Mrs. Otis rather irreverent toward sacred things — like its Brahmin caste.[42]

During his visit to New England Tocqueville did not hesitate to give Ticknor and his friends the supreme compliment: "Society, at least the society in which we have been introduced, and I think that it is the first, resembles almost completely the upper classes of Europe." Ticknor and many of his friends had grown up in a Federalist Boston which had little patience with social democracy. Respect for authority, propriety of manners, and severe standards of morality were hallmarks of that society. These traits persisted and were apparent to Tocqueville. Henry Adams observed that

The Boston to which Mr. Ticknor returned in 1838 had a physiognomy quite its own . . . Its characteristic quality was perhaps provincialism, but provincialism based on Puritanism, stirred within fixed limits by great activity of mind, and lit up, though hardly enlightened, by some notable men. The logical social results of republican institutions had not yet worked themselves out. Lingering tradition and close-woven associations seemed solid and sure to continue. There were leaders in Israel, — people whose natural vocation it was to decide on important questions, — and who took the crown of the causeway in things intellectual as surely if not as consciously as any red-cloaked Glasgow merchant of the old days.[43]

The traditional leaders in Federalist Boston had been ministers, lawyers, judges, merchants, doctors, and professors. Henry Adams said that professional men continued to dominate the community as he grew up in the 1840's: "Down to 1850, and even later, New England society was still directed by the professions. Lawyers, physicians, professors, merchants were classes, and acted not as individuals, but as though they were clergymen and each profession were a church." Although expanding economic ventures drew young Brahmins into banking, manufacturing, and other avenues of business, the learned professions continued to attract — and create — patricians and remained the chief source of social and political leadership. Eminent lawyers, especially, constituted an untitled elite. "If I were asked where I place the American aristocracy," commented Tocqueville, "I should reply without hesitation that it is not among the rich, who are united by no common tie, but that it occupies the judicial bar and bench."

Not only did successful professional men maintain high esprit de corps and severe intellectual standards within their guilds, but they also aspired to broad cultivation. Oliver Wendell Holmes, a doctor who was also poet and essayist; Joseph Story, the learned constitutional commentator and littérateur; William Ellery Channing, preacher and literary critic — these were but outstanding examples of a host of other Boston professional men who gave Latin toasts at their clubs, who wrote local history, who read Thackeray and Milton. Such men, together with cultured businessmen, were the core of Brahmin society.[44]

Of the many determinants of social rank, wealth was the most tangible and the most significant in the long run. "There is nothing in New England corresponding at all to the feudal aristocracies of the Old World," commented Oliver Wendell Holmes, Sr. "What we mean by 'aristocracy' is merely the richer part of the community, that live in the tallest houses, drive real carriages (not 'kerridges'), kid-glove their hands, and French-bonnet their ladies." Fortunes made in the professions, commerce, banking, insurance, manufacturing, and transport bought the outward symbols of high social position, leisure time to enjoy or at least display wealth, assured handsome dowries to magnify the attractions of daughters, and provided education and a family business for sons.

Yet wealth alone was not apt to create a cohesive and lasting social group. While the sons of shopkeepers, farmers, and mechanics were becoming rich, a few families that had been wealthy for two or more generations were losing their fortunes, either by subdivision or faulty management. Holmes contended, with some exaggeration, that the "trivial and fugitive fact of personal wealth does not create a permanent class . . . one does not need to live a very long life to see most of the rich families he knew in childhood more or less reduced, and the millions shifted into the hands of the country-boys who were sweeping stores and carrying parcels when the now decayed gentry were driving their chariots."

Rags to riches to rags was a familiar fear in Boston before the Civil War. One of Boston's favorite charities was the support of individuals reduced "by the Providence of God from Affluence to Penury." In *The Barclays of Boston,* a patrician lady confessed that her "deepest sympathies are not aroused for merely the poorly poor; they incline vastly towards the class that has seen better days . . . The head that was once uplifted as high as any in the land, now fallen by the adverse fortunes of commercial ventures, fills my heart with compassion, and many a one there is." Recurrent financial panics harassed the well-to-do; the very possibility of financial ruin, with all it entailed, aroused an anxiety out of proportion to probable disaster.[45]

The impermanence of wealth was not the only source of anxiety. From all sides came criticisms that the pursuit of wealth was becoming a low passion, that Boston was becoming a town of Scrooges. George Hillard described the results of worshipping Mammon in his lecture to young businessmen, *The Dangers and Duties of the Mercantile Profession:* "Every power, every affection, every taste, except those which . . . [the merchant's] particular occupation calls into play, is left to starve. Over the gates of his mind he writes in letters which he who runs may read, 'No admittance except on business.' " The result: "In time he reaches the goal of his hopes; but now insulted Nature begins to claim her revenge . . . The spring of his mind is broken. He can no longer lift his thoughts from the ground . . . He cannot purge his voice of its fawning tone, or pluck from his face the mean, money-getting mask." [46] William Ellery Channing complained to Ticknor of "the mournful effects of the infinite, intense thirst for gain and accumulation here. It takes so much the form of insanity, that one may on that account charge on it the less immorality . . . This people will find out at length that money is not the supreme end of the social compact, that republican institutions in particular have liberty and improvement and the development of human nature for their objects."

Something more than wealth was needed; benevolence and cultivation alone could redeem a commercial bourgeoisie. Even the most earnest self-made men were apt to be green fruit culturally. When Abbott Lawrence accepted his diplomatic post as Minister to England, Prescott confided to Bancroft that his businessman son-in-law felt "some natural mistrust as to taking an office in which . . . he is obviously deficient. I thought he must feel this the other day at dinner, for the conversation took a literary turn." [47]

If wealth alone was too impermanent and the pursuit of riches too narrowing to produce a class of gentlemen, then what other attributes would designate the socially elect? "There is . . . in New England an aristocracy, if you choose to call it so," wrote Holmes the Autocrat, "which has a far greater character of permanence" than the wealthy. This "aristocracy," which he called the *"Brahmin caste of New England"*, was a group of scholars, generally of moderate wealth, which had perpetuated itself through several generations. Perhaps it was cultivation and good family that marked the true gentleman and created a "harmless, inoffensive, untitled aristocracy" which could leaven the republican mass. Tocqueville sensed the influence of Holmes' "caste." In Boston the manners of the upper class "are distinguished," he said, "their conversation turns on intellectual matters, one feels oneself delivered from those commercial habits and that financial spirit that render the society of New-York so vulgar. There are already in existence in Boston a certain number of persons who, having no occupation, seek out the pleasures of the spirit." [48]

The idea of distinguished heredity, of a cultivated and influential family perpetuating itself through several generations, appealed to Bostonians, to whom genealogy was a sacred science. Holmes declared "that, *other things being equal,* in most relations of life, I prefer a man of family." A "man of family" was the descendant of "four or five generations of gentlemen and gentlewomen; among them a member of his majesty's Council for the Provinces, a Governor or so, one or two Doctors of Divinity, a member of Congress, not later than the time of long boots with tassels." His heredity would show itself in his features: "Money kept for two or three generations transforms a race," Holmes commented, " — I don't mean merely in manners and hereditary culture, but in blood and bone." [49]

This notion of hereditary yet untitled gentility was attractive but for one consideration: it bore little relation to reality. Wistfully, Ticknor appreciated the importance "of good kith and kin . . . I have lived long enough to believe a good deal in such matters." But heredity could threaten as well as comfort. James Russell Lowell wrote to a friend of a retort Thackeray made to Ticknor: "Ticknor was telling him that one mark of a gentleman was to be well-looking, for good blood showed itself in good features. 'A pretty speech,' cries Thackeray, 'for one brokennosed man to make to another.' All Boston has been secretly tickled with it." And once an Englishman singled out Wendell Phillips and Edmund Quincy, who had been disbarred from polite society for their abolitionist views, as "the only men I have ever seen in your country who look like gentlemen." [50]

Handsome appearance, then, could be an embarrassing criterion of gentility. So, too, genealogy. Ticknor's friend James Savage was a diligent pioneer in the pious craft — or crafty piety — of genealogy, but Ticknor dismissed his researches as a "vain" quest. How many Bostonians could profess to be men of family as Holmes defined the breed (a definition doubtless made with tongue in cheek)? Ticknor's own grandfather was a poor farmer, probably barely literate, and his father a grocer and school teacher. Webster's father was an impoverished farmer in the wilds of New Hampshire. Ticknor and Webster typified the patrician clan of Boston more than the handful of persons who could, like Dana and Robert Winthrop, claim illustrious forebears in the colonial period. Most of Ticknor's friends were descended from sturdy yeomen like Prescott's ancestors: "men of strongly marked character but small estates, and devoted to mechanical or agricultural pursuits, — circumstances which fitted them as nothing could so well have done for the trials and labors incident to their settlement in this Western wilderness." No genealogical alchemy could transform such ancestors. Until the influx of immigrants most Bostonians could claim equal ancestral distinction. The rapid social rise of the patricians — the Cabots, Eliots, Grays, Perkins, Storys, Appletons, Lawrences, Bowditches, Dexters, Wards, Forbes, and the rest — testified to the possibility of acquiring high social position without a distinguished family tree.[51]

Very early, Bostonians developed a sense of reverence for the family founder, commonly a merchant who established the fortunes of the family in the years following the Revolution or the early decades of the nineteenth century. The sons started a school of filio-pietistic biography aimed at giving a marmoreal polish to the earthy founder and a sense of family solidarity and tradition to his descendants, present and future. Some patricians, like Prescott's father, even entailed their estates. After his marriage, Prescott continued to live with his parents. Susan Prescott, the historian's wife, lived for twenty-seven years of her married life in a household which her mother-in-law administered; at the age of eighty Catherine Prescott finally wrote her son that "it is proper . . . that your wife should be the mistress of your family. Your children should consider her the head to direct and guide in every thing." It was common for extended families to live together in the large mansions which symbolized their rank. Harrison Gray Otis built a house on Beacon Street roomy enough for himself and three of his married children, and complete with a floor for joint entertaining.

Clearly, though, it was difficult to create a sense of family continuity through time either backward or forward. Through intermarriage, the social equivalent of the financial directorate, the Boston Associates, it was possible to develop a sense of *lateral* genealogy, to consolidate a family's social position, wealth, power, education, and cultivation during one or two generations. The Ticknors were related by marriage, for example, to the Eliots, Dwights, Dexters, and Nortons; the Prescotts to the Amorys, Dexters, Lawrences, and Peabodys. Intermarriage created an interlocking Brahmin directorate.[52]

A severe code of sexual morality also protected the extended patrician family. Francis Lieber, a German scholar who had emigrated to Boston, told Tocqueville that the morals of the elite "are as perfect as it is possible to imagine them. I don't believe that there is a single intrigue in Boston society. A woman would be lost." Even the location of bedrooms frustrated romantic liaisons. The women of Boston were coquettes "because they know that they cannot go beyond a certain point, and that no one believes that they overstep that bound. After all, I like still better our women of Europe with their weaknesses, than the glacial and egotistical virtue of the Americans." Tocqueville and Beaumont enjoyed flirting with the young ladies of Boston: "the faces are always new, and I think, God pardon me, that we always tell them the same things, at the risk of complimenting a brunette on the whiteness of her skin, and a blond on the ebony of her hair. But that is a bagatelle and occupies but a very small place in the lives of two young men of politics, utterly devoted to speculations of the most elevated order." Their learned investigations disclosed that Lieber was right. "American morals are . . . the purest existing in any nation," Tocqueville decided.

This purity he attributed to religious conviction, preoccupation with making money, the American "physical constitution" (as characteristic of "a northern race"), early marriage, and the "rational" education of girls. He reported the opinion of a southerner that "the young blood of the city frequents" prostitutes, but added that "the evil stops there, without ever crossing the domestic threshold or troubling the families." Prudery had its roots as much in prudence as in smugness. Amid the fluctuations of wealth, the maelstrom of politics, the worries of a group consolidating its position, sexual purity was a bastion of the family and the family a bastion of the patrician class.[53]

One avenue to social eminence was pedigree by foreign association. The pedigree by association was important especially for bachelors, like Charles Sumner. Henry Adams commented that "social success in England and on the Continent gave to every Bostonian who enjoyed it a halo never acquired by domestic sanctity." Tocqueville noticed that all the men of the "first society" of Boston had been to Europe, but few had been so successful there socially as Ticknor. The mere fact of being entertained at a British country seat or being presented at a foreign court imparted glory. Frederick Marryat, a Tory observer of American follies, snorted that "it will be a curious anomaly in the history of a republic, that, fifty years after it was established, republicans should apply to the mother country whose institutions they had abjured, to obtain from her a patent of superiority, so as to raise themselves above that hated equality which . . . they profess." Americans did not wish to be reminded that their "aristocracy" was merely a bourgeoisie in European eyes.[54]

Still, there were pitfalls in the pedigree by association: it exaggerated cultural and social provincialism. And provincialism was not entirely a welcome fact even in Boston. "Everett thinks of London too much," Prescott wrote to George Bancroft in 1847. "His wife and daughter talk of it a good deal . . . don't stay abroad long enough to lose one's relish for home." "After all, there is nothing more silly," Longfellow commented, "than this aping of foreign nations; — the love of foreign nobility." Obsequiousness to nobility seemed pretentious and absurd to many Bostonians of high standing. When the Duke of Saxe-Weimar visited Boston, Josiah Quincy, Jr., noticed that he "seemed to have a full understanding of the value of money, and said many things which showed that his possessions were by no means equal to his rank. He asked some questions about Stuart's paintings, and added, 'Is he very dear?' " Quincy smiled at Everett's pomposity in addressing the Duke as "Your Highness" in "a reverence of voice which appeared to me, to say the least, superfluous. I suppose Mr. Everett wanted to show that he was accustomed to the manners of Europe." [55]

The close association of Brahmin Boston with Harvard also helped to define the Boston elite, especially the members of the second generation. True, some of the patricians were self-educated, and some had gone to other colleges. But the great majority of proper Bostonians went to Harvard, as Henry Adams said, "because their friends went there, and the College was their ideal of social self-respect." Harvard offered an extra-curricular course in the Brahmin life-style. This style, as Adams described it, was "quietly penetrating and aggressively commonplace; free from meanness, jealousies, intrigues, enthusiasms and passions; not exceptionally quick; not consciously sceptical; singularly indifferent to display, artifice, florid expression . . . with not much humor . . . negative to a degree that in the long run became positive and triumphant . . . their judgment . . . a sort of gravitation." Harvard even taught the Bostonian to hold his liquor — "though the mere recollection of [his drinking] . . . made him doubt his veracity." [56]

Since in a sense Harvard was a social extension of the Brahmin family, Ticknor had been especially concerned about the morals as well as the cultivation of the students. A prime purpose of higher education, Ticknor believed, "consists in adjusting a young man, during the most flexible part of his life, to his place among the associates who can best help him onward." Ticknor and his fellow Brahmins had no desire to make Harvard a closed corporation for the wealthy, only a patrician finishing school. They admired the poor rustic scholar, "the large uncombed youth" as Holmes put it, who startled the "hereditary class leaders by striding past them all." Ticknor also wanted the Boston Public Library to help people raise themselves culturally by their bootstraps. It was only right, however, that the Brahmin clan should establish the tone and direction of such institutions. [57]

Ticknor's friend Sir Charles Lyell wrote that the mingling in Boston "of the [Harvard] professors, both literary and scientific, with the eminent lawyers, clergymen, physicians, and principal merchants of the place forms a society of a superior kind; and to these may be added several persons, who, having inherited ample fortunes, have successfully devoted their lives to original researches in history and other departments." The existence of a group of respectable professors and gentlemen of letters, the influence of Harvard and a refined clergy, the prominence of men of affairs with literary tastes — these increased the intellectual density of Boston society. Especially in the 1840's and 1850's when the social arteries were hardening, "the social arbiters of Boston — George Ticknor and the rest" — were able to convince many people that a gentleman must be cultivated as well as rich, polished as well as powerful. Indeed, scholarship, a pedigree by association, genteel manners, and a reverential attitude might admit a man like George Hillard to the "caste" even though he had neither wealth nor distinguished family.[58]

Lyell thought that the literary tone of Boston high society was welcome in a country "where the public mind is apt to be exclusively absorbed in politics." Ever since the fall of Federalism Ticknor had displayed an ambivalent attitude towards politics, as had many of his fellow Brahmins. Ticknor affected disdain for the daily machinations of politicians: in his biography of Prescott he praised his friend for dealing "with political discussions only when they related to events and persons at least two centuries old." A fellow patrician ridiculed the country bumpkins who represented the sovereign state of Massachusetts in the General Court — "members who advocate 'mackerel inspection,' cider presses, fences, raising potatoes, and brewing small beer." "The positive fact is," said another to Francis Grund, "that few of our representatives are gentlemen." Tocqueville, as usual, had an explanation: "the rich frequently abandon the lists, through unwillingness to contend, *and frequently to contend in vain,* against the poorer classes of their fellow citizens. As they cannot occupy in public a position equivalent to what they hold in private life, they abandon the former and give themselves up to the latter; and they constitute a private society in the state which has its own tastes and pleasures." Tocqueville's description aptly characterized Ticknor's stance: he chose not to do battle in the political arena.[59]

This disdain for partisan politics hardly meant that Ticknor and his fellow Brahmins were uninterested in statesmanship or in the destiny of the nation. Henry Adams observed that "it was the old Ciceronian idea of government by *the best* that produced the long line of New England statesmen." A number of Ticknor's circle were active in Whig politics: Daniel Webster, Edward Everett, Robert Winthrop, Abbott Lawrence, Rufus Choate, and Nathan Appleton. Webster, in particular, was a Brahmin idol until the slavery contest, and his defense of the fugitive slave law split the patrician group into warring factions.

The nature of American partisan politics, especially on the national stage, made it difficult for the Brahmins to translate their economic, social and intellectual authority into political power. From this fact stemmed Ticknor's ambivalence towards politics and the ambiguity of the patrician's political role: the people often did not want *"the best"* to lead them. Consequently Ticknor and a number of his conservative friends sought to bypass parties and legislatures and to influence the course of the nation in other ways. They sought to control institutions — schools, churches, libraries, the legal system, the republic of letters — which would stabilize society. "What force can now unclench the giant grasp of the People?" asked James Hillhouse. "The young Titan has risen up . . . Though he cannot be deprived of his power, may not his eyes be enlightened, his heart be refined, his purposes and aims be made more beneficent and wise? Therein lies our hope!" Gentlemen of letters might carry out this task of enlightenment and refinement, "performing the functions of an Aristocracy, without its intolerable appendages." Such was Ticknor's goal.[60]

4. *High Priest*

The literary critic Edwin Whipple wrote that Ticknor's social position "was so assured that one of his friends, Nathan Hale, pleasantly suggested that the name of Boston be changed to Ticknorville. In New York, and other cities, the good society of Boston was long regarded as the select circle of ladies and gentlemen in which Ticknor moved, and to which he almost gave the law." Ticknor took seriously his obligation to civilize Boston. Oliver Wendell Holmes, Sr., called Ticknor's library the "headquarters of scholarship and hospitality." "You may well believe that the influence of this amiable and accomplished family has been most salutary on our little society," Prescott wrote to a Parisian count. "Indeed it has contributed much to raise the character of social enjoyment by giving a more intellectual character to it." [61]

Mrs. Ticknor did her share. Kate Gannett Wells, a daughter of Ticknor's minister Ezra Gannett, thought her "the one Boston woman — with the exception of Emily Marshall" — worthy of being called a social queen. "From the beginning of her married life until her death she was a queen. There was only one Mrs. Ticknor, by implication, and greatly honored were those who had access to her house, — to the parlor and to the library upstairs, the throne room as it were. There she and Mr. Ticknor received nightly . . . The nobility and the scholars of Europe met there as no where else . . . I have never seen any society equal to what was there, great cordiality shading off into degrees of welcome, high-bred courtesy in discussion and courtly grace of movement." Remembering his own youth as an aspiring scholar without wealth or social distinction, Ticknor, as did *The Barclays of Boston,* entertained "poor scholars, artists and others, to whom a well-appointed repast was a boon indeed, and the charm of social intercourse, a greater one still." [62]

Eminent foreign visitors came automatically to Nine Park Street. Mrs. Basil Hall, wife of the crabbed Tory who blistered America in his *Travels,* could find nothing to disdain at the Ticknor's table, where the "conversation . . . was really worthy of a London dinner." After closely observing a ball which the Ticknors gave, she concluded that "they are both of them animated and intelligent persons, and he never says *Madam;* he might indeed pass current for a well-informed, well-bred Englishman." A visiting Frenchman thought that Ticknor could pass for a well-bred Parisian: "he has French manners, and speaks our language without the slightest accent." [63]

"The Paris of Louis Philippe, Guizot, and de Tocqueville, as well as the London of Robert Peel, Macaulay, and John Stuart Mill, were but varieties of the same upper-class *bourgeoisie* that felt instinctive cousinship with the Boston of Ticknor, Prescott, and Motley," Henry Adams observed. Ticknor's role as high priest of the Brahmin caste bridged the worlds of Boston, London, and Paris. Lord Morpeth visited Boston in 1841 and found Ticknor "well-bred and cordial", Mrs. Ticknor "a very superior person." He ate in the broad-arched dining room at Nine Park Street "well-furnished with chintzes," attended by "five men-servants"; "the whole process would have bespoken refinement in any society; travel had enabled them to combine what was pleasant in all." Thackeray, too, often visited the "great city magnate and litterateur" Ticknor, listened to music in the morning room while winter winds blew outside, and sat "in that library . . . with that good supper and talk afterwards." [64]

Ticknor's role as social and cultural arbiter in Boston embarrassingly resembled that of the French court he had so vehemently attacked in his lectures on French literature. Praise or criticism emanating from Nine Park Street carried weight in Brahmin circles. Francis Grund satirized this Brahmin guardianship of taste. On one occasion he attended a concert of an English singer — "her morality being endorsed by three responsible merchants" — and ventured to say to his cicerone that she sang without feeling or taste. In alarm his companion exclaimed, "Do not say that loud enough for other people to hear you . . . Our elite would never forgive such a difference of opinion . . . This is a *free* country, sir! every man may do or think what he pleases, only he must not let other people know it." Theodore Parker thought "Boston . . . a queer little city; the Public is a desperate tyrant there, and it is seldom that one dares to disobey the command of public opinion." [65]

Indeed the custom of casting out heretics had not died with Puritanism. Just as the Federalists practiced social ostracism as a normal form of political policy, so Ticknor and many of his friends excommunicated men whose influence or opinions they condemned. Thus when Ticknor's friend George Bancroft turned Jacksonian democrat, or others became abolitionists, they placed themselves beyond the pale of Nine Park Street. Charles Sumner incurred the same ban for a variety of indiscretions. This was no minor privation for Sumner. His friend and biographer Edward Pierce commented that "to be admitted to such a house as Mr. Ticknor's was a test of culture and good breeding; to be shut out from it was an exclusion from what was most coveted in a social way by scholars and gentlemen who combined the fruits of study and travel." When George Hillard, a friend of both Sumner and Ticknor, protested this ostracism, Ticknor replied that the principles of Boston society "are right, and its severity towards disorganizers and social democracy in all its forms, is just and wise. It keeps our standard of public morals where it should be . . . and is the circumstance which distinguishes us favorably from New York and the other large cities of the Union, where demagogues are permitted to rule, by the weak tolerance of men who know better, and are stronger than they are." [66]

Ostracism, after all, wasn't the same as the faggot and rack. In a society ruled by public opinion, such sanctions were essential. Some thought otherwise: John Sibley, the Harvard librarian, wrote angrily in his journal that "when such 'Old Fogies' as George Ticknor, who would not admit Charles Sumner's bust to the Boston Public Library . . . have passed away, there will be a generation I trust who will rise above such bigotry and narrow mindedness." [67]

Himself reproachful, Ticknor invited reproach. Sumner dismissed his former guide as "the personification of *refined* idleness," a man who "sits in his rich library, and laps himself in care and indulgence, *doing* nothing himself, treating unkindly the works of those who *do,* looking down upon all, himself having no claim to be regarded, except as a man of *promises* — never, in a life no longer short, redeemed." Viewed from outside, Nine Park Street looked barren and cheerless.[68]

Seen from below, Beacon Hill struck many as pretentious. One of the most outspoken critics of the Brahmin caste was the anonymous author of *Our First Men,* a book predicated on "the inalienable right of all Yankees to inquire into, and to thoroughly sift and examine, their neighbor's affairs." Ruthlessly, he reminded the Boston elite "that they were once poor themselves, or their fathers were" and that their "money which so puffs them up, and makes them feel so big, came to them through toil and labor, and close sharing, and tight economy; and now and then, perhaps, a little cheating." He divided the rich into a "yearling aristocracy" and a "two-year-old aristocracy," asserting that the "vulgar, violent, robust and hard-hearted" entrepreneurs of the "yearling aristocracy" reminded him of the saying "that all that is necessary for success in this world is a good constitution and a bad heart." The "two-year-old aristocracy" were second-generation rich men characterized by rigid propriety and a veneer of refinement which glossed over the true bases of their power. "To those within this charmed circle, it appears for the most part very delightful . . . But to those without it looks forbidding, arrogant, cold, comfortless." [69]

Charles Gordon Greene, editor of the Democratic *Boston Morning Post,* was decidedly outside the "charmed circle." In 1840 he broadcast what Longfellow called a "scurrilous attack on Ticknor . . . A shameful invasion of the security of private life." Greene assaulted Ticknor's snobbery in a favorable review of Orestes Brownson's *Boston Quarterly Review*. According to Greene, Lord Brougham asked Ticknor what he knew about Brownson. Spurning "Brownson as a vulgar loco-foco," Ticknor replied, " 'We don't think much of him in Boston. Indeed, I am not acquainted with him.' 'Then,' replied Lord Brougham, 'I advise you to become acquainted with him as soon as you get home. Let me tell you, sir, he is one of the first thinkers and writers, not merely of America, but of the present age.' " Greene went on to assert that Ticknor was "one of the sleepy drones . . . a man more distinguished for his petty dilettantism than for any good accomplished for his race." [70]

5. *Labor Ipse Voluptas*

Although Ticknor could dismiss Greene as a vulgar upstart, he still wished to justify his career as a man of letters. The problem of vocation plagued intellectuals of the period. Thoreau's *Walden* offered one solution, Brook Farm another, but neither would do for a proper Bostonian. Emerson, who also agonized over his role, once reminded himself in his journal of the sorry results of forced literary labor: "I have been writing with some pains essays on various matters as a sort of apology to my country for my apparent idleness. But the poor work has looked poorer daily, as I have strove to end it." Unlike many intellectuals, Ticknor lacked neither time nor money, but he, like they, had to prove that he was a useful and industrious citizen.[71]

The "yearling aristocracy" and the average man sometimes questioned the value of the professional purveyors of culture. Kid gloves and cultivation were fine for women; but men should forget such "moonshine" and get down to the true business of "our *cool, calm, calculating, money-making* Yankees." Francis Grund asked a yearling why, if this was so, Boston should be called "the Athens of the United States." " 'That appellation,' replied he, 'refers to our women, not to our gentlemen. Our ladies read a great deal. And why should they not? What else have they to do? And we have, besides, a lot of literary twaddles, manufactured by the wholesale at Cambridge, who attempt to turn the heads of the young girls with the nonsense they call "poetry," which fills nearly all our papers, instead of clever editorials. If we have one poet among us, we have at least fifty, the joint earnings of whom would not be sufficient to keep a dog. But then poets don't turn *our* heads, you see; we are too much occupied with business.' " [72]

Secure within the Brahmin caste, Ticknor might disregard the jibes of those outside — even though they may have piqued him. But one demand he could not ignore was the command common to all classes that a respectable man must work. Tocqueville found that in America it was more honorable to labor than to enjoy elegant leisure, turning the European "point of honor quite round . . . I have sometimes met in America with young men of wealth, personally disinclined to all laborious exertion, but who had been compelled to embrace a profession. Their disposition and their fortune allowed them to remain without employment; public opinion forbade it, too imperiously to be disobeyed." Ticknor agreed that one must work — his signet read *Labor Ipse Voluptas* — but for him the chief problem was to prove that pleasure was work, not that work was pleasure. And in the study as in the cotton mill, one had to maintain production.[73]

The moral which informed Ticknor's biography of Prescott was that the historian's life had been one of "almost constant struggle — of an almost constant sacrifice of impulse to duty." "Struggle," "sacrifice," "duty," — only a formidable effort of will enabled the genial, pleasure-loving Prescott to satisfy the conscience of the community and his own. Prescott hated to get up in the morning, yet early each day the servant knocked on the door, Prescott counted to twenty, and "resolutely sprang out of bed; or, if he failed, he paid a forfeit, as a memento of his weakness, to the servant who had knocked at his chamber-door." Despite his near blindness, which gave him as good an excuse as any for idleness, he sentenced himself to a lifetime of hard labor; "it is of little moment whether I succeed in this or that thing, but it is of great moment that I am habitually industrious." When he found his work flagging while composing *Ferdinand and Isabella,* he made a bond with his secretary that he would pay $1,000 if he should not write 250 pages within the next year. He continued to make such wagers, and again and again in his literary memoranda he chided himself for looking out the window, or staying out too late to work efficiently the next day, or for being lazy.

To the end, Ticknor declared, "work was often painfully unwelcome to him . . ." In the midst of his torment, while he was writing his first history, he would often meet a relative who "affectionately urged him to undertake some serious occupation as a thing essential to his happiness, and even to his respectable position in society." His whole life, Ticknor said, taught those "whose social position makes no demand on them for exertion" to shun "a life of dainty, elegant idleness." [74]

Prescott's scholarly output was indeed impressive: the edition of his works, including Ticknor's biography, published by Lippincott in 1904 totaled twenty-two volumes, including the *History of Ferdinand and Isabella, History of the Conquest of Mexico, History of the Conquest of Peru,* and *History of the Reign of Phillip the Second.* The large number of published works of several other New England scholars — multi-volume men like Sparks, Bancroft, Motley, Parkman, Longfellow, and Lowell — also testified to the industry of Yankee men of letters. How did Ticknor compare with his peers in the American literary republic? The theme of willful industry permeated the biography of Ticknor; he did not yield, his daughter said, "to the allurement of a life of unprofitable leisure." Prescott's testimony was somewhat different. He believed that Ticknor worked in his youth "with an assiduity which has few parallels in this country," but that after retiring from Harvard he began to court the Muses "with something more of a Platonic love than in his earlier days." [75]

It appears that after 1835 Ticknor did clip coupons on his previous scholarly investment. Before then, Ticknor worked hard enough to satisfy the most exacting critic. He published hundreds of pages of reviews and essays. His lectures on French and Spanish literature represented laborious, pioneer American scholarship. His translations of Sophocles, Aristophanes, Sallust, Xenophon, Winckelmann, Lessing, and Goethe show how carefully and diligently he prepared himself for his teaching. And the many pages of notes he took for his lectures on Shakespeare and studies of Milton and Dante might easily have issued in competent critical works; Count Circourt wrote Prescott that Ticknor's unpublished notes on Dante were "of the highest interest. Few persons in the world are so intimately acquainted with the old bard; and nowhere, perhaps, such a combination of profound learning, acute criticism, and serene elevation of mind can be found as in this highly gifted and excellent man." Yet Ticknor published none of his translations, and his handful of essays in literary criticism all appeared before 1828, with the exception of his *History of Spanish Literature.*[76]

Moreover, many of the guidelines and ideas of his *History,* published in 1849, appeared in the 1820's in his Harvard lectures. His subsequent work largely filled out this basic structure. As the time for publication drew near, Ticknor grew less and less willing to part with the manuscript which justified his scholarly existence, more and more eager to polish it and add another bibliographical detail. Washington Irving wrote Ticknor that "I am glad you brought it out during my life time . . . I began to fear that it would never see the light of day, or that it might fare with you as with that good lady, who went thirteen years with child and then brought forth a little old man, who died in the course of a month of extreme old age." Ten years later Prescott said, "I suppose that Ticknor will never write another book." When Prescott died it was Ticknor's sad duty to write another book, his fine biography of his best friend, a volume which gives an inside glimpse of the Brahmin mind. But at the age of seventy-two, Ticknor confessed to a self-made scholar that "it makes me ashamed to think that, with all the means vouchsafed to me, I have yet done no more. I assure you, I feel this painfully at the moment I write it." [77]

Why was it that after 1835, with *Labor Ipse Voluptas* as his motto, Ticknor wrote so little? His *Life of Prescott* and his correspondence show that he retained mental clarity and vigor well into his seventies. He knew that scholars and creative writers commonly were judged by their books rather than their reputation as cultural entrepreneurs; that morally, in the eyes of the community, it was publish or perish. He rebuked his friend Francis Calley Gray for not allowing "the world to profit more than it does by the large resources of . . . [your] accurate and tasteful learning." He knew that Boston and Cambridge considered Richard Henry Dana, Sr., a lotus-eater. Charles Francis Adams pronounced New England's stringent verdict on the old poet: "The elder Richard Henry was born a dreamer." Becoming a man of letters at about the same time as Ticknor, Dana hung out his professional shingle in a short-lived periodical ironically titled "The Idle Man" and blazoned on its front the lines of Cowper: "How various his employments, whom the world/Calls idle." James Russell Lowell painted a harsh portrait of Dana in "A Fable for Critics":

Here comes Dana, abstractly loitering along,
Involved in a paulo-post-future of song,
Who'll be going to write what'll never be written
Till the Muse, ere he thinks of it, gives him the mitten, —
Who is so well aware of how things should be done,
That his own works displease him before they're begun, —

. . . .

That he once was the Idle Man none will deplore,
But I fear he will never be anything more.

Ticknor, too, tried to prod the reluctant poet by reporting that Wordsworth admired his work "and said, he thought it a great pity, that the author of the Lines on Greenough's Statues, did not write more." [78]

On the surface, at least, Ticknor had little of Dana's diffidence and self-distrust. He could not understand why his friend Washington Allston could not complete his master painting on the feast of Belshazzar: "Let his distrust, his anxiety — whatever it is," he wrote to Dana (Allston's brother-in-law), "be shook to dust." Yet underneath Ticknor perhaps felt much the same anxiety. His social and scholarly position before publishing his *History* was so eminent that he would have little to gain if the book succeeded, and much to lose if it fell flat. He well knew how severe the international judges of scholarship could be, and perhaps feared their high expectations. Perhaps, too, he became more interested in being a *gentleman* of letters after his second European trip. Did not a maid in *The Barclays of Boston* think "her master the very first gentleman in Boston, for she asked, 'Was he not doin' most noffin from mornin' till night?'" With ample wealth to cool his passion for print, without the kind of neurotic compulsions of Parkman who quelled his "enemy" by working obsessively, with a desire to be absolutely authoritative, he was in no hurry. It was true that in the 1850's Ticknor spent much of his time building the Boston Public Library. But whatever the reasons or extenuating circumstances, Ticknor was distressed by the gap between the Boston ideal of industry and the results of his own life's work.[79]

At Göttingen Ticknor had learned that to become a scholar of the German mold, any "man must be completely *upset* . . . he must learn to give up a love of society." This he was unwilling to do. Endowed with a strong taste and aptitude for social life, he enjoyed instead an eminent career as arbiter of Boston literary society. He was one of those who strove to make Boston a city where, as Dickens said, "The golden calf they worship . . . is a pigmy compared with the giant effigies set up in other parts of that vast counting-house which lies beyond the Atlantic, and the almighty dollar sinks into something comparatively insignificant amidst a whole Pantheon of better gods." [80]

VI

Clouded Destiny

Passion, appetite, seem to have self-reliance and reality; but
Whiggery is a great fear.   *Ralph Waldo Emerson*[1]

"The Civil War of '61 has made a great gulf between
what has happened before it in our century and what has happened
since," George Ticknor anxiously observed in 1869. "It does not seem to
me as if I were living in the country in which I was born, or in which I
received whatever I got of political education and principles." Although
he often professed disdain for politics, Ticknor followed the course of
the American experiment with close attention, and, toward the close of
his life, with horror. Never was he able to lose the conviction acquired
in his youth that the American social order was precarious. In an era
of optimism, he was commonly a pessimist. In an age when men spoke
of manifest destiny, he believed that the fate of America was clouded.
In a period of ebullient egalitarianism, he sought ways to curb the
sovereign people. In a time when men proclaimed that the United States
rode the Providential escalator of Progress, he suspected that America
might be implicated in Europe's decay.[2]

Born not long after one revolution and living to see the second
American revolution, he viewed events from a perspective far different
from that of most of his countrymen. To the end he counted himself a
Federalist, though he recognized that as a party Federalism died after
the Hartford Convention. Persistently, he continued to judge events by
the political canons of his youth, no matter how anachronistic these
ideas seemed to others. Since he realized that Federalism could no longer
be proclaimed from the stump, he sought in other ways to inculcate a
conservative persuasion.

But it was not the Federalist creed alone that colored his interpretation of the American experiment. His experience in Europe and his
extensive correspondence with friends in the Old World also informed

his reading of American politics. Ticknor was well aware that American republicanism occupied but a small portion of the wide spectrum of European political belief and practice. He knew how eagerly European conservatives awaited the collapse of the "grand experiment of a free government in the United States." Often to friends abroad he had to explain and defend American policies — indeed, the whole nature of the American democratic process. He habitually explained American events in terms comprehensible to Europeans.[3]

Whether he interpreted events historically — in the light of the crises of the early republic — or comparatively — in terms of contemporary European experience — his opinions often clashed with views dominant in that age of the common man. Rarely did he find European observers wiser in their judgments than his optimistic countrymen. Perhaps Alexis de Tocqueville came closest to understanding both the strength and the weakness of democracy in America as Ticknor understood it, for Tocqueville saw that American society was an aberration, a deviation from traditional patterns of human association. Like Ticknor he placed his analysis of American society within a comparative and historical framework. Ticknor found much in common with this handsome and idealistic young aristocrat who visited Boston in the fall of 1831; he saw Tocqueville frequently then and during his two subsequent visits to Europe.[4]

Tocqueville found a nation thriving without the institutions which linked past to present and class to class in Europe: monarchy, aristocracy, and an established church. "It is as if a man removed the main supports of a massive structure," Marvin Meyers has commented, "and felt its terrible weight in his own hands; then withdrew and saw it still standing." Like Ticknor, Tocqueville probed for the hidden supports of the republic, and found them not in political parties, but in the forces which expressed and shaped the national character: a heritage of customs, law, education, religion, and "the physical circumstances of the country." [5]

Ticknor and his fellow conservatives never developed an explicit and systematic political ideology comparable to the theory Tocqueville set down in *Democracy in America*. Yet starting as a displaced Federalist elite, and desiring to create a conservative persuasion in a nation where the people was sovereign, they wove a tapestry of conviction and hope, doubt and despair, which became a conservative testament. Much of their political thought was an elaborate gloss of Washington's "Farewell Address." [6]

The doctrine of national character shaped Ticknor's political beliefs. He saw the commonwealth as an organic whole, the expression of a national character and social tradition with roots deep in the past, not as a transitory artifact, "an encampment of tents on the great prairie, pitched at sundown, and struck to the sharp crack of the rifle next morning." Despite fatalistic overtones in his conception of the national character, he actively supported such institutions as schools and libraries which could shape the public mind to a conservative mold. His program to produce harmony in the body politic resembled the Greek conception of *paideia;* on this total education of the mind and character the fate of the republic ultimately rested. Complementing these agencies of socialization was a body of organic law, a means of protecting the people against themselves. [7]

Ticknor hoped that the American republic might prove durable, but as the years went by he became less and less sanguine. By 1848 he was convinced that all Europe was in decay, gradually in some nations and violently in others: "it looks, as if the decaying civilization of our times, like that of the fourth and fifth centuries of the Roman empire were to go through a series of convulsions. How we are to be affected by it is wholly beyond conjecture. But in the present state of the world, half Christendom cannot suffer without carrying many mischiefs and griefs through the rest of it." "I saw England . . . at the heighth of her power and pride," Ticknor had written Jefferson in 1815; "I saw Holland, too, a fallen and ruined nation . . . the ominous ripeness of the one and the dotage and decrepitude of the other." Europe might be "in a state of general conflagration," Jefferson replied, but "what a divine contrast is the calm of our condition to the volcanic state of that. How our little party bickerings and squabbles shrink to nothing compared with the fire and sword, havoc and desolation of that arena of gladiators!" In time the possibility of American apocalypse became the key question for Ticknor, who had studied the rise and fall of the great empires of France and Spain: was America bound to the same cycle of decay as the rest of Christendom? [8]

Ticknor adopted the pose of the apolitical scholar. He succeeded so well that people were surprised to find that he voted at elections. His friend Alexander Everett chided him for being "the very Atticus of the times — who always boasted, and like Johnson's friend, thanked God, for your ignorance of politics." Political parties he distrusted. Yet he was the friend of almost all the leading conservative politicians of New England and a scholar who fulfilled the role of the model intellectual of the Anthology Society as "a judicious biographer of the great, and a persecutor of the ambitious." Again and again in his correspondence during his later years he expressed concern about politics; his predictions were more often ominous than optimistic. He was, of course, not alone in stark prophecy. His friend Nathaniel Bowditch had "evil forebodings" in the 1830's. In 1864 Ticknor recalled that "Dr. Bowditch said to me, above thirty years ago, in a manner so impressive that I remember the spot where we stood, and rarely pass it without recalling the circumstances, 'We are living in the best days of the republic.' " [9]

As Ticknor witnessed the development of the United States, his hope for a conservative persuasion darkened into confusion, then subsided into alienation and despair. Demagoguery, panics, riots, repudiation of debts, subversive immigrants, the awful slavery issue, and finally the catastrophe of disunion and war — did these not destroy the value of prosperity and the westward march of empire? And did not Ticknor sometimes wish to ask with Mallet du Pan, whom he had avidly read as a boy, "What can we say to men who sleep on beds of roses, surrounded by hundreds of assassinations; and who, with the ruins of Persepolis or of Carthage before their eyes, have never, even for a moment, conceived that empires were perishable?" [10]

1. *The American Character and the American Revolution*

"As to the present French and continental convulsions, which some persons regard with favorable eyes," Ticknor wrote George Hillard in the turbulent year 1848, "I can only say, that during a life of seven or eight years in Europe, I never was in any country where I should have thought it wise, or Christian, to join in any such movement . . . republics, I much fear, cannot grow on the soil of Europe . . . There is no nourishment for them." Unlike Edward Everett, who boasted that if the Old World copied the United States, "it is not too much to say, not only that Europe would be regenerated, but that the empire of civilization might again be pushed into Africa and Asia," Ticknor never believed that the American experiment was exportable. On the contrary, he feared that if liberals battled the old order on the continent "with the vain hope of obtaining free governments . . . nothing but a decay of civilization will be the result." [11]

To "the most intense Hunker in Boston," as one of Ticknor's critics called him, no existing government was really desirable, yet the American political system was at least the best of a bad lot. Why, then, didn't Ticknor want other nations to emulate America? Government, like literature, reflected the national character and stemmed from long tradition. Thus European republicans would only corrupt their nations by disseminating ideas hostile to their national character and their political heritage. No wise man could hope, Ticknor wrote his friend Prince John of Saxony, that an illiterate and politically inexperienced European nation could found a republic "in which the people, by severe organick laws, would limit its own powers; — in which labour and capital would rest in the same foundations; — and in which the rights of the minority would be protected by the same principles that give the majority all its control of the state." What might be a reality in America could only be a delusion elsewhere. [12]

The concept of national character was even more obscure in politics than in literature. Glibly, Ticknor had described the national character of other countries, but he never systematically analyzed the American national character, even though he assumed that there was one. At times his notion of national character had biological or racial overtones. He never doubted the superiority of the Anglo-Saxon "race" to the Negro or the Indian. He deplored the possibility that the United States might absorb Mexico, for he knew not "what we shall do with such a miserable conglomerate of undesirable peoples based on an effete civilization." The English and Americans were "children of one family; connected by original qualities that will never permit us to get very far apart, even if we try." Ticknor used biological imagery when he spoke of America's "youth" or expressed the fear that the American nation might "prove to be like fruit imperfectly formed and nourished, which rots without ripening." [13]

Ticknor believed that nations, like individuals, were bound to a Providential cycle of growth and decay. Rufus Choate agreed with Ticknor that the most profound questions which a philosopher might ponder were how an ordered yet free country "may be preserved through a full lifetime of enjoyment and glory, what kind of death it shall die, by what diagnostics the approach of that death may be known, by what con- juration it is for a space to be charmed away, through what succession of decay and decadence it shall at last go down to the tomb of nations." In this obscure quest there are "some things we know," Choate declared:

A nation, a national existence, a national history, is nothing but a production, nothing but an exponent, of a national mind. At the foundation of all splendid and remarkable national distinction there lie at last a few simple and energetic traits: a proud heart, a resolute will, sagacious thoughts, reverence, venera- tion, the ancient prudence, sound maxims, true wisdom; and so the dying of a nation begins in the heart. There are sentiments concerning the true idea of the State, concerning law, concerning liberty, concerning justice, so active, so mortal, that if they pervade and taint the general mind, and transpire in prac- tical politics, the commonwealth is lost already.[14]

The *History of Spanish Literature* taught that the Inquisition and the worship of despotic rank had corrupted "the general mind" of the Span- ish people. For Ticknor, as for Choate, the concept of national character was both a descriptive metaphor to categorize uniformities and a device to explain events. God in his Providence chose to act in history through this medium of national character. Within the broad Providential cycles men could shape the national character as a gardener might cultivate fruit, but at best these efforts could only temporarily hasten growth or arrest decay; they could not alter the larger cycle.

This concept of a national character conforming to its own seeds of development and shaped by its long heritage was conservative in its political implications. It argued against changes based on radical ideol- ogy rather than gradual evolution. This organic interpretation of the body politic portrayed society not as discrete individuals, classes, or sec- tions, but as a unified whole — a view Edward Everett shared in refer- ring to "the State, the great, complex, social being, which we call Massa- chusetts, the genial mother of us all." [15]

As a conservative, Ticknor believed that tradition and the counsel of men wise and experienced were the best guides in politics. Thus the bur- den of proof was upon anyone who believed that change was desirable. "The welfare of the society is less the work of ourselves and our contem- poraries than we are sometimes willing to believe it to be," wrote Tick- nor. "The foundations, on which alone the chief interests and moral soundness of a community can safely rest, must be laid in the past." The commonwealth was a complex organism evolving through history;

it was far more comprehensive than the political state with its conflicting parties. Like Ticknor, the Whig senator Rufus Choate maintained that successive generations were not "flights of summer flies, without relations to the past or duties to the future." Americans should be taught that all generations are "one moral person, — one for action, one for suffering, one for responsibility, — that the engagements of one age may bind the conscience of another; the glory or the shame of a day may brighten or stain the current of a thousand years of continuous national being." [16]

Ironically, America was born in revolution. "Our history *begins* with the disruption of time-honored things," Ticknor's conservative friend James Hillhouse warned. Americans should "sit like watchful sentinels" to determine "whether our government contains the principles of perpetuity, or whether it carries in it the seeds of decay." But Ticknor's nephew, George Ticknor Curtis, a brilliant lawyer and bluff Tory, concluded that the American Revolution had not really been a revolution at all in the usual sense. In his oration, "The True Uses of Revolutionary History," he explained that "the age for declamation upon the American Revolution has passed away." Although he could not deny that the conflict established "the right in mankind to change or abolish the government over them," he cautioned that "you shall take this abstract question [of the right of revolution] and sit down in the closet to debate it in the seriousness of an honest heart, and you will find that there are few questions in moral or political science more difficult of solution."

Ticknor and Curtis agreed that the revolutionists had acted from the purest motives. Not self-interest, not metaphysical theories, not a fit of rebellious temper, but a desire to preserve the rights of all Englishmen impelled the colonists to oppose their beloved mother country. They acted upon "some of the most solid principles of the British Constitution," and established them "for future ages." Above all, the American Revolution spared more than it destroyed: "Certain and manifest it is . . . that when the country was freed by the final accomplishment of Revolution, society did not have to be reconstructed from its foundation; that only a form of government had to be framed; and that immediately and, as if from a goal on the race course, the young giant started on his career." We inherited the law, the literature, the economic structure, and the mores of England since we had waged war only "against the king's government and not against the institutions of the country." The elder Josiah Quincy told Tocqueville that "Massachusetts was nearly as free before the Revolution as to-day. We have put the name of the people where was the name of the king; otherwise nothing has been changed with us." [17]

As Curtis told the story, the revolutionists were not subversives overthrowing a government but decorous models of American character. "The history of a people bears the same relation to their present condition, tone, character, and future destiny, as that of an individual bears to his . . . All that it has done and suffered; opportunity wasted or gloriously improved . . . these have made the man . . . So may we image the general heart and mind and present state of a whole nation." Thus the men of '76 cast the national character. "The institutions of no country, severed from its history . . . can ever be rightly understood . . . If they are free, what are the limits of that freedom, as prescribed at their formation and settled by usage?" The "true" use of the Revolution, therefore, was to "prescribe" the boundaries of liberty. The most characteristic virtue of the revolutionary generation was the nationality of its patriotism . . . it is the cultivation of that spirit which is to save this vast republic from falling into speedy dissolution." Paradoxically, the lesson of the Revolution for Americans of all classes and sections was to exercise restraint and to live together harmoniously.[18]

This interpretation became a conservative Whig litany. Ticknor hoped that Americans might escape sectional and class conflict through agreement on the patriotic principles of the revolutionists. He commended Webster's "loftiest tone of national feeling, entirely above the dim, misty region of sectional or party tone or prejudice" when he appealed to the nationalism of the Revolution. Ticknor's eulogy of Lafayette stressed that the visit of the General in 1824 "turns this whole people from the bustle and divisions of our wearisome elections . . . the troubles and bitterness of our manifold political dissentions; and instead of all this, carries us back to that great period in our history, about which opinions have long been tranquil and settled . . . It brings, in fact, our revolution closer to us, with all the high-minded patriotism and self-denying virtues of our forefathers." It pleased Ticknor that the nobleman Lafayette, who normally would have been one of "the most natural and powerful allies of a splendid despotism" had chosen to join disinterested republicans locked in an "obscure and almost desperate contest for freedom in a remote corner of the world." [19]

Rufus Choate, an avid student of early American history, urged Americans to write romantic histories about the revolutionary period in the style of Scott, since such a literature might help "to perpetuate the Union itself . . . [by creating] a treasure of common ancestral recollections . . . Reminded of our fathers, we should remember that we are brethren." Edward Everett contrasted the French Revolution with the American in a speech which Ticknor thought his noblest effort: "After sickening over the horrors of that dreadful period, the butchery, I do not say of kings and queens, but of gray-haired men, of women, of priests; the atrocities of human tigers . . . I am fain to turn for relief to the pages of our own revolutionary history; to gather renewed hope for constitutional freedom . . . new lessons of true patriotism . . . new faith in humanity . . . from the spotless career of George Washington." [20]

Thus in the strange logic of Ticknor and his fellow conservatives the Revolution should teach Americans to value the continuity of their institutions.[21] They believed that Americans had inherited British characteristics and institutions, and they thought that what was distinctively national in the American character had been formed in the past, in the contests of the Revolution. It was no accident, then, that the Revolution and the formation of the Constitution were pervasive themes in Webster's, Choate's, and Everett's orations. The right of revolution, said Choate, should be hidden "in the profoundest recesses of the chambers of the dead, down the deep vaults of black marble, lighted by a single silver lamp." Reform should be personal, not political. The government should stay "substantially as it is; jurisprudence substantially as it is . . . the Constitution and the Union, exactly as they are, — this is to be wise, according to the wisdom of America." [22]

2. *The Rule of Law*

Tocqueville believed that American "lawyers, as a body, form the most powerful, if not the only, counterpoise to the democratic element . . . qualified . . . to neutralize the vices inherent in popular government." The counselors to whom Ticknor most often turned for political guidance — and whom he assuredly considered an aristocracy of virtue and talent — were almost all lawyers and judges: Daniel Webster, whom he counted the greatest statesman in America; Jeremiah Mason, the desponding ex-Federalist; Robert C. Winthrop, Speaker of the U.S. House of Representatives, punctilious patrician descendant of John Winthrop; Rufus Choate, dean of Boston lawyers, orotund speaker and amateur historian; Hugh Swinton Legare, Southern Whig congressman and Secretary of State under Tyler, brilliant legal philosopher and Unionist; Joseph Story, ally of Harvard battles, Supreme Court Justice and author of the legal classic, *Commentaries on the Constitution*; and Ticknor's two nephews, George Ticknor Curtis, a rock-ribbed conservative who had married Judge Story's daughter; and Benjamin R. Curtis, Justice of the U.S. Supreme Court, a stern man with a square jaw and piercing eye.[23]

It was not surprising that the "aristocracy" of lawyers had a high regard for the rule of law. Indeed, they seemed sometimes to contend that the government was an appendage of the legal system. In an address titled "The Position and Functions of the American Bar, As an Element of Conservatism in the State," Rufus Choate asked his fellow lawyers, "Are you not . . . statesmen while you are lawyers, and because you are lawyers?" He argued that lawyers must preserve "our organic forms, our civil and social order, our public and private justice, our constitutions of government, — even the Union itself." It must be "the praise of the American Bar, that it helped to keep the true idea of the State alive and germinant in the American mind; that it helped to keep alive the sacred sentiments of obedience and reverence and justice, of the supremacy of the calm and grand reason of the law over the fitful will of the individual and the crowd." He saw conservation as "the chief end, the largest duty, and the truest glory of American statesmanship." [24]

To these conservative lawyers the Constitution was holy writ. "The Constitution of the United States was the means by which republican liberty was saved from the consequences of impending anarchy," wrote George Curtis in his *History of the Formation and Adoption of the Constitution of the United States*. This study delighted Ticknor, to whom the book was dedicated. "You know how conservative Curtis is," Ticknor wrote his English friend Sir Charles Lyell, "and how frank and fearless he is in expressing his opinions; but the main characteristic of

the book is a wise and statesmanlike philosophy, profitable to all."
Theodore Parker, who heartily disliked Ticknor and was amused at the
mutual admiration society of the two Tories, ridiculed Ticknor's favorable review of Curtis' volume, observing that "it was most characteristic.
G.T.C. dedicated the Book to G.T. and speaks of *ties* which are a
source of Pleasure to him — I suppose the two sit and *turn up their noses
at each other* mutually." [25]

The Constitution embodied the sound principles of the revolutionists
and made them permanent in the form of a government. Above all, the
Constitution represented that favorite virtue of Ticknor's, common
sense: "we are a practical people, — eminently so, — and it was not
possible metaphysics should become a part of our Constitution," he told
Maria Edgeworth. After reading Madison's account of the Constitutional
Convention, he "was struck with the moderate amount of talent, knowledge, and practical skill in government that was shown in the whole body.
Nor was I displeased to see that it was so; for it gave so much the more
prominence and value to their honesty . . . it was their honesty, their
sincere desire to fulfil the great duty for which they were appointed,
which . . . gave us the best form of government that was ever made."
A strange description of a group which included James Madison, Alexander Hamilton, George Washington, Benjamin Franklin, George Wythe,
and John Dickinson! Yet Ticknor was determined to regard the Constitution as an expression of the national character, not as a construct
of a few brilliant men.[26]

Once ratified by the states, the Constitution bound the nation in a
fashion more permanent than monarchy. "The history of this Constitution is not like the history of a monarchy," said Curtis, "in which some
things are obsolete . . . The Constitution of the United States is a
living code, for the perpetuation of a system of free government, which
the people of each succeeding generation must administer for themselves. Every line of it is as operative and as binding today as it was
when the government was first set in motion by its provisions." [27]

The Constitution was thus the organic law by which all questions of
fundamental politics should be decided. Once Joseph Story, who had
been a rabid Democrat in his erring youth, mentioned to friends at Ticknor's house that he had reread a Fourth of July oration he had given
long ago. " 'Well, sir,' said Webster in his deep and impressive bass, 'now
tell us honestly what you thought of it.' 'I thought the text was pretty,

sir,' replied the Judge: 'but I looked in vain for the notes. *No authorities were stated in the margin.*'" An *authoritative* judicial interpretation of the Constitution and the common law must regulate society. Tocqueville was surprised that a democracy would give the prerogative of judicial review to the bench: "Armed with the power of declaring the laws to be unconstitutional, the American magistrate perpetually interferes in political affairs. He cannot force the people to make laws, but at least he can oblige them not to disobey their own enactments and not to be inconsistent with themselves." [28]

A secondary line of defense of the American "lexocracy," another form of "severe organic laws," was the tradition of common law. Story regarded the common law as "the bulwark of our public liberties, and the protecting shield of our private property." Originally, the common law was designed to protect the people against arbitrary acts of the sovereign. Now that the people itself was sovereign, it could protect the minority against the tyranny of the majority. The result of a long quest for ordered freedom, the common law was a heritage precious to conservatives. The interpretation of precedents by judges and the education of the populace through jury duty further buttressed the republic.

The aristocracy of Whig lawyers was eager to divert political issues from the caucus to the bench. They considered Webster's role as a constitutional lawyer as vital as his service in the U.S. Senate. Horrified by the power of demagogues, perturbed by the "metaphysical" contentions of those who spoke of a "higher law than the Constitution," they tried to resolve complex and emotion-laden issues into legal questions. But Ticknor knew that the rule of law demanded popular support. The people must share the conservative persuasion, and to do so they must be properly educated. No matter how sound and stately the Constitution may be, said Judge Story, "it may . . . perish in an hour by the folly, or corruption, or negligence of its only keepers, THE PEOPLE. Republics are created by the virtue, public spirit, and intelligence of the citizens." [29]

3. *The Role of Public Schools and Libraries*

From the beginning of the nation, conservatives had sought to stabilize the republic through public instruction. The Federalist teacher and textbook writer Noah Webster urged the formation of an Association of American Patriots for the Formation of the National Character. Ticknor and his circle looked on the public schools as political instruments of the first importance, far more vital than party politics. In his article, "National Education," Joseph Cogswell wrote that "we have declared that freedom is a common right — we must endeavor [through education] to prove it a blessing." Ticknor's friend, the Maine Whig Charles Daveis announced that in a land where the people was king, it was essential to educate the sovereign: "it is vain to seek in the positive structure of society for those securities, which must depend in the main upon its spirit. Who shall take care of the keepers?" [30]

In 1834 Judge Story told a group of teachers that it was their duty to inculcate correct doctrines of political science in the rising generation, for otherwise faction and demagoguery would shatter the precarious structure of the constitutional republic. Teachers should do their best to "repress the inordinate love of innovation of the young, the ignorant, and the restless." He did his part by writing a textbook for the upper grades of the common schools, an adaptation of his *Commentaries on the Constitution*. At the close of his tract for the times he praised the legacy of the founding fathers but warned that the "future is that, which may well awaken the most earnest solicitude, both for the virtue and for the permanence of our Republic." The history of other republics showed how easily false leaders could undermine "all solid principles and institutions of government." Ticknor's friends William Sullivan and George Hillard joined the throng of conservative New Englanders who edited textbooks. These books taught veneration for the Whig heroes, especially Washington, and inculcated conservative principles of *ordered* liberty, freely quoting Webster and Everett.[31]

"In his political views in regard to the prospects of his own government, Mr. Ticknor was not an optimist," commented his lifelong friend Jacob Bigelow. "He had grave doubts about the possible despotism of an ignorant, uneducated, and unscrupulous majority; nevertheless he was unable to indicate any other country to which he would willingly transfer his allegiance and his home, and, like other men of sense, he settled down into a willingness to accept what is practicable . . . and fell back on universal education, intellectual and moral, as the greatest safeguard for national progress and prosperity." Or, put more simply by Ticknor in the guise of Mr. Lewis in Paris, speaking of the French Revolution,

"Poverty and injustice are apt to make people cross, and they grow savage when they are not only poor and angry, but ignorant." Ticknor believed that the schools should give "all instruction that is necessary to preserve the order and purity of society." He wrote to an English acquaintance that the principle of publicly supported education "is as firmly settled in New England as any principle of the British Constitution is in your empire . . . though I do not foresee the effects, it requires no spirit of prophecy to show that they must be great; and can they be anything but good? . . . Boston is a happy place to live in because all the people are educated." [32]

Ticknor practiced what he preached. Following in his father's footsteps, he became a member of the Boston Primary School Board and the treasurer of the Farm School for boys. In the *North American Review* he commended James G. Carter's *Letters to the Hon. William Prescott on the Free Schools of New England,* a tract which helped to pave the way for the reforms of Carter and Horace Mann. Applauding Carter's plea for state aid to local schools, Ticknor declared that the best proof of the excellence of the Boston public schools was the fact that the rich could find no better. [33]

To Ticknor the career of Daniel Webster alone justified public education, "this characteristic trait of New England policy." Because the public school sought him out in the forests of New Hampshire, Webster first started on his eminent career. "Undoubtedly, in any other country, the sufferings, privations, and discouragements inevitable in such a life, would have precluded all thoughts of intellectual culture," Ticknor observed. "But, in New-England, ever since the first free-school was established amid the woods that covered the peninsula of Boston in 1636, the school-master has been found on the border line between savage and civilized life, often indeed with an axe to open up his own path, but always looked up to with respect, and always carrying with him a valuable and preponderating influence." [34]

Who could explain "the very principles and foundations on which the free-schools rest" better than Webster, who was himself shaped by them? In his famous speech at Plymouth Rock in 1820 Webster declared that every man, whether or not he had children, benefited from public schools, for they secured "property, and life, and the peace of society . . . by inspiring a salutary and conservative principle of virtue and of knowledge in an early age." Instruction of all could "purify the whole moral atmosphere . . . We hope for a security beyond the law, and above the law, in the prevalence of an enlightened and well-principled moral sentiment. We hope to continue and prolong the time, when, in the villages and farmhouses of New England, there may be undisturbed sleep within unbarred doors. And knowing that our government rests directly on the public will, in order that we may preserve it we endeavor to give a safe and proper direction to that public will." [35]

Like Webster, Edward Everett stoutly justified public education on republican grounds. During one of his terms as governor of Massachusetts the State Board of Education was formed, and its first secretary, Horace Mann, chosen. Like Webster, Everett and Mann had been poor in their childhood and had begun their careers in the common schools. Although in public orations Everett and Mann waxed lyrical about education and the glorious progress of mankind, their zeal for free schools stemmed at least as much from fear as from hope. In 1839 Emerson found Mann "full of the modern gloomy view of our democratical institutions, and hence the inference to the importance of schools." [36]

Everett hoped that through education America might "aim at a new development of national character." In his oration, "The Importance of Education in a Republic," he pointed out that the duties of the citizen required common schooling. Voting "cannot be discharged with rectitude, unless it be discharged with intelligence . . . The good citizen, who is not willing to become the slave of a party because he is a member of it, must make up his mind for himself on all . . . great questions." Otherwise citizens will be "at the mercy of anyone who has the interest and the skill to delude them." Service in the militia was another duty, Everett observed, "of fearful import . . . the time may come when this duty also is to be performed. It will not then be a matter of indifference whether the honor and peace of the community are committed to an ignorant and benighted multitude . . . or to an educated and intelligent population . . . able to discriminate between constitutional liberty and arbitrary power on the one hand, and anarchy on the other." All citizens were eligible for jury duty: "Look into the anxious faces of those whose estates, whose good name, whose all, is at stake, hanging on the intelligence of those twelve men, or any one of them. What assurance is there, but that which comes from our schools, that these men will understand and do their duty?" In America any man, Everett concluded, might be elected or appointed to public office. Three options were open. "We must have officers unqualified for their duties; or we must educate a privileged class, to monopolize the honors and emoluments of place; or we must establish such a system of general education, as will furnish a supply of well-informed, intelligent, and respectable citizens, in every part of the country and in every walk of life, capable of discharging the trusts which the people may devolve upon them." In the age of the common man, Everett could choose only the last.[37]

The old Federalist leaders had acted like schoolmasters instructing unruly and ignorant pupils. In the neo-Federalist conception of education, the schoolmaster became, in effect, the central political leader. Amid the earthquakes of partisan politics the courthouse and the schoolhouse stood firm.

To these institutions Ticknor, Cogswell, and Everett sought to add another: the public library. Cogswell was the founder — with the Astor fortune — of the New York Public Library. Ticknor and Everett were the prime agitators for establishing the Boston Public Library. They had long believed that the common schools of Boston were an unfinished structure. A public library should be the capstone of the system, "one more added to the school-houses of the city, at which Boston boys and girls, when they have outgrown the other schools, will carry on the education which has there commenced." Ticknor's "idea was that which he felt lay at the foundation of all our political institutions," his daughter commented, "namely, that in order to form and maintain our character as a great nation, the mass of the people must be intelligent enough to manage their own government with wisdom; and he came . . . to the conclusion that a very free use of books, furnished by an institution supported at the expense of the community, would be one of the effective means for obtaining this result." As an instrument of conservative republicanism the public library should purify character and diffuse "general information . . . so . . . that the largest possible number of persons should be induced to read and understand questions of social order." [38]

As early as 1822 Ticknor became interested in a charitable society whose purpose was "to furnish wholesome religious, moral, and improving reading of all kinds to the poor, cheaper than they now get fanatical or depraved reading." A minister in Portland, Maine, requested from him a list of books to buy for a circulating library. Ticknor replied that he had chosen popular books — "if people will not come to your library you may as well establish none" — but that he had also tried "to select such books, as would gradually raise the tone of thought and character in any place, where they may be generally read." [39]

From his youth he had envied the scholarly libraries of Europe. During his voyage to study "not men, but books," he had written to an American friend, "I feel a gratification always in sending home good books, for I know I can in no way so directly and efficiently serve the interests of letters in my native country." On his return to Boston he tried to persuade the leading men to combine the Boston Athenaeum, a large subscription library, with "all the public libraries in town; such as the Arch Library, the Medical Library, the New Scientific Library . . . and then let the whole circulate, Athenaeum and all . . . open to the public according to the admirable direction in the Charter of the University of Göttingen, *quam commodissime, quamque latissime.*" He failed, for each library wished to keep a separate identity. Not daunted, Ticknor continued to dream of a large public library in Boston which would satisfy and stimulate both the general public and scholars. Such an institution could be a fulcrum for moral and intellectual reform. [40]

In 1848, when John Jacob Astor gave $400,000 for a public library in New York City, a number of Bostonians came to agree with Edward Everett that their city also "must have a great public library, or yield to New York in letters as in commerce." The same year the General Court of Massachusetts authorized a library, but work moved slowly. In 1852 Ticknor and Everett, who had been exchanging ideas about the public library for over a year, were appointed to the Board of Trustees. Ticknor persuaded the reluctant Everett that to become a genuinely popular institution the library should circulate its books freely — that is, citizens should be allowed to take books home rather than having to read them at the library. Ticknor believed that a library adapted "to our peculiar character" would "differ from all free libraries yet attempted; I mean one in which any popular books, tending to moral and intellectual improvement, should be furnished in such numbers of copies that many persons, if they desired it, could be reading the same work at the same time." If this meant investing in popular books, fine; this was investing in the republic, for soon the public taste would "be carried much higher than is generally thought possible." [41]

Everett was not so confident as Ticknor. "I cannot deny" he wrote Ticknor, "that my views have, since my younger days, undergone some change as to the practicability of freely loaning books at home from large public libraries. Those who have been connected with the administration of such libraries are apt to get discouraged." As director of the Astor Library in New York, Cogswell sided with Everett and complained that "the young fry . . . employ all the hours they are out of school in reading the trashy, as Scott, Cooper, Dickens, Punch, and the 'Illustrated News.'" "It would have crazed me," he told Ticknor, "to have seen a crowd ranging lawlessly among the books." Cogswell set the minimum age at seventeen for permission to use the reading room. In contrast to Cogswell, who was eager to preserve the books and the system, Ticknor was a wild-eyed anarchist.[42]

On the Board of Trustees Ticknor found others as skeptical as Everett and Cogswell. As in so many spheres of his life, Ticknor bucked the current, but curiously enough, now the old Tory stood alone because he trusted the people more than his fellow conservatives. He had accepted the position as trustee on condition that the library would circulate its books freely and would "be dedicated . . . to satisfying the wants of the less favored classes of the community" rather than scholars alone.

Earlier he had proposed that Harvard become more than a closed corporation for the fortunate few by opening itself into a university available to all who wished to attend. In 1853, in a similar vein, he proposed that another quasi-private institution, the Athenaeum, be merged with the Boston Public Library. In an article originally published in the *Boston Daily Advertiser* he argued that the city could not properly support two large libraries — the Athenaeum was one of the five largest libraries in the nation at the time, having over 50,000 volumes. He claimed that the Athenaeum was not really a substitute for a popular institution since it had few duplicate copies and pointed out that a union of the two libraries would strengthen each financially. But Ticknor's appeal to the proprietors of the Athenaeum failed when Josiah Quincy launched a counterattack charging that if the two institutions were merged, the Athenaeum would be the sport of "a political body, annually shifting its members, and changing principles and policy with every turn of party or passion." [43]

Ticknor wrote the major portion of the eloquent 1852 report of the Trustees of the Boston Public Library that etched a bold blueprint for a liberal institution. The first superintendent, Charles C. Jewett, wrote gratefully to Ticknor that "few persons alive know as well as you and I do, that with regard to the great features of the plan, — the free circulation of books, and the paramount importance of the popular department, — Mr. Everett had from the beginning, serious misgivings, and that he yielded his doubts only to your urgency." [44]

Ticknor's report caught the attention of Joshua Bates, a self-made banker who had grown up in Boston and who had become a partner in the London firm of Baring Brothers. While reading the plea for a popular library Bates recalled the evenings he had spent as a poor boy reading in a bookstore. He decided to give the city $50,000 to buy books for the library provided that it construct a suitable building. "Let the virtuous and industrious of the middle and mechanic class feel that there is not much difference between them," he wrote. "Few but worthy young men will frequent the library at first; they may draw others from vice to tread in the same paths; and with large, well-lighted rooms, well-warmed in winter, I feel sure that the moral effect will keep pace with the mental improvement, and it will be carrying out the school system of Boston as it ought to be carried out." Bates's view appealed to the self-made men of Boston. When Everett delivered his address at the opening of the newly built library on Boylston Street, he eulogized that greatest self-made Bostonian of all, Benjamin Franklin.[45]

Bates's gift launched the library on its prosperous career. During the 1850's Ticknor devoted his energy and time to ensuring the success of the plan he had persuaded the trustees to adopt. On his insistence, the privilege of borrowing books was extended to school children who had won the Franklin prizes and to an equal number of pupils selected by public school teachers. With his own money Ticknor bought multiple copies of Florence Nightingale's *Notes on Nursing*, Samuel Smiles's *Self Help*, William Thayer's inspirational biography of Amos Lawrence, Edward Everett's *Life of Washington*, and other works calculated to improve the young. He was determined that the index of popular works in the lower hall of the library should be published before the entire catalogue was compiled — the latter was a more impressive tome, but not so useful to the "less favored classes." Anxiously, Ticknor watched the first day of operation of the new library to see how the experiment would work, and was delighted to note that the first volume signed out was Southey's *Commonplace Book*. At the end of the day he went home satisfied, having seen not "a moment's trouble or confusion." By 1858 the annual circulation of books in the lower hall reached 179,000 volumes.[46]

After Ticknor was assured of the success of the popular circulating library, the "lower hall," he turned his attention to the upper chamber of his bicameral system, the reference library for the senators of learning. The scholars' portion of the library was, in fact, on the second story of the Boylston Street building, a high-ceilinged, ornate, dark, and ostentatiously inconvenient structure with room for 200,000 books. Up to this time Ticknor had helped his friends to collect books and had lent volumes freely from his own superb library, excellent in all departments of belles lettres and superb in Spanish literature. In 1860 he set a precedent for other scholar-princes by giving 2,400 choice books to the library, most of which went to the upper chamber as non-circulating reference works. In his will he bequeathed his Spanish collection to the library.[47]

In 1856 he went abroad as envoy extraordinary to discuss Bates's offer to buy more books for the library and to purchase works in the bookmarkets of England and the continent. Before leaving, he collected lists of appropriate books from his scholarly friends — Louis Agassiz, the famous naturalist; Benjamin Pierce, an outstanding mathematician and professor at Harvard; Judge Benjamin Curtis, and others — and put his skill as a bibliographer at the service of the library during his fifteen-month visit to the Old World.

Both in his plea for a library broadly useful to the public and in his efforts to build a scholars' treasurehouse, Ticknor was far more successful than he had been earlier in his abortive attempt to reform Harvard. Just as Jefferson spent his last years creating the University of Virginia, of which he was proud to call himself the father, Ticknor could rightly be called the moving spirit behind the Boston Public Library. He still shared the trust of the founding fathers in the diffusion of knowledge. For the anxious Tory, it was an act of faith to enlist in this cause, for he hoped that it would help to stabilize the republic and to keep America from being a second Carthage.[48]

4. *Antaeus*

Political faction threatened to disrupt the conservative persuasion inculcated by public schools and libraries. It was a fixed part of Ticknor's creed that "mere party politics . . . are always odious." George Washington had warned in his "Farewell Address" of the "fatal tendency" of political parties; "they serve to organize faction, to give it an artificial and extraordinary force; to put, in the place of the delegated will of the nation, the will of a party, often a small but artful and enterprising minority of the community; and, according to the alternate triumphs of different parties, to make the public administration the mirror of the ill-concerted and incongruous projects of faction, rather than the organ of consistent and wholesome plans digested by common counsels and modified by mutual interests." But despite Washington's warnings factions did arise, and Ticknor feared their consequences. "The character of Washington and Jefferson, like the good and evil principles in Persian mythology," William Prescott wrote to a European acquaintance, "have given a pervading coloring to the policies of the country." [49]

Disbarred from political careers by the Hartford Convention and the collapse of the Federalist party, Ticknor and most of his scholarly friends made a virtue of necessity. In 1831 Ticknor rejoiced that his friend Bancroft had failed to win the Jacksonian nomination for the Senate, telling him that "you are not made by your talents or your affections: by your temperament or your pursuits to be either the leader or the tool of demagogues." Prescott, the ideal gentleman of letters in Ticknor's eyes, "took little interest in the passing quarrels of the political parties that, at different times, divided and agitated the country." [50]

The Whig idolatry of the early American heroes — Washington foremost among them — suggested that only dead politicians could be regarded as statesmen. There was, however, an exception to this; one man Ticknor canonized during his lifetime as a model of the representative American leader. This was Daniel Webster. Joseph Story lamented in an article on statesmen that the United States had all too few leaders of ripe education, experience, and "lofty ambition," though it had "party men and party leaders in abundance . . . politicians . . . and demagogues." The "busy, inquisitive, and . . . meddlesome" American people thought all were qualified for office and seemed unaware that our government was a tenuous experiment whose "failure will spread a gloom over the human race, as well as involve our own ruin." "We have our all at risk in the voyage without insurance; and we must always keep on board the ship of state, not only a competent crew to work the ship, but the most cautious of the skillful, as well as the truest of the best, to keep her in good trim, and secure her from shipwreck on the new coasts of the ocean, which we traverse without experienced pilots, upon a voyage partly of discovery, and partly of profit." Webster was surely a safe pilot. "Has he been devoted to the mere objects of party," Story asked, "or to sectional and local interests? Or has he, — as public duty required, — represented the nation, and maintained the integrity of its interests at home and abroad?" The answers to these questions, Story said, were manifest in Ticknor's biography of Webster, a work written "by one of the ripest scholars of the age, and in a manner which cannot be surpassed."

Ticknor's short biography of Webster was first published in the *American Quarterly Review* in 1831 and reprinted with additions as *Remarks on the Life and Writings of Daniel Webster of Massachusetts.* In this study Ticknor portrayed Webster as the representative man, a successor to Washington, a statesman and orator who expressed an American consensus. Two concepts informed his biography: that Webster "can be shown as one who, from the whole course of his life, is continually connected with the mass of the people, their character, their condition and hopes"; and that "it can be shown that he belongs to no party; but that he has uniformly contended for the great and essential principles of our government on all occasions." Consequently Ticknor stressed "how completely his talents and lofty national bearing disarmed all political animosities . . . No man has been found tall enough to overshadow him." Instead of talking of party struggles in the Jacksonian period, Ticknor spoke of orations at Plymouth Rock and Bunker Hill, of the Webster-Hayne debate, and Webster's exposition of the republican catechism. And when Ticknor did write of charged political issues — the United States Bank, the tariff, or nullification, for example — he presented Webster's position on these questions as the only conceivable patriotic one.[51]

Was Ticknor deceptive or hypocritical in speaking thus? Surely he knew about Webster's presidential ambitions. Surely he knew about Webster's "honoraria" and retainers from businessmen while he was in the Congress. Surely he knew that the interests of New England and the rest of the nation were not necessarily the same. Ticknor owned stock in the Bank of the United States, which Webster defended, and was investing in new manufacturing companies protected by the tariff policy Webster advocated. Webster served the interests of Ticknor's class and section, but Ticknor's support of the godlike Daniel went beyond economic self-interest. Ticknor was politically naive and unconcerned about the particular configurations of parties, the tricks and knifings of the stump and caucus room. When his politician friends wrote to him about political issues, they assumed a lofty tone, for they knew that he was interested in rhetoric and philosophy more than in political footwork. As an unreconstructed Federalist, at no time did Ticknor really take Whiggery seriously.[52]

His idealization of Webster, though, gave him a way to reconcile himself to the polity of his country. He could escape the indignities of American political life through following the representative yet king-like leader. He could reconcile popular rule with the dictates of the wise and good. Webster had grown up in poverty on the frontier. Shaped by American institutions, he represented the proper — conservative — principles of the American character. When we recognize in Webster's speeches, Ticknor observed, "how completely Mr. Webster has identified himself with the great institutions of the country, and how they, in their turn, have inspired and called forth the greatest efforts of his uncommon mind, we feel as if the sources of his strength, and the mystery by which it controls us, were . . . interpreted. We feel that, like the fabulous giant of antiquity, he gathers his power from the very earth that produced him." [53] Webster's rhetoric reinforced the conservative persuasion and left a living record of American greatness.

An Antaeus, a giant who maintained his strength only when touching his native soil, Webster was thus the representative republican and the leader-hero. His orations, "marked throughout with the best characteristics of a generous nationality," glorified the nation and were its glory. "I was never so excited by public speaking in my life," the usually coldblooded Ticknor exclaimed after hearing Webster's oration at Plymouth Rock. "Three or four times I thought my temples would burst with the gush of blood . . . When I came out I was almost afraid to come near him. It seemed to me as if he was like the mount that might not be touched and that burned with fire." [54]

With hair "coal black, & coarse as a crow's nest," large burning eyes, a deep sepulchral voice that made "noble explosions of sound," Webster was the idol of all New England. After seeing Webster, Sydney Smith exclaimed "Good heavens, he is a small cathedral by himself." Henry

Adams remarked that there was a poetic quality in the reverence for Webster of Whigs who might have said: "We that loved him so, followed him, honored him;/Lived in his 'dark' and magnificent eye." A lion to the public, he could be "as playful as a kitten" when relaxing with his friends.

Emerson believed that "Webster's speeches seem to be the utmost that the unpoetic West has accomplished or can." Longfellow gave no such provincial boundaries to Webster's talent. In 1840 he wrote in his journal, "Read five cantos in Dante's Inferno — Daniel Webster is the only man of the living, who I can conceive of as writing such a poem." People were not surprised to learn that Washington Allston had used Webster's massive head as a model for the head of the Biblical Daniel in his unfinished masterpiece, "Belshazzar's Feast." Choate thought that Webster "had wisdom enough to have guided the counsels of Austria as Metternich did . . . skill enough to have saved the life of Louis the Sixteenth." In Everett's sketch, "Daniel Webster as a Man," the statesman emerged as a Natty Bumppo, raised "upon the verge of civilization" and imbued with "love for that pure fresh nature in which he was cradled!" Never more at home than when wading in the Marshfield River or drifting in his rowboat near Green Harbor, he was at one with nature. Everett sensed "a manifest sympathy between his great mind" and the vast sea, and recalled how Webster often discussed the ocean "and its great organic relations with other parts of nature and with man." Fitting it was that Webster should have composed his Bunker Hill oration while hunting in the wilds on Naushon Island.[55]

Antaeus, Dante, Metternich, the prophet Daniel, the Great Man in sympathy with Nature — Webster was the incarnation of the aspirations and the fears of anxious men. "Webster is the Atlas of the country now," Charles Sumner wrote in 1841, "and on his shoulders rests the great weight of affairs." Through all trials Ticknor would remain faithful to his idol, for Webster to him was more than a friend. He was a second Washington, the only sort of Representative Man who could save the republic from the folly of its representatives.[56]

5. *The American Experiment*

In 1841 the ruddy, jovial Lord Morpeth sat down to dinner with Ticknor, Judge Story, Jeremiah Mason, and some of their neo-Federalist friends. Their political opinions shocked him. "The conversation approached very nearly to treason," he wrote in his diary. They claimed that the constitutional safeguards were crumbling, "especially with regard to the election of fit men for the office of President . . . they talk much as Lord Grey would talk of the present proceedings of the Reform Parliament." [57]

Everywhere Ticknor went on his return from his grand tour in 1838 — by the glow of oak logs in fireplaces on Beacon Hill, on the piazzas of summer homes at Nahant where crickets sang, in the noise and smoke of the merchants' exchange — he heard desponding talk. While abroad he had tried to cheer the political pessimists by telling them that things were worse in Europe. Joseph Cogswell, who had also visited the continent in 1836–37, exclaimed after his return to America that "I never saw our blessed condition with such clear eyes before . . . I have done nothing but preach hope and confidence in republics, whenever I have been in Boston, to which even the desponding listen with some satisfaction, and in which a few join heartily." Slowly, Ticknor and Cogswell would change their minds.[58]

The election of Jackson, with its train of woe, alarmed the keepers of the Federalist conscience. Even George Bancroft, soon to be the intellectual ornament of Jacksonian democracy, scorned a levee at the White House: "there was a throng of apprentices, boys of all ages, men who were not civilized enough to walk about the rooms with their hats off; the vilest promiscuous medley, that ever was congregated in a decent house . . . pouncing with avidity upon the wine and refreshments . . . starvelings, and fellows with dirty faces and dirty manners; all the refuse that Washington could turn forth from its workshops and stables." That man in the White House — at least all earlier presidents had been gentlemen. "By the way," Bancroft added, "I forgot to mention, that General Jackson is a great stickler for virtue and truth; he declares that our institutions are based upon the virtue of the community, and added, that the moment 'demagogues obtain influence with the people our liberties will be destroyed.' I was excessively edified by so chaste and apposite a remark." [59]

Ticknor's old legal mentor, William Sullivan, agreed that demagogues could destroy American liberties. And who was a greater despot than King Andrew? "With a head and heart not better than Thomas Jefferson had, but freed from the inconvenience of that gentleman's constitutional timidity," Jackson made his will the law of the land. His admirers called him "born to command," an epithet "which he has spared no pains, and has halted at no legal, or constitutional obstacle, to verify." Jackson's attempt in his war on the Bank of the United States to separate "mere numbers from intelligence and property," to stir up class conflict, was "a profitable field to cultivate, because it is manured with all the perversions of which human nature is capable. There has never been, in the world, any community, in which it was so entirely false, that the members of it have separate and distinct interests." [60]

Jacksonians had aroused the ogre of party passion, and fed its greed through the spoils system. Sullivan urged young men not to vote under influences "such as spring up in the hot-bed of party excitement." What do "nine hundred and ninety-nine men in every thousand" care "who is the Governor of a state, or the President of the United States, so that he is an able, virtuous, and conscientious man, and disdains the influence of corrupting party"? All "constitutionalists" should unite to elect a president "who may be able to bless this country with an administration like that of WASHINGTON." [61]

What could one expect in America but Jacksonianism, grumbled the prophet Jeremiah, the tall, caustic old Federalist senator, Jeremiah Mason? Stability in government requires a bond between wealth and political power; "after all the real power must mainly rest in property. In our country, it is quite apparent that most of our troubles arise from the right of universal suffrage. This is our radical error." Judge Story agreed that the future looked gloomy: "the great difficulty is to make the mass of the people see their true interests, there being so many political demagogues, and so many party presses, that are in league to deceive them." In the midst of Jackson's war on the Bank, Story declared that "I seem almost, while I write, to be in a dream, and to be called back to the last days of the Roman republic, when the people shouted for Caesar, and liberty itself expired with the dark but prophetic words of Cicero." Even the Supreme Court, that faithful Federalist band, deserted to the tents of the wicked in 1835, when Jackson appointed Roger Taney to replace Chief Justice John Marshall. [62]

The old prophets predicted cataclysm, but Jackson came and went and the nation still stood. It did not stand still, however. Much of the anguish of the Federalist old guard stemmed from the declining influence of New England in Congress and the transfer of commercial hegemony from Boston to New York. Annoyed with the nay-sayers, William Ellery Channing wrote to Ticknor in 1836 that "we are very unreasonable. We choose to have a popular government, but are not willing to accept its essential condition, viz., that it shall have the imperfections of the people . . . If instead of croaking, we would try to improve our sovereign, we should then show a little comprehension of our situation." [63]

A serious problem remained: was there now a sign over the door of the White House saying "No Patricians Need Apply"? The election of 1840, when patricians joined with common politicians to bamboozle the people, dismayed many of Ticknor's friends. Someone exulted to Jeremiah Mason that the Whigs had swept the country like a hurricane. He wryly replied, "I don't like these hurricanes. In less than a year, it will blow like hell the other way." Like Tocqueville, Francis Grund observed that in egalitarian America conservatives have "tried to *smuggle* [themselves] . . . into power . . . They are no longer the plain honest men who come out with their principles in broad daylight; they do not advocate openly and manly the system they once gloried in, but only certain detached parts of it. They administer their politics to the people, like some disagreeable medicines, in exceedingly small doses, in order not to disgust the public stomach." Having no political ambitions, Ticknor and his Federalist cronies could ignore the new style in political leadership. Webster could not. [64]

In 1840 Webster returned from a triumphal tour of English high society to don linsey-woolsey and to bloviate from the stump. *He* did not have the good fortune to be born in a log cabin, he confessed, but his younger brother and sister were so favored. He threatened to punch anyone who called him an aristocrat. In London Webster had rebuked John Kenyon for talking in too liberal a vein about universal suffrage, putting his hands on Kenyon's shoulders and saying, "Don't talk so. Depend on it, if you put the property into one set of hands, and the political power into another, the power won't rest till it has got hold of the property." At home he became the friend of the workingman, hard cider, and log cabins. He and his fellow Whigs played their parts well. Soon Tippecanoe entered the White House, and shortly after Tyler too. [65]

But where did it all lead? Following Harrison's early death Webster stayed on as Tyler's Secretary of State after the rest of the cabinet had deserted. This decision earned Webster the enmity of many of his former supporters and helped lead to a split in the Massachusetts Whig party. In drafting the platforms for the Massachusetts Whigs in 1840 Webster had declared that "party spirit . . . when it gains such ascendency in men's minds as leads them to substitute party for country . . . not only alloys the true enjoyment of . . . [free] institutions, but weakens, every day, the foundations on which they stand." A party platform abusing the party spirit was a novel note. By 1842 Webster was attacking partisanship within his own party — Abbott Lawrence was trying to unseat him — and he wrote to Edward Everett that "our system of self-government is now undergoing an experiment, which amounts to torture. Party and personal rancor, recklessness and animosity, seem to make havoc of all just feelings, all practical expediency, and all really patriotic feeling. I hope for better times, but the present darkness is thick and palpable."

In the nominating conventions of 1840, 1848, and 1852 the Whigs bypassed Webster, in Ticknor's view the most able man in the party, for popular military heroes: Harrison, Taylor, and Scott. Ticknor wrote King John of Saxony that Webster's "absolute fitness for the Presidency" was unquestionable and that only "faction prevented" his election. In 1852 a bitter Webster wrote to George Ticknor Curtis urging him to investigate party conventions: "Where do they get their authority? See how the choice of the people is absolutely restricted to two individuals. Go back to the Constitution and see what that meant. It is difficult, I know, to say what is the remedy, but the first step towards the removal of an evil is to expose it." Washington was right: parties menaced the republic. Metternich was right: democracies shun able leaders.[66]

Ticknor deplored the fact that his hero Webster never attained the presidency, but he dismissed the footwork and juggling of the political stage as vaudeville. You politicians should be paid, he wrote his Whig friend Hugh Legare, "for all the time you are *not* in Washington, cutting off all your rations the instant you go there, and begin to talk and act." Ticknor wrote to Lord Fitzwilliam that the important task was to "keep the relations of domestic life as true and pure as they are now, and continue the advancement and diffusion of knowledge and intelligence through the whole people . . . Our free institutions will then have a fair chance; and if they fail, they will fail from the inherent faults of such institutions, and not from the unfavorable circumstances under which the experiment will be tried." Ticknor took "a deep personal interest" only in political questions which revealed whether "the original Anglo-Saxon materials of the national character [were moving] to some good result." [67]

One such issue, which caused Ticknor embarrassment abroad, was the repudiation of state debts. Following the Panic in 1837 a number of states refused to pay their debts and some disavowed their bonds. This nonpayment infuriated many of Ticknor's European friends who had invested in state securities, and led Sydney Smith to attack America bitterly as a nation of pickpockets. Ever conscious of the United States as being "the observed of all observers," Ticknor wrote to Longfellow, who was in Europe, that "the situation of the country is indeed so discreditable, that its disgrace . . . must annoy you and other of our travellers abroad." By the next summer Ticknor announced to an English friend that Americans were beginning to understand the moral issue of repudiation of debts. "What Prince Metternich once said to me, in reproach of our democratic institutions, is entirely true: we must first suffer from an evil before we can apply the remedy; we can have no preventive legislation upon such subjects. But then, on the other hand, when the people *do* come to the rescue, they come with a flooding force, which your societies, where power is balanced between governments and the masses, know nothing about." The only guarantee of your investments — and the only guarantee of the republic — is not shifting political parties, but "the character of the people." The sovereign citizens have made mistakes, but "neither half so numerous, nor half so grave as the wisest and best men thought they would, seventy years ago, when we were beginning the world." [68]

A more searching test of American character and institutions was the large influx of immigrants in the 1840's and 1850's. In the early days of the American experiment the Federalist General Court of Massachusetts had proposed that naturalized citizens be disbarred from office for fear that immigrants might "contaminate the purity and simplicity of the national character." Harrison Gray Otis "considered the native American germ to be amply sufficient for the production of such scions as were worth cultivating," and he believed it wrong "to invite hordes of wild Irishmen, and the turbulent and disorderly of all parts of the world, to come here with a view to distract our tranquility, after having succeeded in the overthrow of their own governments." If republicanism was impossible in Europe because the masses of the Old World had no experience in self-government, how would the mob of Irish and Germans affect the American republic when they streamed to this country at mid century? [69]

Writing to Prince John of Saxony in 1851, Ticknor claimed that immigrants were partly to blame for lawlessness in the United States. The Germans were often "active red republicans and avowed unbelievers in Christianity"; the Irish, "less enlightened and more prone to brute violence, but . . . more manageable." He believed that Americans should "receive kindly the multitudes who come to us every year and — (what was never known before) assimilate their masses to our own national character, and bring them in willing subjection to our own institutions. In this way, the Irish Celts, — (who have kept their distinctive nationality so long . . .), — melt away and are mingled with our people; giving up through the softening influences of prosperity, that nationality which adversity and suffering had only hardened in them." The Germans were more difficult to assimilate — "the least religious, the least moral, the least loyal to law." Ticknor did not want the immigrant flood to increase; indeed, he wondered why "their present numbers do not more affect our national character." [70]

As time passed, Ticknor began to worry more about the task "never known before" of assimilating masses of immigrants to American ways. He believed homogeneity of conviction and "blood" essential to the success of popular government. During a visit to Ireland in 1835 he foresaw an Irish rebellion against England, for Ireland was "a country wholly divided by ancient hereditary hatreds, divided by religion, by condition, by blood and political parties, and yet capable of being excited and kindled in a mass to violence by the slightest causes." To some extent Boston inherited this problem. Ticknor often visited the terrible Irish slums on Broad Street where whole families jammed one dark cellar room, where desperately poor immigrants died of cold and starvation. Ethnic conflicts broke out in once placid Boston, and the old Yankee hatred of Catholicism erupted in the burning of the Charlestown convent.

In New York at the Astor Place riots in 1849, Ticknor noted that "every person injured, killed, or arrested was a foreigner; so were three-fourths of those present, and nineteen-twentieths of the active mob." During his visit to Boston in 1824 Lafayette had asked Mayor Josiah

Quincy, " 'Have you ever been in Europe, Mr. Quincy?' . . . 'No, never,' [replied Quincy]. 'Then you have no idea of what a crowd is in Europe. I declare, in comparison the people of Boston seem to me a picked population out of the whole human race.' " Immigration destroyed this apparent homogeneity of the chosen people of Boston.[71]

By 1854 Ticknor had decided that the vast immigration "at no time, consisted of persons who, in general, were fitted to understand our free institutions or to be entrusted with the political power given by universal suffrage." Though he disliked the secrecy of the Know-Nothing Party, he thought it wise "to give no office or employment or political influence to any persons not born in the United States or who favor and support the political claims of those, who are of foreign blood and sympathies." As a party the Know-Nothings might die, but "the principle, that none but persons born in America, — bred in its peculiar institutions and attached to them by habit as well as choice — shall govern America, is — with reasonable limitations — so just and wise, that the party founded on it will surely leave its impress on a government as popular as our's is." [72]

Immigration, antagonism between rich and poor, partisan politics, the inability to prevent mistakes like repudiation of debts, the failure of democracy to elect the ablest leaders — these defects endangered the republican experiment and disrupted the harmonious and organic commonwealth of Whig ideology. But America had a more fatal flaw, one which all the agencies of conservatism could not cure. This flaw was slavery.

6. *Slavery and Disunion*

In 1824 on a trip to Washington and Virginia, Ticknor first began to fear that slavery might one day shatter the union. He talked then with Jefferson who had written that the recent debate about slavery during the Missouri Compromise "like a firebell in the night, awakened and filled me with terror." Ticknor met Calhoun, Clay, and other politicians at the Capitol. He sensed that the federal government could not be *E Pluribus Unum* as the Commonwealth of Massachusetts might be organically one. The national government was an ingeniously constructed and delicately balanced artifact, but there was a cleft in this structure: slavery. "Here is a stupendous fabric of architecture . . . the Capitol at Washington," said Rufus Choate. "It rests grandly on its hill by its own weight kept steadfast, and seemingly immovable; Titan hands might have built it; it may stand to see the age of a nation pass by. But one imperfection there is . . . a real vertical fissure, parting by an imperceptible opening from top to foundation the whole in two. The builder saw it, and guarded against it as well as he might; those who followed, to repair, with pious and skillful hands, tried by under-pinning, by lateral support, by buttress and buttress alternately, to hold the disjointed sides in contact." But the wedge of agitation over slavery could easily topple this precarious structure so carefully constructed. Many foresaw this disaster: "A sad foreboding of what would ensue, if war should break out between North and South, has haunted me through life," Everett declared in his speech at Gettysburg.[73]

Expansion of the United States westward and southward put new strains yearly on the structure of government. Like most of his Whig friends Ticknor opposed the annexation of Texas and the Mexican War. Every new mile of territory, especially slave territory, added to the task of fusing the disparate states into a harmonious commonwealth. Webster tried to create a mystical sense of nationalism, of reverence for the Constitution and the Union, but this centripetal influence barely matched the centrifugal forces at work. By 1850 Ticknor saw "trials and disasters . . . in store for us; — the heaviest of which, I think, will be found to come from . . . [slavery], the gravest of our national curses and wrongs." Again and again such words as "fear," "anxiety," "alarm," and finally "horror" crept into his letters about the state of the nation.[74]

In the middle of the sectional crisis of 1850, Webster tried again to bridge the widening gap between North and South. Webster had always opposed the extension of slavery. He condemned the "peculiar institu-tion" as "a continual and permanent violation of human rights." Still, he knew not how it could be uprooted without risking an even greater evil, civil war. "I cannot cooperate in breaking up social and political systems, on the warmth, rather than the strength, of a hope that, in such convulsions, the cause of emancipation may be promoted. And, even if the end would justify the means, I confess I do not see the relevancy of such a means to such an end. I confess . . . that, in my judgment, confusion, conflict, embittered controversy, bloodshed, and civil war, would only rivet the chains of slavery the more strongly."

Henry Clay had devised measures to settle the angry disputes over slavery in the new territories wrenched from Mexico. On the stormy evening of January 21, 1850, Clay, anxious, old, and sick, visited his Whig rival Webster to persuade him to support his compromise proposals. From that time to the seventh of March Webster came to believe that the nation was heading for civil war.[75]

Early on the morning of March seventh, crowds jammed the floor and galleries of the Senate to hear Webster. That day in Boston rain fell somberly on the cobblestones. As Webster rose to speak, he felt that he was about to launch his "skiff from the shore alone, considering that . . . if she foundered, there would be but one life lost." "I wish to speak today," he began, "not as a Massachusetts man, nor as a Northern man, but as an American . . . It is not to be denied that we . . . are surrounded by very considerable dangers to our institutions and government. The imprisoned winds are let loose. The East, the North, and the stormy South combine to throw the whole sea into commotion, to toss its billows to the skies, and disclose its profoundest depths. I do not affect to regard myself . . . as holding, or as fit to hold, the helm in this contest with the political elements; but I have a duty to perform . . . I speak today for the preservation of the Union." [76]

After reviewing the dispute over the new territories and the opposing religious views of slavery, North and South, Webster said that too many men wore the blinders of moral absolutism. "There are men who . . . do not see how too eager a pursuit of one duty may involve them in the violation of others . . . They deal with morals as with mathematics . . . They are apt, too, to think that nothing is good but what is perfect, and that there are no compromises or modifications to be made in consideration of difference of opinion or in deference to other men's judgments. If their perspicacious vision enables them to detect a spot on the face of the sun, they think that a good reason why the sun should be struck down from heaven." Let us take off the blinders of sect and section and look at the full range of public duties. Most important for the future was "the preservation of the Constitution and the harmony and peace of those who are to live under it." [77]

We must compromise our differences, for we cannot allow the great experiment to fail. As for the new territory acquired from Mexico, geography and climate have effectively excluded slavery there. Why taunt the South with the Wilmot Proviso? The Constitution clearly demands — in Article IV, Section 2, Clause 3 — that states return fugitive slaves. How can a Northerner refuse to do his Constitutional duty? Let us stop the torrent of recrimination pouring from pulpit and press and political forum. Let the abolitionist cease his agitation, for it only rivets the fetter on the slave. The Southerner must stop talking of secession. "Secession! Peaceable secession! Sir, your eyes and mine are never destined to see that miracle! The dismemberment of this vast country without convulsion! . . . Who is so foolish . . . as to expect any such thing?" So some talk of a secession convention at Nashville? Such a meeting held "over the bones of Andrew Jackson!" No, we must no longer speak of secession or dwell "in those caverns of darkness." [78]

Webster believed "that the whole world is looking to see whether this great popular government can get through such a crisis." He also knew that the eyes of Massachusetts were upon him. "Thursday we had the great Speech which, I may say in confidence, would have killed any man in New England but Daniel Webster," declared Robert Winthrop. "Yet many of its most obnoxious things were undeniable truths, which we must all acknowledge and sustain." [79] Webster alienated many of his constituents by his defense of the fugitive slave law. All his life Webster had opposed slavery; was he now a traitor, a "fallen archangel"? The Free-Soilers of Massachusetts bitterly assailed him. The usually temperate Charles Francis Adams wrote in his diary that "it is a deep and damning spot on the good name of Massachusetts that a profligate adventurer from another state shall be able to come into this and beslave so many honest citizens with his bitter poison. For thirty years he has done much to corrupt the hearts of the young and the minds of the older community."

Antislavery men disagreed about Webster's motives for making the speech. Some thought that Webster had made a corrupt bargain with the South to pass a tariff in return for his support of the fugitive slave bill. Others believed that Webster had his eye on the 1852 election and had thrown Massachusetts principles to the wind to gain the vote of the South. But all of them were sure that Webster had sinned against his conscience, that the terms "Cotton Whig" and "Conscience Whig" were polar.[80]

Ticknor and his conservative friends leapt to defend Webster, for they saw nothing inconsistent in Webster's speech. Quite the contrary, they called it an extraordinary "example of moral independence" for Webster "to stand between two highly-excited sections of a great and free country, whose institutions are purely popular, and to speak in terms which might disappoint the expectations of his own particular region." Did not Webster demonstrate his courage when he bluntly told the citizens of Boston that "the simple question is, whether Massachusetts will conquer her local prejudices, will shrink from, or will come up to, a fair, reasonable, and moderate performance . . . of her sworn obligations?" [81]

Eager to defend his idol, Ticknor began writing articles for the daily press. How could anyone be surprised at Webster's acceptance of the fugitive slave law, Ticknor asked, since Webster was "a servant of the Constitution of the United States, and nothing else"? It was folly to place "conscience" above Constitution, for Southerners, too, thought that they were obeying God's will. A citizen should "follow his own interpretation of the law of God against a provision of the supreme law of the land" only if he believed it "his duty to begin a revolution." Ticknor chided his fellow Bostonians that "if a man like Mr. Webster cannot be sustained, when he is performing this hard and anxious duty, then we say, God help the country! for human wisdom cannot save it. But he will be sustained — he *is* sustained in it . . . fifty years hence, this great, calm speech will be recognized as the most statesman-like effort of his life; as the crowning glory of his public service." No "ghostly abstractions," no metaphysical sense of duty to the slave alone could diminish Webster's reverence for the Constitution and the rule of law. Ticknor believed that if Webster had attacked the South, "the whole North would have gone with him, and the breach would have been much widened, if not made irreparable." [82]

Ticknor's minister agreed that Webster was right. Ezra Gannett "was too good a Peace-man to be an Abolitionist; for he saw what some abolitionists could not, and others would not," observed his son, "that disunion almost certainly meant war. And that meant, besides all other horror, failure of the Republic and shock to the great cause of popular government throughout the world. — And finally, apart from that reason for his devotion to the Union, the whole strength of his nature, conscious and unconscious, was reverent to organic order and visible law." Talk of "higher law" than the Constitution was nonsense — dangerous nonsense. Webster was just as much a "conscience Whig" as his opponents.

Just as the liberal Christian rested his faith in God in the historical evidence of revelation rather than in some mystical inner light, so in political affairs Gannett and Ticknor and Webster wanted to guide their actions by a constitutional canon. Religion taught them to consult common sense, not "the crotchets of a transcendentalist philosophy." Slavery was evil — Gannett wept bitterly when he heard that the fugitive slave Anthony Burns had been surrendered to his owner — but the law was the law.[83]

At a public meeting on November 26, 1850, called to support Webster and dampen antislavery agitation, Rufus Choate assailed the philanthropists and politicians who were stirring up hatred against the South. We ought to be grateful that some statesmen like Webster "remembered that they had a country to preserve as well as a local constituency to gratify." The real danger lies with the politicians and reformers who "will talk and write us out of the Union while the people sleep." We must oppose the philanthropy of the abolitionists whose "means are bad faith, abusive speech, ferocity of temper, and resistance to law." They "drive pitch-pine knots" into the flesh of the South and ignite them. Every citizen "in his party, in his social, or his literary, or his religious circle, in whatever may be his sphere of influence, [should] set himself to suppress the further political agitation of this whole subject." [84]

Ticknor marshalled the ranks of proper Boston in its battle against antislavery agitation. The slave question split Boston and Cambridge intellectual circles into opposing camps. Ostracism was a two-edged sword. Ticknor once told a young Harvard instructor, Nathaniel Shaler, that if he were intimate at Nine Park Street, he would inherit "certain disabilities. He went on to say [Shaler commented] that my frequent presence there would lead to my being excluded from the society of a certain group of people whose acquaintance would probably be of more value to me than his own; that I should find my way to the homes of the Lawrences, to those of Mr. George Hillard and Judge Parker and Professor Parsons of Cambridge, but that I should not enter those of the Lowells or the Quincys or that of Mr. Longfellow." [85]

One by one Ticknor saw his friends in the republic of letters adopt the Free-Soil or abolitionist heresies. It was especially painful to see the sons of his friends Bowditch and Dana desert the Websterian doctrine on slavery, but they, too, must be ostracized. "I was unwilling to be treated as Charles Sumner told me he was treated by Mr. Ticknor, before whom all had to deferentially bow on this subject of slavery in the South," Henry Bowditch declared. "Mr. Sumner told me . . . that Mr. Ticknor treated him so outrageously after his avowal of anti-slavery sentiments that self-respect prevented him from ever entering that cold, aristocratic, but charming abode." To Ticknor, the abolitionist virus was a disease fatal to the republic, and must be quarantined.[86]

Ticknor believed that slavery was a curse, no less to the white than to the Negro. But he believed that abolition of slavery would not only shatter the Union but also harm the Negro. "The truth is," Ticknor wrote in 1851, "that the question of race underlies all the other questions and, in its remote results, will be more important than all of them. The black man has been on the soil of the United States — bond and free — [a] hundred years but has no where taken a natural and healthy root; — he has no where found a home or become a part of society. In nearly half the states he is a slave. In most of the rest his rights are very imperfect. In all he is in an inferior social position." In New England Negroes have "never thriven . . . and though they have had the same school, and the other means of advancement open to them that are open to the poor Irish and Germans . . . they remain and always will remain an inferior caste; — a shiftless, inefficient race of men; — disliked and even hated by the inferior classes of whites, especially the Irish, with whom they come most directly in competition." Elsewhere, as in the Mississippi Basin, and on the Pacific Coast, states are either banning free Negroes or putting heavy penalties on them to drive them away. "The negro, it is certain, will hereafter be more and more excluded from every free state in the Union from which it is still possible to exclude him. He will become more and more unwelcome and degraded in all the other free states. He will, in time, be felt as a curse alike in the slave-holding states and in the free states." [87]

The reason for this "condition of things," Ticknor claimed, "is not accidental. It comes from deeply seated causes. It comes from the inherent and ineffaceable differences of character between the Anglo-Saxon race and the black race. And, as these differences are becoming more developed as our population becomes more dense, we find that the black race is more and more a disturbing element in our political system, and therefore, we — the white race, to protect ourselves increase their disabilities in different ways, and, on the whole, render their position everywhere less favorable." Ticknor did not justify the suppression of the Negro; he simply accepted it as a fact.[88]

What, then, was to be the fate of the Negro? "I see no alternative left for him," Ticknor predicted, "except emigration or extermination. Every where in these United States I look upon the African as a doomed man." Like the Indian, the Negro will be a vanishing race retreating before the encroaching Anglo-Saxons, "and if they cannot be forced to go [emigrate], they will be exterminated. A war of the races will, in some form or other come on, and the black race, as the inferior, will be its inevitable victims. All history shows that this will be the case." It was a sad and somber destiny, to be sure, and right-thinking men should do all they could to help the Negro to emigrate; but immediate emancipation would only hasten the war of the races.[89]

Ticknor's opinions about the Negro were by no means unique. Few Americans of the period grappled with the problems of full equality for the freed slave. William Lloyd Garrison himself thought immediate political equality "not practicable." Lincoln told a group of Negro leaders who visited him at the White House that "there is an unwillingness on the part of our people, harsh as it may be, for you free colored people to remain with us." As President he tried to set up separate colonies for Negroes either at home or abroad. Few penetrated beyond emotional attack or defense to consider the future condition of the Negro in America. Racist assumptions deeply permeated the entire outlook of Ticknor's circle. Lord Morpeth noticed that "Mrs. Ticknor (a very enlightened woman) could not suppress a shudder when the conversation turned upon meeting the black race in society." He commented that even the genial Prescott "did not quite seem to feel upon slavery as I could have wished, however that is never a matter of wonder here." [90]

Instinctively, Ticknor supported the existing social order in the South, as in Boston. Nathaniel Shaler, a Kentuckian, noticed that Ticknor admired "the tone of the Southerners. It may have been that his studies of Spanish history and literature had developed in him a fancy for the medieval type of man and society; he himself was clearly of that fashion." Southerners were frequent guests at Nine Park Street. In the midst of the nullification crisis of 1833 Ticknor wrote to a friend in Charlestown to learn the southern point of view. One of his closest friends and a favorite political informer was the brilliant Whig from South Carolina,

Hugh Swinton Legare, Attorney General under Tyler. Legare died in Ticknor's arms after becoming sick on a visit to hear Webster give his second Bunker Hill oration in 1843.[91]

In 1852 America lost its Representative Man. For almost forty years Ticknor had turned to Webster as pilot on the stormy seas of the republic. In October he visited the dying Webster at the Marshfield farm where they had spent many happy days. There Webster had gone fishing on the bay with Seth Peterson, a weatherbeaten lobsterman, and brought back mackerel and cod for the dinner table. There on hot summer days he had sat under the huge elm tree in the yard talking with Ticknor about Cicero. There he had worked in the field, ditching and plowing. Now, in the Indian summer, as he was dying of catarrh and diarrhea, he had his sailboat with the flag nailed to its mast moored in the bay where he could watch it from his bed. At night a lantern shone on the flag waving in the breeze. Sensing the end approaching, he looked at the people around him and asked, "Have I, on this occasion, said anything unworthy of Daniel Webster?" [92]

Ticknor was there as the rough New England farmers, Webster's neighbors, carried his coffin to the "peaceful, sea-girt grave" past a line of ten thousand mourners. Emerson heard the bells tolling at Plymouth. Though he had by now disavowed his former hero, he wrote in his journal that "Nature had not in our days . . . cut out such a masterpiece. He brought the strength of a savage into the height of culture . . . Cities had not diminished him; he held undiminished the power and terror of his strength, the majesty of his demeanor." Ticknor attended a memorial meeting of three thousand people in darkened Faneuil Hall, "unlike any other that was held of so many persons, anywhere; not a sound being heard except the voices of the speakers, and the sobs of the audience of *grown men,* and the response of *Aye* to the resolutions coming up, at last, like a moan." There is now "a feeling of anxiety about the future in our political position," Ticknor wrote Everett soon after. "The hunter beyond Superior; the fisherman on the deck of the nigh night-foundered skiff; the sailor on the uttermost sea, — will feel, as he hears these tidings," lamented Choate, "that the protection of a sleepless, all-embracing, parental care is withdrawn from him for a space, and that his pathway henceforward is more solitary and less safe than before." [93]

Nothing had been too difficult for this man, and when he died at the age of seventy, it seemed a shock that he was mortal. In 1859, in one of the annual dinners devoted to the apotheosis of Webster, Choate called, "Oh for an hour of Webster now! Oh for one more roll of that thunder inimitable! One more peal of that clarion! One more grave and bold counsel of moderation! One more throb of American feeling!" And Ticknor wistfully wrote in 1870 that "by a wise statesmanship, our cruel Civil War from 1861 to 1865 might have been prevented . . . if Mr. Webster had been President it would have been prevented." [94]

After Webster's death the contests between North and South became more and more bitter. In 1852 the Whig candidate General Scott carried only four states, and during the next four years Whiggery disintegrated. Ticknor and his friends had nowhere to go politically. Edward Everett, Senator at the time of the Kansas-Nebraska Act of 1854, resigned because of illness and because he saw "no course left for men of moderate counsels between extremists at both ends of the scale." Everett had opposed the Kansas-Nebraska Act, as did almost all the conservatives of Boston; Ticknor called it "a shameful violation" of the Missouri Compromise which "will tend to a dissolution of the Union more than any measure ever did." Ticknor believed that the passage of this act would make antislavery agitation "fiercer among the people, and cause the formation of sectional parties; — the thing of all others most to be deprecated in our government." [95]

In 1856 most of the Cotton Whigs supported the Know-Nothing candidate for President, Millard Fillmore, the old friend and ally of Webster, who sought to divert attention from the slavery issue. Ticknor thought that the Know-Nothings might "do good by rebuking the violence and unprincipled selfishness of the old organizations and their managers, and by breaking down their power." He maintained that "the old parties have . . . so misbehaved as to have lost the confidence of the great majority of our people . . . who insist on having a Government, — sound, faithful and wholesome — under whose protection they can fulfil the duties of life safely and die in peace, leaving an inheritance of similar wellbeing to their children." [96]

Rufus Choate predicted in 1856 that the victory of the Republic candidate Frémont would split the Union. Since he thought that Fillmore could not win, he urged Whigs to vote for the Democrat, Buchanan. He dismissed as wishful thinking the hope that the South would stay in a government dominated by a Northern party. "The question is not what ought to endanger the Union, but what will do it? Is it man as he ought to be, or man as he is, that we must live with or live alone? . . . Do you make no allowance for passions, for pride, for infirmity, for the burning sense of even imaginary wrong?" A Republican victory would be "the beginning of the end," for it could only result in fratricide.[97]

The events of the next four years— the Dred Scott decision, the caning of Charles Sumner on the Senate floor, the bloody struggle in Kansas, John Brown's raid, and all the rest — horrified Ticknor and his fellow conservatives. Like Choate they foresaw the probable outcome of this agitation more clearly than most of their zealous or apathetic countrymen. Many Republicans refused to believe that the blustering South would secede; many Southern fire-eaters thought that the pusillanimous North would never oppose secession by force.

Webster's heirs turned to pitifully inadequate, yet characteristic, measures to save the Union. Everett toured the nation giving an inspirational lecture on George Washington. All of Washington's sacrifices would be in vain, he cried, if "brothers' hands be imbrued in brothers' blood." He quoted Jefferson's remark to Washington that "North and South will hang together while they have you to hang to." Reviving the suggestion made a half century ago by a member of the Anthology Society, he urged that there be an annual festival on Washington's birthday to unite the nation. Meanwhile, Choate appealed to the memory of that other conservative idol, Webster, as a means of averting disaster.[98]

In 1860 the only refuge for Boston conservatives was the Constitutional Union Party, which campaigned on a single plank that aptly summarized the conservative persuasion in its impotent last days: "The Constitution of the Country, the Union of the States, and the Enforcement of the Laws." Reluctantly, Edward Everett accepted the nomination for Vice-President: "I make a painful sacrifice of inclination to what I am led to believe is a public duty." Ticknor deplored the contest "of sectional and geographical parties; — the most dangerous parties undoubtedly that can be formed in a confederated republic." The Constitutional Union Party never had a chance in that year of raw nerves and recrimination.[99]

Desperately, Ticknor and his friends sought to stem the tide of secession after the election of Lincoln. In December 1860, Ticknor met with Everett, Robert Winthrop, Benjamin R. Curtis, Amos Lawrence, George T. Curtis, William Appleton, and others to discuss how they might halt the disruption of the Union. The first step, they agreed, would be to repeal the personal liberty law of Massachusetts which barred the return of fugitive slaves, thereby infuriating the South. In characteristic legalistic fashion, they decided that Chief Justice Lemuel Shaw and Judge Curtis should write an "unanswerable" opinion on the unconstitutionality of this law. Ticknor argued that only Shaw's and Curtis' names should be on the public statement so that it would be incontrovertible and above faction. The more canny politician Winthrop cautioned that the plan might "be in danger of being regarded as too much of a Beacon Street, a Bell and Everett affair, and might prevent the very result we all desire to accomplish." Despite his warning, the group rushed ahead with a petition to the legislature, and failed when the antislavery forces opposed compromise. "It is a funny chapter in the history of Back Stairs Politics," Winthrop commented sadly. "I had perceived that George T. Curtis was not pleased that I had not chimed in with his arrangements. He is undoubtedly the wire puller of the whole affair, — a man of ability and integrity, but with an unhappy tendency to believe that there are only three men in Massachusetts, Mr. George Ticknor and his two nephews." [100]

Grasping at straws, Everett and Winthrop went on a futile "peace delegation" to Washington in the spring of 1861 to persuade Congress to adopt the Crittenden Compromise. George T. Curtis thought the failure of the Crittenden Compromise a tragedy, since it "was as reasonable a proposal as could have been made, considering the situation of the Union at that time." The leaders of both sections had misled the people by fatal misreadings of the Constitution and by agitation about slavery.[101]

Webster had been right. Agitators had destroyed the Union, and his own state had played an evil part. "The war of words which led to the war of blows was too much a Massachusetts and South Carolina affair," lamented Winthrop, " — and if the fire-eaters and the fire-blowers of those two states could have been extinguished four years ago, we should have had no Civil War . . . Paris and Helen were not more responsible for the fall of Troy, than Sumner and Brooks, and their compeers on both sides, for the conflagration which threatens our nation." As the war fever took hold, Winthrop attacked the prevalent "spirit of defamation . . . involving all who do not chime in with the extravagances of the hour."

A friend of Ticknor's recalled that "at the outbreak of the Civil War, Mr. Ticknor was regarded as a Secessionist, and at the time when Seward was 'ringing his battle bell,' there was talk of imprisoning him in Fort Warren, where a number of men of distinction from the Southern states had been confined." Ticknor was opposed for re-election as Trustee of the Boston Public Library because people thought he was opposed to "the popular military spirit of the times." Now Ticknor found himself more in the minority than ever, and was losing his sway even over Beacon Hill. He distrusted the newly organized Union Club and told Everett, its president, that "it was regarded by conservative men as an abolition concern, and stigmatized as a 'Jacobin Association.' " Ticknor refused to go to a dinner party at Everett's house; Everett responded that "Mr. Ticknor intimates that it was on account of my own political 'condition,' which, considering that he was greatly troubled at the origination of the Union Club, because it threatened social ostracism, is rather cool." Ticknor grew ever more lonely and alienated as darkness settled over the land.[102]

Ticknor had written to King John in 1859 that a civil war would be "a great calamity, all whose disastrous consequences no human eye can see." Like Thucydides he watched from the exile of old age "the fiercest and most cruel [conflict] between people speaking the same language that had been seen since the days of the Greek Republics." Ticknor supported the North — indeed he found some comfort in the people's willingness to pay the terrible cost of preserving the Union — but he keenly felt "the terrible evils that are oppressing my country and tearing it to pieces." From his library window he could see soldiers march by the State House and hear the shouts of excited crowds.[103]

One of the casualties of the war, Ticknor believed, was the Constitution. "I recollected," he wrote a friend in 1861 "that the acute lawyer who was at your house one evening with the mayor of your city did not hesitate to say that we no longer have any Constitution . . . I could not gainsay him." Men were claiming that the Constitution was effete, that it was proper that "the President is substantially made an irresponsible Dictator," for the times demanded a strong hand. Where will we be going, Ticknor asked George T. Curtis, "when we get to the other side without a Constitution?" In a Fourth of July oration in 1862 Curtis admitted the North's constitutional duty to bring the South back into the Union, but pointed out that the abolitionists had long been guilty themselves of waging "open and undistinguished war upon the Constitution . . . because its founders, for wise and necessary purposes, threw the shield of its protection over the institutions of the South." [104]

Curtis and Ticknor believed it unconstitutional to emancipate the slave. Soldiers were fighting to defend "the Constitution as it is, and the restoration of the Union of our forefathers," not to free the Negro. Curtis shared Ticknor's conviction that freed slaves would still be inferior and burdensome to the whole nation. Twenty years after emancipation Curtis wrote that "the church, the press, society and benevolence have to encounter such questions as these: — Whether the negro is by nature vicious, intractable, thriftless — the women incurably unchaste, the men incurably dishonest; whether the vices and failings . . . are to be attributed to centuries of slavery, or are taints inherent in the blood. Who can doubt that all such questions could have been satisfactorily answered, if the Christianity of the South had been left to its own time and mode of answering them." In 1869 Ticknor wrote to King John that the freed slaves were "an inferior caste in the midst of a superior race, which looks down upon them at best with pity, but oftener — especially since they have received political power — with dislike and distrust. Can these two races live together in peace and prosperity — one of them, our own Anglo-Saxon, — being the most intolerant and encroaching on the face of the earth." [105]

The Emancipation Proclamation had come, and with it further erosion of the Constitution. Ticknor feared that the perfervid patriotism and "insane hatreds" of the sections would block reunification. Like many of his friends he supported General McClellan as the Democratic candidate in 1864. After the re-election of Lincoln, Ticknor wrote to Robert Winthrop asking him, General McClellan, and Millard Fillmore to go to Richmond to "see what can be done for union and peace" — asking Winthrop not to show his letter to anyone. Charles Francis Adams disliked the machinations of the Copperhead Democrats and unreconstructed conservatives, and he claimed that "talk as treasonable as it was idle was daily and hourly heard in the fashionable clubhouses of Beacon Street." [106]

Actually, Ticknor remained quite consistent over the years in his attitude toward slavery and the Union. He believed that the war was tragic and needless. It was only right to try to end it as soon as possible on terms which would reconcile the South to union again. The Negro, he thought, could never achieve genuine equality. He believed that the radical Republicans were carrying out a punitive plan of reconstruction rather than reconciliation; they were motivated, he thought, by partisan politics or "metaphysical" ideology. The assassination of Lincoln filled him with dread: "I never dreamed, in my worst fears, of living through such a period of horrors." When, shortly after the war, William Dean Howells attended a party at Ticknor's house, he commented, "There were two English noblemen there that night, who had been traveling in the South, and whose stories of the wretched conditions they had seen moved our host to some open misgivings." When Howells "ventured to say that now at least there could be a hope of better things, while the old order was only a perpetuation of despair, he mildly assented, with a gesture of the hand that waived the point, and deeply sighed, 'Perhaps; Perhaps.' " [107]

7. *Prospect and Retrospect*

"We are in the breakers," Ticknor wrote in anguish in 1866 to his nephew, Judge Benjamin Curtis. The next year Joseph Cogswell exclaimed to Ticknor that "we have fallen on perilous times and still more perilous seem to be impending . . . I have no confidence in the wisdom of rulers or people. The former are rogues and the latter dupes . . . You see the leaven of old Essex Juntoism has never got out of me. I am a full believer in what Calhoun once confessed to me, 'The old Federal party is the only honest party the country has ever had.' " Perhaps the organic commonwealth of Boston conservatives was only a dream; surely the present was a nightmare. In the midst of the violent draft riots in New York in 1863 Cogswell wrote:

Since Monday our city has been besieged by an enemy vastly more to be dreaded than the rebels, and now I write in the uncertainty of being able to transmit my note to you. For the moment the rioters are silenced, but it is certain that the riot is not ended . . . We understood yesterday that Governor Morgan's house was to be sacked and fired last night, and as it is directly opposite the Library, we naturally feared for its safety. It has no protection against violence, and nothing but iron shutters to protect it against conflagration . . . I was too anxious to feel the want of sleep, and remained on the roof, meditating on the scene, until I found my clothes saturated with the damps of night, warning me to go below.[108]

During the war Ticknor assailed the "incompetency and corruption of the men at Washington." After the war political standards slid to a new low. The best men, Ticknor told Charles Eliot Norton, no longer can bear the political strife and corruption of the Capitol: "Mr. Bartlett tells me that he will never go to Washington again." What choice did a conservative have in 1868? Grant was the presidential candidate of a corrupt and vindictive party, Seymour the nominee of a party "avowedly unsound on the question of our public debt . . . it needs no spirit of prophecy to foresee that we are to have disturbed times; — alienation, strife and financial troubles of the most serious sort." Since both parties were "radical" in Ticknor's view, the result of the election could only depress him: "I express my opinions without reserve but I mean to be a faithful citizen and obey the constitutional majority as I have always done, though I have always or almost always been in the opposition and never more earnestly and anxiously than now . . . We shall grow more and more radical every year . . . the authority of law in its practical forms will be lessened." [109]

Everywhere Ticknor looked he saw the politics of discord: the dismal attempt to impeach President Johnson, whom Judge Curtis ably defended; "grudges and hatreds" between the United States and England which would probably lead to war; an angry clamor for the punishment of the South; and squabbles over the spoils of office. Congress became an underworld. For Ticknor Webster had been "the last of the Romans." Henry Adams, visiting the Senate in 1850, had also thought that "Senators . . . were Romans." But in the Grant era Adams was told, "A Congressman is a hog!" Adams wondered, "If a Congressman is a hog, what is a Senator?" [110]

Even in Massachusetts, 1868 was a time of infamy for the patrician in politics. That year the Brahmin Richard Henry Dana, Jr., ran against the upstart son of a boardinghouse keeper, Benjamin Butler, in the heart of the old Federalist territory. Skilled in the art of ethnic politics and shrewd in using patronage, Butler derided Dana as a condescending, kid-gloves politician, and bullied his way to overwhelming victory. All

Dana needed to do to lose the election was to open his mouth: according to Butler, Dana confessed that he did sometimes wear white gloves, but assured the workingmen of Lynn that when he sailed before the mast, he "was as dirty as any of you." [111]

Standards in business were little better. Long ago Ticknor had written to Longfellow that "if we are ruined in America, it will be by our prosperity — not by fires or failures." In 1859 he had predicted the Crédit Mobilier scandal, saying that it "will be made a stupendous job, involving great corruption, in Congress and out of it." Compared with the postwar lust for riches, the earlier love of money was platonic. Attacking the cult of millionaires, Cogswell said in 1866 that the "man who does not come up to that figure is accounted a pauper, and now when we hear of defalcations, swindlings, and robberies, it is always in millions." A British reviewer of the *Life, Letters, and Journals of George Ticknor* remarked that Ticknor's sanguine comments in 1838 on the moral purity of Americans had an unreal and archaic flavor after the Civil War: "Commercial probity has become a by-word at New York; corruption has invaded every department of the government; and domestic life no longer rests on that great basis of purity which he supposes to be a myth on this side of the Atlantic." [112]

Did not this all mean Ticknor's worst fears were being realized? In a letter in 1867 to King John he speculated in his despair: "When I look at this unsettled and uncertain condition of things everywhere, I sometimes think we live in a decaying civilization. It seems to me, — in such dark moments, — as if we are all gradually ruining, as, I suppose, all the known civilizations of the world — from the Assyrian down — have been ruined." On New Year's Day, 1871, he discussed this clouded destiny with Charles Francis Adams. Two days later he showed the first signs of the paralysis which ended his life. On the twenty-sixth of January, 1871, at the age of seventy-nine, George Ticknor died as decorously as he had lived. [113]

For New England intellectuals coming to maturity in the postwar years, Ticknor was a symbol of an age and a social order buried by the cataclysm of the Civil War and its aftermath. Henry Adams and Charles Eliot Norton agreed on the meaning of Ticknor as a symbol, though they had different views of Ticknor the man. Norton knew Ticknor as Uncle George, who romped with the children and played blind man's bluff at Shady Hill, who helped his nephew find his way as apostle of culture. During the bitter prewar decade Adams knew Ticknor as the frosty baron of Nine Park Street — "Ticknor's iceberg" as it was called by some — who ostracized his father and his idol, Charles Sumner. Norton saw Ticknor's biography as a record of "permanent value as a vivid illustration of the conditions of the most cultivated society of New England during a period of rapid national development, which even now, though so recent, seems to belong to a somewhat remote past." Adams wrote, "No other life will be lived in America like Mr. Ticknor's, and this gives an historical value to the memoir quite different from its current agreeableness."

Adams conceded that in Ticknor's later "years there was more dissonance between the man and his surroundings than in the happier earlier period," but both he and Norton believed the prewar society of Ticknor's Boston was "far less perplexed with difficult political and social problems, far less unsettled than the present." For them, as for George Ticknor Curtis, the Civil War was "one of those catastrophes which make a wide chasm in the history of a nation, and which separate periods not actually remote from each other, as if a century had intervened." For those who felt alienated in the postwar period, it was tempting to regard the pre-war years as a lost, golden age, a secure patrician era symbolized socially and culturally by George Ticknor.[114]

Surely Ticknor's life was in many respects a fortunate one. His blessings were many: sympathetic parents, a happy marriage, good friends, wealth, health, secure social standing, moral and religious certainty. He was able to transform his love of letters into his profession. The great adventure of his life, his first trip to Europe, became the foundation of his literary and social accomplishment. Though disappointed in his grand plan for reforming Harvard, he could take pride in his achievement within his own department, and he helped to open a way for the work of his nephew, Charles William Eliot. His *History of Spanish Literature* proved to the world that an American could produce a lasting monument of scholarship. He could take justifiable pride in the founding of the Boston Public Library, for he more than any other individual was responsible for its plan and its success. As Brahmin high priest he enjoyed social triumphs at home and abroad.[115]

Yet over the scene of private happiness fell the shadow, at first faint and distant, finally black and threatening, of public apocalypse. Ticknor's Federalist education, his travels, his literary studies, his somber observation of changes in America taught him to distrust the complacent doctrine of progress. Like Henry Adams, he sometimes felt that he had been educated to live in another century. Like Charles Eliot Norton, he found that his studies and his experience in the Old World had alienated him from the broader society around him, though emotionally he never became an expatriate. Rigidly, he retained the traits of character and the political and social assumptions acquired in his youth. The older he became, the more archaic these traits and assumptions seemed to others. Through travel and correspondence he gained a perspective on American society shared by few of his countrymen, and in his later years this perspective more often created confusion and despair than clarification and hope. This very confusion, this despair, this anachronism illuminate the accelerating social changes in America during Ticknor's long career; these transformations assumed a sharp and painful meaning in the life of this patriotic provincial and republican Tory. It is thus as observer, as outspoken critic, as a man often out of step with his countrymen that Ticknor reveals most to us today about himself, his circle, and his time.

Bibliography

ABBREVIATIONS

BPL Boston Public Library

DCL Dartmouth College Library

FL Manuscript of Ticknor's Lectures on French Literature, in Harvard University Archives

HL Houghton Library, Harvard University

HUA Harvard University Archives

LC Library of Congress

MHS Massachusetts Historical Society

MSJ Manuscript Journals of Ticknor's first European trip, in Dartmouth College Library

TJ Typescript of Manuscript Journals of Ticknor's first European trip, in Dartmouth College Library

TL Ticknor Letters, in Harvard University Archives

TP Ticknor Papers, in Harvard University Archives

A Note on Manuscript Sources

The largest and most valuable collection of manuscripts by Ticknor and relating to Ticknor is deposited in the Archives of the Dartmouth College Library. Besides the manuscript volumes noted below the collection includes a large number of letters by Ticknor and his family, his wife's journals, and ten filing boxes of letters from eminent people, many of them to Ticknor, which he collected and entitled "Autograph Collection."

In addition to a number of Ticknor's letters the Massachusetts Historical Society has several manuscript collections which cast light on Ticknor's career, the most notable of which are the Bancroft, Prescott, Everett, and Winthrop Papers.

In its Rare Books Room the Boston Public Library has a valuable collection of manuscripts, newspaper clippings, and documents relating to Ticknor, including many Ticknor letters, his drafts and revisions of the *History of Spanish Literature,* manuscripts and published writings describing Ticknor's role in creating the Boston Public Library, and useful files and lists of obituaries and reviews of Ticknor's works. Ticknor's collection of Spanish books was deposited in the Boston Public Library, though most of his general library was bequeathed to the Dartmouth College Library.

Houghton Library at Harvard has some of Ticknor's letters and a number of important collections, especially the Sumner, Sparks, and Longfellow Papers, which provide an important perspective on Ticknor. The Harvard University Archives contains a large number of manuscripts and documents describing Ticknor's work at Harvard, the most important of which are collected in a bound volume of Ticknor letters and a box of Ticknor's papers.

Other sources of manuscripts illuminating Ticknor's career are indicated in the notes.

Ticknor's Writings

Lessing, Laocoön or the Limits of Painting and Poetry (first 8 chs.).

Sallust, An Abstract of the History of Catiline. 1811.

Sophocles, Oedipus Tyrannus. 1809.

Tacitus, Manners of the Germans. 1810.

Winckelmann, Thoughts on the Imitation of the Greeks in Painting and Statuary.

Xenophon, Apology of Socrates before the Judges.

Translations into German. One volume of various short pieces. DCL.

Varia. 2 vols. DCL.

These volumes contain short literary essays and notes, garnered from readings and lectures.

PUBLISHED WORKS

COLLECTIONS OF PUBLISHED LETTERS AND JOURNALS

Briefwechsel König Johann von Sachsen mit George Ticknor, ed. Johann Georg. Leipzig and Berlin, 1920.

A fascinating correspondence between a monarch who was also a gentleman of letters and a republican conservative, concerning the political and literary developments of their time.

George Ticknor's Travels in Spain, ed. George T. Northrup (University of Toronto Studies, Philological series, 2). Toronto, 1913.

In this book Northrup edited, with commentary and notes, parts of Ticknor's Journals written while he was in Spain in 1818 which were not included in the *Life, Letters, and Journals of George Ticknor.*

Letters to Pascual de Gayangos; from Originals in the Collection of the Hispanic Society of America, ed. Clara L. Penney. New York, 1927.

Letters of Ticknor to a Spanish scholar who helped him to collect his magnificent Spanish library; they are chiefly of bibliographical interest.

Life, Letters, and Journals of George Ticknor, ed. George S. Hillard, Mrs. Anna Eliot Ticknor, and Miss Anna Eliot Ticknor. 2 vols. Boston, 1876.

George S. Hillard prepared the first ten chapters and Mrs. Ticknor and her daughter the remainder. Mrs. Ticknor asked Charles Eliot Norton to complete the work when Hillard became ill (letter of Mrs. Anna E. Ticknor to Charles E. Norton, June 6, 1874, and another undated letter to Norton, HL). Miss Ticknor did the bulk of the task of editing Ticknor's manuscripts and writing the connecting narrative. This work is, for the most part, a primary source composed of Ticknor's Journals, a brief autobiography (Ch. 1), and letters from him and to him. The *Life* illustrates the care with which Ticknor wrote even trifling manuscripts: indeed, in all of Ticknor's writings which I have seen, both published and unpublished, I have almost never seen an awkward sentence or phrase. At times Hillard and the two Anna Ticknors distorted Ticknor's manuscripts by deleting earthy expressions or phrases which betrayed Ticknor's occasional naiveté, self-doubts, pessimism or misinformation; but on the whole they executed their task of transcription accurately and with commendable candor, considering their relation to Ticknor. The connecting narrative is likewise clear and well written. Although Victorian filiopietistic biographies have received more criticism than praise from scholars, I believe that this is an honest book and valuable source material for the student of the social and intellectual history of Ticknor's time.

West Point in 1826, ed. H. Pelham Curtis. Boston, 1886.
    This is a collection of letters written by Ticknor to his wife during his visit to West Point in 1826.

JOURNAL ARTICLES

"Annotations on Milton's Paradise Lost," *General Repository and Review,* II (1812), 66–84.
    In all likelihood this is the work referred to in the *Life, Letters, and Journals of George Ticknor,* II, 507. A scholarly effort, tracing many of Milton's allusions to their Latin and Greek sources, a natural outgrowth of Ticknor's studies with the Rev. John Gardiner.

"Biography of Michael Stiefel," *North American Review,* IV (1817), 166–176.
    The evidence of Ticknor's authorship is the reference in the *Life, Letters, and Journals of George Ticknor,* II, 507; the references to German texts in the body of the article; and the manuscript notation in the copy of the article in the DCL, which says that the article was written by Ticknor while he was at Göttingen.

"Early Spanish Drama," *American Quarterly Review,* IV (1828), 308–349.
    Henry Grattan Doyle ascribes this article to Ticknor, a hypothesis which seems very probable because of the learned quality of the article and Ticknor's move from the *North American Review* to the *American Quarterly Review.*

"Essays on Scenes in Italy," *North American Review,* XVIII (1924), 192–204.
    This review of a travel book contains a section of Ticknor's Journal which discusses the disease-ridden Campagna. A brief but interesting essay on the moral impact of Europe on an American. A part of this

was published in the *Life, Letters, and Journals of George Ticknor,* I, 168–169.

"Free Schools of New England," *North American Review,* XIX (1824), 448–457.

A sympathetic review of a plea by James Carter for better common schools.

"Griscom's Tour in Europe," *North American Review,* XVIII (1824), 178–192.

Another review of a book of travel, John Griscom's *A Year in Europe* . . . Griscom, like Ticknor, was interested in European educational systems.

"Joshua Bates," *American Journal of Education,* VII (1859), 270–272.

An appreciative account of the major donor of the Boston Public Library.

"Lafayette," *North American Review,* XX (1825), 147–180. Reprinted as *Outlines of the Principal Events in the Life of General Lafayette* (Boston, 1825). Also translated into French as *Histoire du Général de la Fayette par un Citoyen Américain* (Paris, 1825).

A well-written short biography of Lafayette and a useful source for Ticknor's political ideas.

"The Leper of Aost," *North American Review,* XXI (1825), 243–245.

A brief review of *The Leper of Aost; Translated from the French of Lemaistre* (Boston, n.d.).

"Memoirs of the Buckminsters," *Christian Examiner,* XLVII (1849), 169–195. Reprinted as *Review of Memoirs of the Rev. Joseph Buckminster and the Rev. Joseph Stevens Buckminster* (Cambridge, 1849).

This article gives an excellent portrait of Ticknor's idol, Buckminster, and a clear picture of Boston during his youth and of his religious opinions.

"Mr. Sullivan's Address," *North American Review,* XXI (1825), 225–230.

This review of William Sullivan's *An Address to the Members of the Bar of Suffolk, Mass., at Their Stated Meeting on the First Tuesday of March, 1824* (Boston, 1825) gives a clear view of Ticknor's jaundiced opinion of the law as a career.

Monthly Anthology and Boston Review. Ticknor's contributions:

"Baldness," X (1811), 169.
"Cosmeticks," X (1811), 329.
"Criticks," VIII (1809), 22.
"Eclogues," X (1811), 96–97.
"Etymology," VIII (1810), 243.
"Firmness," VIII (1810), 168.
"Friendship," IX (1810), 19.

"Hypercriticism," X (1811), 243.

"Literary Fastidiousness," IX (1810), 323–324.

"Martial," X (1811), 16.

"Milton and Addison," IX (1810), 239–241.

"Montesquieu," X (1811), 14.

"Passion and Fancy," IX (1810), 322–323.

"Poetry of Cicero," X (1811), 96.

"Population," X (1811), 396.

"Ridiculous Literary Blunders," IX (1810), 87–88.

"Savage and Dermody," VIII (1810), 102.

"Sir Richard Steele," VII (1809), 311–312.

"Study of the Law," X (1811), 169.

"Voltaire," X (1811), 327.

Untitled reviews: X (1811), 33–40, 114–116, 426.

>These brief articles are interesting chiefly as a prefiguration of the conflicting principles of literary criticism which Ticknor witnessed and expressed as a member of the Anthology Society.

"Moore's Anacreon," *General Repository and Review,* I (1812), 102–114.

>This appears to be the article referred to in the *Life, Letters, and Journals of George Ticknor,* II, 507. Ticknor here displays again his classical erudition in the magazine edited by Andrews Norton, an organ of emergent Unitarianism or "Liberal Christianity."

"Thacher's Sermons," *Christian Examiner,* I (1824), 136–143.

>Despite the discrepancy in the date, this must be the work referred to in the *Life, Letters, and Journals of George Ticknor,* II, 507. It is a review of the sermons of Ticknor's friend Samuel Thacher, who, like Buckminster, died at an early age. A useful exposition of Ticknor's view of the role of the church.

"Webster's Speeches and Forensic Arguments," *American Quarterly Review,* IX (1831), 420–457. Reprinted, with some additions, as *Remarks on the Life and Writings of Daniel Webster of Massachusetts* (Philadelphia, 1831).

>An important source for Ticknor's political ideas.

"Works of Chateaubriand," *American Quarterly Review,* II (1827), 458–482.

>This article displays Ticknor's personal knowledge of Chateaubriand and his slight disparagement of him as an extravagant writer.

OTHER PRINTED WORKS

History of Spanish Literature. 4th ed. 3 vols. Boston and New York, 1891. Translated into French by J. G. Magnabal, *Histoire de la Littérature*

Espagnole (Paris, 1864); into German by N. H. Julius, *Geschichte der Schönen Literatur in Spanien* (Leipzig, 1867); into Spanish by Pascual de Gayangos, *Historia de la Literatura Española* (Madrid, 1851); in each case the translator added notes of his own.

The 1891 edition contains all of Ticknor's corrections of the previous editions, the first of which was issued in 1849.

Lecture on the Best Methods of Teaching the Living Languages. Delivered before the American Institute, August 24, 1832. Boston, 1833.

This perceptive lecture illustrates Ticknor's sensitivity to the problems of teaching.

Life of William Hickling Prescott. Boston, 1864.

A balanced and well-written biography of Ticknor's best friend. A useful source for Ticknor's ideas about the role of the scholar in America.

Papers Discussing the Comparative Merits of Prescott's and Wilson's Histories. Pro. and Con., as Laid before the Massachusetts Historical Society. Boston, 1861.

A defense of Prescott against an upstart rival.

The Remains of Nathaniel Appleton Haven. With a Memoir of His Life. Cambridge, Mass., 1827.

A short biography of one of Ticknor's friends, showing what moral qualities Ticknor appreciated in his countrymen.

Remarks on Changes Lately Proposed or Adopted in Harvard University. Boston, 1825.

An important summary of Ticknor's educational views.

Syllabus of a Course of Lectures on the History and Criticism of Spanish Literature. Cambridge, Mass., 1823.

A foreshadowing of the *History of Spanish Literature.*

"Tribute to Edward Everett," Massachusetts Historical Society, *Proceedings, 1864–1865* (Boston, 1866), 130–141.

A valuable picture of Ticknor's relation with Everett including their odyssey in Göttingen.

Union of the Boston Athenaeum and the Public Library. Boston, 1853.

See discussion, part VI.

"William Hickling Prescott," in Evert A. and George L. Duyckink, *Cyclopaedia of American Literature* (2 vols.; New York, 1855), II, 235–242.

General Bibliography

Adams, Charles Francis, *Richard Henry Dana: A Biography* 2 vols. Boston, 1891.

Adams, Henry, *The Education of Henry Adams,* Modern Library ed. New York, 1931.

⸻ *History of the United States.* 9 vols. New York, 1889–1891.

⸻ "Life, Letters, and Journals of George Ticknor," *North American Review,* CXXIII (1876), 210–215.

Adams, Herbert B., *Thomas Jefferson and the University of Virginia.* Washington, D.C., 1888.

Adams, John Quincy, *Life in a New England Town: 1787, 1788, Diary of John Quincy Adams While a Student in the Office of Theophilus Parsons of Newburyport.* Boston, 1903.

Ames, Seth, ed., *Works of Fisher Ames; with a Selection from his Speeches and Correspondence.* 2 vols. Boston, 1854.

Amory, Cleveland, *The Proper Bostonians.* New York, 1947.

Ampère, Jean-Jacques, *Promenade en Amérique.* 2 vols. Paris, 1855.

Appleton, Nathan, *Letter to the Hon. William C. Rives of Virginia on Slavery and the Union.* Boston, 1860.

Bancroft, George, *History of the Formation of the Constitution of the United States of America,* 6th ed. 2 vols. New York, 1889.

Barnard, Henry, "Documentary History of Normal Schools," *American Journal of Education,* XVI (1866), 75–77.

Bassett, John S., "The Round Hill School," The American Antiquarian Society, *Proceedings,* New Series, XXVII (1917), 18–62.

Berthoff, Rowland, "The American Social Order: A Conservative Hypothesis," *American Historical Review,* LXV (1960), 495–514.

Bilderback, William, "The Cotton Whigs of Massachusetts: A Conservative Reaction to the Slavery Crisis," unpub. B.A. diss. Reed College, 1961.

Blanshard, Frances Bradshaw, *Letters of Ann Gillam Storrow to Jared Sparks* (Smith College, Studies in History, VI, 3). Northampton, 1921.

Boswell, James, *Journal of a Tour to the Hebrides with Samuel Johnson, LL.D.,* ed. F. A. Pottle and C. H. Bennett. New York, 1936.

Bowditch, Nathaniel I., et al., *Remarks Concerning the Late Dr. Bowditch by the Rev. Dr. Palfrey with the Replies of Dr. Bowditch's Children.* Boston, 1840.

Bowditch, Vincent Y., *Life and Correspondence of Henry Ingersoll Bowditch.* 2 vols. Boston, 1902.

Brooks, Van Wyck, *The Flowering of New England, 1815–1865.* New York, 1936.

———— *Opinions of Oliver Allston.* New York, 1941.

Brown, Cynthia Stokes, "Discovery of the German University: Four Students at Göttingen, 1815–1822," unpub. diss. Johns Hopkins University, 1964.

Brown, Samuel, *The Life of Rufus Choate.* Boston, 1885.

Calhoun, Daniel, *Professional Lives in America: Structure and Aspiration, 1750–1850.* Cambridge, Mass., 1965.

Channing, Edward, "On Models in Literature," *North American Review,* III (1816), 202–209.

Channing, William Ellery, *Works,* 14th ed. 6 vols. Boston, 1855.

Charvat, William, *The Origins of American Critical Thought.* Philadelphia, 1936.

Chase, Frederick, and John K. Lord, *A History of Dartmouth College and the Town of Hanover, New Hampshire.* 2 vols. Cambridge, Mass., 1891.

Choate, Rufus, *Addresses and Orations.* Boston, 1887.

———— *The Romance of New England History.* Old South Leaflet, 10. Boston, n.d.

Circourt, Adolphe de, *"Life, Letters, and Journals of George Ticknor," Bibliothèque Universelle et Revue Suisse,* LVIII (1877), 509–525, 693–712.

Clark, Harry H., "Literary Criticism in the *North American Review,* 1815–1835," Wisconsin Academy of Sciences, Arts, and Letters, *Transactions,* XXXII (1940), 299–350.

———— ed., *Transitions in American Literary History.* Durham, N.C., 1953.

Clarke, James Freeman, *Autobiography, Diary, and Correspondence,* ed. Edward Everett Hale. Boston, 1899.

Clive, John, *Scotch Reviewers: The Edinburgh Review, 1802–1815.* Cambridge, Mass., 1957.

Cogswell, Joseph G., "National Education," *New York Review,* III (1838), 149–194.

———— "On the Means of Education, and the State of Learning, in the United States of America," *Blackwood's Edinburgh Magazine,* IV (1819), 546–553, 639–649.

———— *Outline of the System of Education at the Round Hill School with a List of the Present Instructors and of the Pupils from its Commencement until this Time, June, 1831.* Boston, 1831.

———— "University Education," *New York Review,* VII (1840), 109–136.

———— and George Bancroft, *Prospectus of a School to be Established at Round Hill, Northampton, Massachusetts.* Cambridge, Mass., 1823.

Commager, Henry Steele, "Leadership in Eighteenth Century America and Today," *Daedalus,* Fall 1961, 652–671.

Crane, Theodore, ed., *The Colleges and the Public, 1787–1862*. New York, 1963.

—————— "Francis Wayland: Political Economist as Educator," Brown University, *Papers,* XXXIX. Providence, 1962.

Crawford, Mary C., *Famous Families of Massachusetts*. 2 vols. Boston, 1930.

—————— *Romantic Days in Old Boston*. Boston, 1910.

Current, Richard N., *Daniel Webster and the Rise of National Conservatism* (Oscar Handlin, ed., Library of American Biography). Boston, 1955.

Curtis, George T., *History of the Origin, Formation, and Adoption of the Constitution of the United States; with Notices of its Principal Framers.* 2 vols. New York, 1860.

—————— *Life of Daniel Webster,* 2nd ed. 2 vols. New York, 1870.

—————— *Life of James Buchanan.* 2 vols. New York, 1883.

—————— *The Merits of Thomas W. Dorr and George Bancroft as They are Politically Connected.* Boston, n.d.

—————— *The True Uses of Revolutionary History. An Oration Delivered before the Authorities of the City of Boston, on Monday, the Fifth of July, 1841, Being the Day Set Apart for the Celebration of the Sixty-Fifth Anniversary of American Independence.* Boston, 1841.

Dahl, Curtis, "The American School of Catastrophe," *American Quarterly,* XI (1959), 380–390.

Dana, Richard H., Jr., *An Autobiographical Sketch (1815–1842),* ed. Robert Metzdorf. Hamden, Conn., 1953.

Dana, Richard H., Sr., *Poems and Prose Writings*. Boston, 1833.

Daveis, Charles, *An Address Delivered on the Commemoration at Fryeburg, May 19, 1825*. Portland, Me., 1825.

Davis, Richard B., "The Early American Lawyer and the Profession of Letters," *The Huntington Library Quarterly,* XII (1948), 191–205.

—————— *Francis Walker Gilmer: Life and Learning in Jefferson's Virginia.* Richmond, 1939.

Dickens, Charles, *American Notes and Pic-nic Papers*. Philadelphia, n.d.

Dole, Nathan H., "The Anthology Club," The Bibliophile Society, *Eighty Year Book*. n.p., 1909.

Donald, David, *Charles Sumner and the Coming of the Civil War*. New York, 1960.

—————— *Lincoln Reconsidered: Essays on the Civil War Era*. New York, 1961.

Doyle, Henry G., *George Ticknor; Together with Ticknor's "Lecture on the Best Methods of Teaching the Living Languages."* Washington, 1937. A reprint from the *Modern Language Journal,* XXII (1937), 3–37.

Du Pan, Mallet, *Considerations On the Nature of the French Revolution; and on the Causes which Prolong its Duration*. Trans. from the French. London, 1793.

Dwight, Timothy, *Travels in New-England and New-York*. 4 vols. New Haven, 1821–1822.

East, Robert, *Business Enterprise in the American Revolutionary Era.* New York, 1938.

Ekirch, Arthur A., *The Idea of Progress in America, 1815–1860.* New York, 1944.

Eliot, Charles W., *Report* [on Harvard University] *for 1883–84.* Cambridge, Mass., 1885.

Eliot, Samuel, and Elizabeth Cary Agassiz, eds., *Society to Encourage Studies at Home, Founded in 1873 by Anna Eliot Ticknor.* Boston, 1897.

Elson, Ruth M., *Guardians of Tradition: American Schoolbooks of the Nineteenth Century.* Lincoln, Neb., 1964.

Emerson, Ralph W., *English Traits.* Centenary ed., vol. V. Boston and New York, 1903.

———— "Historic Notes of Life and Letters in New England," *Works* (X, 323–370). Boston, 1883.

———— *The Journals and Miscellaneous Notebooks of Ralph Waldo Emerson,* ed. William H. Gilman et al. 5 vols. Cambridge, Mass., 1960————.

———— *Journals of Ralph Waldo Emerson,* ed. Edward Waldo Emerson and Waldo Emerson Forbes. 10 vols. Boston, 1909–1914.

———— *Letters,* ed. Ralph Rusk. 6 vols. New York, 1939.

Everett, Edward, "European Politics," *The North American Review,* XXI (1825), 141–153.

———— *A Letter to John Lowell, esq., in Reply to a Publication Entitled Remarks on a Pamphlet. Printed by the Professors and Tutors of Harvard University, Touching Their Right to the Exclusive Government of that Seminary.* Boston, 1824.

———— *Orations and Speeches on Various Occasions,* 2nd ed. Vol. I. Boston, 1850.

———— *The Peculiar Motives to Intellectual Exertion in America; an Oration Pronounced at Cambridge before the Society of Phi Beta Kappa, August 26, 1824.* Boston, 1824.

———— "University of Virginia," *The North American Review,* X (1820), 115–1137.

Fisher, Joshua F., *The Degradation of the Representative System and its Reform.* Philadelphia, 1863.

Forbes, Abner, and J. W. Greene, *The Rich Men of Massachusetts: Containing a Statement of the Reputed Wealth of about Fifteen Hundred Persons, with Brief Sketches of More than One Thousand Characters.* Boston, 1851.

Ford, Richard, "Ticknor's *History of Spanish Literature,*" *Electic Magazine of Foreign Literature, Science and Art,* XXII (1851), 1–24.

Fowle, William B., "Memoir of Caleb Bingham," *The American Journal of Education,* V (1858), 325–349.

Frothingham, Paul R., *Edward Everett, Orator and Statesman.* Boston and New York, 1925.

Gannett, Ezra S., "The Christian Scholar," *Old and New,* III (1871), 516–522.

Gannett, William C., *Ezra Stiles Gannett: Unitarian Minister in Boston, 1824–1871.* Boston, 1875.

Gardiner, Robert Hallowell, *Early Recollections, 1782–1864.* Hallowell, Me., 1936.

Gentz, Friedrich, *The French and American Revolutions Compared,* trans. John Quincy Adams. Intro. by Russell Kirk. Chicago, 1955.

Gray, Francis C., *Thomas Jefferson in 1814; Being an Account of a Visit to Monticello, Virginia.* With notes and introduction by Henry S. Rowe and T. Jefferson Coolidge. Boston, 1924.

Griswold, Rufus W., *The Republican Court, or American Society in the Days of Washington.* New York, 1855.

Grund, Francis J., *Aristocracy in America. From the Sketchbook of a German Nobleman.* New York, 1959.

Hale, James W., *Old Boston Town, Early in this Century; By an 1801-er.* New York, 1880.

Hall, Basil, *Travels in North America in the Years 1827 and 1828,* 3rd ed. 3 vols. Edinburgh, 1830.

Handlin, Oscar, *Boston's Immigrants, 1790–1865: A Study in Acculturation* (Harvard Historical Studies, 50). Cambridge, Mass., 1941.

———— and Mary F. Handlin, "Radicals and Conservatives in Massachusetts after Independence," *The New England Quarterly,* XVII (1944), 343–355.

Hart, Charles H., *Memoir of George Ticknor, Historian of Spanish Literature. Read before the Numismatic and Antiquarian Society of Philadelphia, May 4, 1871.* Philadelphia, 1871.

Hart, Thomas R., Jr., "Friedrich Bouterwek, A Pioneer Historian of Spanish Literature," *Comparative Literature,* V (1953), 351–361.

———— "George Ticknor's *History of Spanish Literature:* The New England Background," *PMLA,* LXIX (1954), 76–88.

Hartz, Louis, *The Liberal Tradition in America.* New York, 1955.

Hawkins, Richmond L., *Madame de Staël and the United States.* Cambridge, Mass., 1930.

Hawthorne, Nathaniel, *The American Notebooks,* ed. Randall Stewart. New Haven, 1932.

Hazelrigg, Charles T., *American Literary Pioneer: A Biographical Study of James A. Hillhouse.* New York, 1953.

Higginson, Thomas W., *Carlyle's Laugh; and Other Surprises.* Boston, 1909.

———— "Göttingen and Harvard Eighty Years Ago," *The Harvard Graduates Magazine,* VI (1897–98), 6–18.

———— *Henry Wadsworth Longfellow.* Boston and New York, 1902.

Hillard, George S., *The Dangers and Duties of the Mercantile Profession. An Address Delivered before the Mercantile Library Association, at its Thirtieth Anniversary, November 13, 1850.* Boston, 1850.

—— *Memoir and Correspondence of Jeremiah Mason.* Cambridge, Mass., 1873.

—— *The Relation of the Poet to his Age. A Discourse Delivered before the Phi Beta Kappa Society of Harvard University on Thursday, August 24, 1843.* Boston, 1843.

—— "Ticknor's *History of Spanish Literature,*" *Christian Examiner,* XLVIII (1850), 121–168. Reprinted as *Review of Ticknor's History of Spanish Literature,* Cambridge, Mass., 1850.

Hillhouse, James A., *Dramas, Discourses, and Other Pieces.* 2 vols. Boston, 1839.

Historical Register of Harvard University, 1636–1936. Cambridge, Mass., 1937.

Hofstadter, Richard, *Anti-intellectualism in American Life.* New York, 1963.

—— and Wilson Smith, eds., *American Higher Education: A Documentary History.* 2 vols. Chicago, 1962.

Holmes, Oliver Wendell, *The Autocrat of the Breakfast Table; Every Man His Own Boswell,* Riverside ed. Boston, 1891.

—— *Elsie Venner; A Romance of Destiny,* Riverside ed. Cambridge, Mass., 1891.

Honeywell, Roy J., *The Educational Work of Thomas Jefferson* (Harvard Graduate School of Education, Studies in Education, 16). Cambridge, Mass., 1931.

Houghton, Walter E., *The Victorian Frame of Mind, 1830–1870.* New Haven, 1957.

Howe, Mark A. DeWolfe, ed., *Journal of the Proceedings of the Society Which Conducts the Monthly Anthology & Boston Review, October 3, 1805, to July 2, 1811.* Boston, 1910.

—— *The Life and Letters of George Bancroft.* 2 vols. New York, 1908.

Howells, William D., *Literary Friends and Acquaintances: A Personal Retrospect of American Authorship.* New York, 1902.

Hunnewell, James M., "The Ticknor Family in America, Being an Account of the Descendants of William Ticknor of Scituate and of Other Immigrants named Ticknor or Tickner." Typescript written in Boston in 1919, in the Library of Congress and the New England Historical and Genealogical Society.

Irving, Washington, *The Sketch Book,* rev. ed. New York, 1849.

James, Henry, *Charles W. Eliot: President of Harvard University, 1869–1909.* 2 vols. Boston and New York, 1930.

Jantz, H. S., "German Thought and Literature in New England, 1620–1820," *Journal of English and German Philology,* XLI (1942), 1–45.

Jefferson, Thomas, *The Papers of Thomas Jefferson,* ed. Julian P. Boyd. 17 vols. Princeton, N.J., 1950——.

Kirker, Harold, and James Kirker, *Bulfinch's Boston, 1787–1817.* New York, 1964.

Kirkland, John T., "Literary Institutions — University," *North American Review,* XX (1818), 270–278.

Kohn, Hans, *American Nationalism: An Interpretive Essay.* New York, 1957.

Labaree, Benjamin, *Patriots and Partisans: The Merchants of Newburyport, 1764–1815* (Harvard Historical Studies, 73). Cambridge, Mass., 1962.

Lawrence, Robert M., *Old Park Street and its Vicinity.* Boston, 1922.

Leach, Richard H., "George Ticknor Curtis and Daniel Webster's 'Villainies,'" *New England Quarterly,* XXVII (1954), 391–395.

Lee, Eliza Buckminster, *Memoirs of Rev. Joseph Buckminster, D.D. and of His Son, Rev. Joseph Stevens Buckminster,* 2nd ed. Boston, 1851.

Levin, David, *History as Romantic Art: Bancroft, Prescott, Motley, and Parkman.* Stanford, Calif., 1959.

"Life, Letters, and Journals of George Ticknor," anon., rev., *The Quarterly Review,* CXLII (1876), 160–201.

"Life, Letters, and Journals of George Ticknor," anon. rev., *The Saturday Review of Politics, Literature, Science, and Art,* XLII (1876), 478–480.

Livermore, Shaw, *The Twilight of Federalism: The Disintegration of the Federalist Party, 1815–1830.* Princeton, N.J., 1962.

Long, Orie, *Literary Pioneers: Early American Explorers of European Culture.* Cambridge, Mass., 1935.

――― *Thomas Jefferson and George Ticknor: A Chapter in American Scholarship.* Williamstown, Mass., 1933.

Longfellow, Henry Wadsworth, "Defense of Poetry," *The North American Review,* XXXIV (1832), 56–78.

――― *Kavanaugh: A Tale.* Boston, 1893.

Longfellow, Samuel, *Life of Henry Wadsworth Longfellow; with Extracts from his Journals and Correspondence.* 2 vols. Boston, 1886.

Lowell, James Russell, *Literary Essays.* Vol. II. Boston and New York, 1892.

――― "Nationality in Literature," *The North American Review,* LXIX (1849), 196–201.

――― *New Letters,* ed. Mark A. DeWolfe Howe. New York, 1932.

――― "The New Timon," *The North American Review,* LXIV (1847), 460–483.

――― *Political Addresses.* Vol. VI. Boston, 1890.

Lowell, John, *Further Remarks on the Memorial of the Officers of Harvard College.* Boston, 1824.

――― *Remarks on a Pamphlet Printed by the Professors and Tutors of Harvard University, Touching their Right to the Exclusive Government of that Seminary by an Alumnus of that College.* Boston, 1824.

Lyell, Charles, *Travels in North America; with Geological Observations on the United States, Canada, and Nova Scotia.* 2 vols. London, 1845.

Marryat, Frederick, *A Diary in America, with Remarks on its Institutions.* 2 vols. London, 1839.

Martineau, Harriet, *Society in America.* 3 vols. London, 1837.

Mérimée, Prospère, "Ticknor's *History of Spanish Literature*," *Revue des Deux Mondes,* X (1851), 275–288.

Meyers, Marvin, *The Jacksonian Persuasion: Politics and Belief.* New York, 1960.

Miller, John C., *The Federalist Era, 1789–1801.* New York, 1960.

Miller, Perry, *Errand into the Wilderness.* Cambridge, Mass., 1956.

―――― *The Raven and the Whale: The War of Words and Wits in the Era of Poe and Melville.* New York, 1956.

―――― "The Romantic Dilemma in America and the Concept of Nature," *Harvard Theological Review,* XLVIII (1948), 239–254.

―――― ed., *The Transcendentalists: An Anthology.* Cambridge, Mass., 1950.

Morison, J. H., "George Ticknor, LL.D.," *The Religious Magazine and Monthly Review,* XLV (1871), 297–303.

Morison, Samuel E., "The Great Rebellion in Harvard College, and the Resignation of President Kirkland," The Colonial Society of Massachusetts, *Transactions,* XXVII (1927–1930), 54–112.

―――― *The Life and Letters of Harrison Gray Otis, Federalist, 1765–1848.* 2 vols. Boston and New York, 1913.

―――― *The Maritime History of Massachusetts, 1783–1860.* Boston and New York, 1921.

―――― *Three Centuries of Harvard, 1636–1936.* Cambridge, Mass., 1936.

Morse, John T., Jr., *Life and Letters of Oliver Wendell Holmes.* 2 vols. Cambridge, Mass., 1896.

Nevins, Allan, *Ordeal of the Union.* 2 vols. New York, 1947.

Norton, Andrews, *The Evidences of the Genuineness of the Gospels.* 3 vols. Cambridge, Mass., 1844.

―――― "Letter to Mr. Ticknor," *The Christian Examiner,* XLVII (1849), 196–203.

―――― *Remarks on a Report of a Committee of the Overseers of Harvard College Proposing Certain Changes, Relating to the Instruction and Discipline of the College.* Cambridge, Mass., 1824.

―――― *Review of Mrs. Hemans' Forest Sanctuary.* Boston, 1826.

―――― *Speech Delivered before the Overseers of Harvard College, February 3, 1825, in Behalf of the Resident Instructors of the College, with an Introduction.* Boston, 1825.

Norton, Charles E., *Letters,* ed. Sara Norton and Mark A. DeWolfe Howe. Boston, 1913.

―――― ed., *Letters of James Russell Lowell.* 2 vols. New York, 1893.

―――― "Life, Letters, and Journals of George Ticknor," *The Nation,* XXII (1876), 148–149.

Orians, Harrison, "The Romance Ferment after *Waverly*," *American Literature,* III (1932), 408–431.

Otis, Eliza Henderson Boardman [Mrs. Harrison Gray Otis], *The Barclays of Boston.* Boston, 1854.

"Our First Men," or a Catalogue of the Richest Men of Massachusetts, Con-

taining a List of Those Persons Taxed in the State of Massachusetts, Credibly Reported to be Worth One Hundred Thousand Dollars and Upwards, with Biographical Notices of the Principal Persons. Boston, 1851.

Parsons, Theophilus, "Comparative Merits of the Earlier and Later English Writers," *The North American Review,* X (1820), 19–33.

Peabody, Andrew P., *Harvard Reminiscences.* Boston, 1888.

Perry, Thomas S., "Life, Letters, and Journals of George Ticknor," *Lippincott's Magazine,* XVII (1876), 629–634.

Phelps, Reginald H., "The Idea of the Modern University — Göttingen and America," *The Germanic Review,* XXIX (1954), 175–190.

Pierce, Edward L., *Memoir and Letters of Charles Sumner.* 4 vols. Boston, 1893.

Pierson, George W., *Tocqueville and Beaumont in America.* New York, 1938.

Pochman, Henry A., *German Culture in America: Philosophical and Literary Influences, 1600–1900.* Madison, Wis., 1957.

Pope-Hennesey, Una, ed., *The Aristocratic Journey: Being the Outspoken Letters of Mrs. Basil Hall Written during a Fourteen Month's Sojourn in America, 1827–1828.* New York, 1931.

Potter, David M., *People of Plenty: Economic Abundance and the American Character.* Chicago, 1954.

Prescott, William H., *Correspondence, 1833–1847,* ed. Roger Wolcott. Cambridge, Mass., 1925.

——— *Papers,* ed. C. Harvey Gardiner. Urbana, Ill., 1964.

——— *Prescott's Literary Memoranda.* Norman, Okla., 1961.

Quincy, Josiah, *An Appeal in Behalf of the Boston Athenaeum Addressed to the Proprietors.* Boston, 1853.

——— *The History of Harvard University.* 2 vols. Cambridge, Mass., 1840.

Quincy, Josiah P., *Figures of the Past from the Leaves of Old Journals,* Intro. by Mark A. DeWolfe Howe. Boston, 1926.

——— "Social Life in Boston: From the Adoption of the Federal Constitution to the Granting of the City Charter," in *The Memorial History of Boston,* ed. Justin Winsor (Boston, 1883), IV, 1–24.

Rahv, Phillip, ed., *Discovery of Europe: The Story of American Experience in the Old World.* Boston, 1947.

Rhea, Linda, *Hugh Swinton Legaré: A Charleston Intellectual.* Chapel Hill, N.C., 1934.

Richardson, Leon B., *History of Dartmouth College.* Hanover, N.H., 1932.

Rudolph, Frederick, *The American College and University: A History.* New York, 1962.

Ryder, Frank G., "An American View of Germany, 1817," and "George Ticknor on the German Scene," *German-American Review,* XXV (1959), no. 3, 16–19, no. 4, 28–30.

——— *George Ticknor's The Sorrows of Young Werther* (University of

North Carolina, Studies in Comparative Literature, 4). Chapel Hill, N.C., 1952.

Saveth, Edward N., "The American Patrician Class: A Field for Research," *American Quarterly,* XV (1963), 235–252.

―――― "Henry Adams: Waning of America's Patriciate," *Commentary,* XXIV (1957), 302–309.

Schlesinger, Arthur, Jr., *The Age of Jackson.* Boston, 1950.

Schouler, James, "The Whig Party of Massachusetts," Massachusetts Historical Society, *Proceedings,* L (1916–17), 39–53.

Schwartz, Harold, *Samuel Gridley Howe: Social Reformer, 1801–1876.* Cambridge, Mass., 1956.

Seybolt, Robert, "Elisha Ticknor," *DAB,* XVIII, 524–525.

Shaler, Nathaniel S., *Autobiography; with a Supplementary Memoir by his Wife.* Boston and New York, 1909.

Shapiro, Samuel, *Richard Henry Dana, Jr., 1815–1882.* East Lansing, Mich., 1961.

Shera, Jesse, *Foundations of the Public Library: The Origins of the Public Library Movement in New England 1629–1855.* Chicago, 1949.

Shlakman, Vera, *Economic History of a Factory Town.* Northhampton, Mass., 1935.

Simpson, Lewis P., "Federalism and the Crisis of Literary Order," *American Literature,* XXXIV (1960), 253–266.

―――― ed., *The Federalist Literary Mind: Selections from the Monthly Anthology and Boston Review, 1803–1811, Including Documents Relating to the Boston Athenaeum.* Baton Rouge, 1962.

―――― "The Intercommunity of the Learned: Boston and Cambridge in 1800," *New England Quarterly,* XXIII (1950), 491–503.

―――― "A Literary Adventure of the Early Republic: The Anthology Society and the Monthly Anthology," *New England Quarterly,* XXVII (1954), 168–190.

―――― "Not Men, But Books," *Boston Public Library Quarterly,* IV (1952), 167–184.

Sizer, Theodore R., *The Age of the Academies,* New York, 1964.

Smelser, Marshall, "The Federalist Period as an Age of Passion," *American Quarterly,* X (1958), 391–408.

Smith, Sydney, "Adam Seybert's *Statistical Annals of the United States,*" *Edinburgh Review,* XXXIII (1820), 69–80.

Spencer, Benjamin T., *The Quest for Nationality: An American Literary Campaign.* Syracuse, N.Y., 1957.

Spiller, Robert, "The Verdict of Sydney Smith," *American Literature,* I (1929), 3–13.

Stearns, Frank P., *Cambridge Sketches.* Philadelphia, 1905.

Storr, Richard J., *The Beginnings of Graduate Education in America.* Chicago, 1953.

Story, Joseph, *A Discourse Pronounced before the Society of Phi Beta Kappa at the Anniversary Celebration on the Thirty-first Day of August, 1826.* Boston, 1826.

———— *A Familiar Exposition of the Constitution of the United States.* New York, 1847.

———— *Lecture Delivered before the American Institute of Instruction, at their Anniversary in August 1834, at Boston.* Boston, 1834.

———— Chairman, Committee of the Overseers, Harvard University, *Report.* Boston, 1824.

———— "Statesmen: Their Rareness and Importance," *New England Magazine,* VII (1834), 89–104.

Story, William W., *Life and Letters of Joseph Story.* 2 vols. Boston, 1851.

Streeter, Robert E., "Association Psychology and Literary Nationalism in the *North American Review, 1815–1825,*" *American Literature,* XVII (1945–46), 243–254.

Stromberg, Roland N., "Boston in the 1820's and 1830's," *History Today,* XI (1961), 591–598.

Sullivan, William, *An Address to the Members of the Bar of Suffolk, Mass., at their Stated Meeting on the First Tuesday of March, 1824.* Boston, 1825.

———— *Familiar Letters on Public Characters and Public Events from the Peace of 1783 to the Peace of 1815.* Boston, 1834.

———— *Specimen of the Political Class Book; Intended to Instruct the Higher Classes in Schools in the Origin, Nature, and Use of Political Power.* Boston, 1832.

Taylor, William R., *Cavalier and Yankee: The Old South and American National Character.* New York, 1961.

Thackeray, William M., *The Letters and Private Papers of William Makepeace Thackeray,* ed. Gordon N. Ray. 4 vols. Cambridge, Mass., 1946.

Thompson, F. L. M., *English Landed Society in the Nineteenth Century.* London, 1963.

Thompson, Lawrance, *Young Longfellow.* New York, 1938.

Ticknor, Miss Anna Eliot, *An American Family in Paris.* New York, 1869.

———— *Health.* Boston, 1878.

———— *Life of Joseph Green Cogswell, as Sketched in his Letters.* Cambridge, Mass., 1874.

Ticknor, Mrs. Anna Eliot, "Polite Travel in the Thirties," *The Atlantic Monthly,* CXL (1927), 56–65.

———— *Samuel Eliot.* Boston, 1869.

Ticknor, Elisha, *English Exercises, in Which Sentences, Falsely Construed, Are to be Corrected; Comprehending All the Rules, Necessary for Parsing the Language; and Arranged in Such a Manner, as Will Greatly Facilitate the Acquisition of Grammatical Knowledge.* Boston, 1792, 1793.

Tocqueville, Alexis de, *Democracy in America,* trans. Henry Reeve. 2 vols. New York, 1958.

Trent, William P., *English Culture in Virginia; a Study of the Gilman Letters and an Account of the English Professors Obtained by Jefferson for the University of Virginia* (Johns Hopkins University, Studies in Historical and Political Science, 7th ser., 6–7). Baltimore, 1889.

"Tribute to the Hon. David Sears and George Ticknor, LL.D.," Massachusetts Historical Society, *Proceedings, 1871–73* (Boston, 1873), 13–30.

Tudor, William, *Letters on the Eastern States*. New York, 1820.

—— "Reflections on the Literary Delinquency of America," *North American Review*, II (1815), 33–43.

Van Deusen, Glyndon G., "Some Aspects of Whig Thought and Theory in the Jacksonian Period," *American Historical Review*, LXIII (1958), 305–322.

Van Tassel, David D., "Gentlemen of Property and Standing: Compromise Sentiment in Boston in 1850," *New England Quarterly*, XXIII (1850), 307–319.

Ward, Julius H., *Life and Letters of James Gates Percival*. Boston, 1866.

Ward, Samuel Gray, *Ward Family Papers*. Privately printed. n.p., 1900.

Wayland, Francis, *Thoughts on the Present Collegiate System in the United States*. Boston, 1842.

Webster, Daniel, *Works*. 5 vols. Boston, 1854.

—— *Writings and Speeches*, National ed. 18 vols. Boston, 1903.

Wecter, Dixon, *The Saga of American Society: A Record of Social Aspiration, 1607–1937*. New York, 1937.

Welter, Barbara, "The Cult of True Womanhood: 1820–1860," *American Quarterly*, XVIII (Summer 1966), 151–174.

Welter, Rush, "The Idea of Progress in America: An Essay in Ideas and Method," *Journal of the History of Ideas*, XVI (1955), 401–415.

—— *Popular Education and Democratic Thought in America*. New York, 1962.

Whipple, Edwin P., "Life, Letters, and Journals of George Ticknor," *International Review*, III (1876), 441–461.

—— "The Webster Memorial," *North American Review*, LXXVI (1853), 263–268.

Whitehill, Walter Muir, *Boston: A Topographical History*. Cambridge, Mass., 1959.

—— *Boston Public Library: A Centennial History*. Cambridge, Mass., 1956.

Whitney, James Lyman, *Catalogue of the Spanish Library and of the Portuguese Books Bequeathed by George Ticknor to the Boston Public Library; Together with the Collection of Spanish and Portuguese Literature in the General Library*. Boston, 1879.

Willard, Sidney, "State of Learning in the United States," *North American Review*, IX (1819), 240–259.

Williams, Stanley T., *The Spanish Background of American Literature*. 2 vols. New Haven, 1955.

[Wilson, Thomas L.], *The Aristocracy of Boston; Who They Are, and What They Were; Being a History of the Business and Business Men of Boston, the Last Forty Years. By One Who Knows Them*. Boston, 1948.

Winsor, Justin, ed., *The Memorial History of Boston, including Suffolk County, Massachusetts 1630–1880*. 4 vols. Boston, 1886.

Winthrop, Robert C., Jr., *A Memoir of Robert C. Winthrop*. Boston, 1897.

Woodward, C. Vann, *The Burden of Southern History*. New York, 1961.

Wright, Conrad, *The Beginnings of Unitarianism in America*. Boston, 1955.

Yale Faculty, "Report on a Course of Liberal Education," *American Journal of Science,* XV (1829), 297–351.

Notes

The bibliography gives full citations for works listed in abbreviated form in the notes. To keep the documentation within modest compass I have omitted names and dates of letters and similar primary sources taken from printed works and have combined several citations in one note.

I. The Formative Years

1. Boswell, *Tour to the Hebrides,* 54.
2. Dwight, *Travels,* IV, 466; Simpson, *Federalist Literary Mind,* 97.
3. Elisha Ticknor, *English Exercises* (1792 ed.), 30. *The Life, Letters, and Journals of George Ticknor* reveals much about the career and character of Elisha Ticknor, especially through the letters exchanged between father and son. George S. Hillard edited the first ten chapters; the remainder was edited by Ticknor's eldest daughter Anna with the help of her mother Anna Eliot Ticknor. This work will hereafter be cited as *Life.*
4. Elisha Ticknor, *English Exercises* (1793 ed.), 7; Seybolt, "Elisha Ticknor," 624–625; Hunnewell, "Ticknor Family"; Elisha Ticknor to Wheelock, April 23, 1785, and Sept. 2, 1786, DCL.
5. Elisha Ticknor to Wheelock, April 23, 1785, DCL; Elisha Ticknor, *English Exercises* (1793 ed.), 6–7; Welter, *Popular Education and Democratic Thought,* ch. ii.
6. Sullivan, *Familiar Letters,* 44; Fowle, "Caleb Bingham," 325–349. Fowle, who knew Ticknor and Bingham personally, commented that their successors as teachers in Boston "sank into a subordinate class and no longer claimed respectability on account of their office" (345).
7. Fowle, "Caleb Bingham," 333; Ticknor to Wheelock, April 23, 1785, DCL; Seybolt, "Elisha Ticknor," 524–525; *Life,* I, 2–3. Henry Barnard, in his "Documentary History of Normal Schools" (75), wrote that he believed that Elisha Ticknor was the first American proponent of schools designed specifically to prepare teachers.
8. *Life,* I, 1–3, 17–18, 21–23.
9. Fred K. Vinton, obituary of Ticknor in *The Capitol,* April 16, 1871; *Life,* I, 5–6, 22.
10. *Life,* I, 6–7; Peabody, *Reminiscences,* 48–49; Ticknor to Freeman, Nov. 2, 1805, DCL.
11. This watercolor is in the Dartmouth College Library and is available in an excellent reproduction made in 1955. *Life,* I, 5; Dwight, *Travels.*

12. *Life,* I, 6–7, 17–18; Elisha Ticknor to Wheelock, June 24, 1805, DCL; Morison, *Harvard,* 189–191.

13. Webster to Ticknor, June 13, 1850, in Webster, *Writings,* XVI, 545; Chase and Lord, *Dartmouth,* II, 116–118.

14. *Life,* I, 6–7; Richardson, *Dartmouth,* I, 246–248, 250–263.

15. Adams, *Life in a New England Town,* 76–77; *Life,* I, 7–8; Ticknor to Charles Daveis, Sept. 16, 1809, MHS.

16. Elisha Ticknor to Wheelock, Feb. 18, 1807, DCL.

17. Ticknor, "Memoirs of Buckminsters," 171–173; *Life,* I, 17–23.

18. Morison, *Maritime History,* ch. ix; Dwight, *Travels,* IV, 449–452, 466–468.

19. *Life,* I, 8–9; Simpson, *Federalist Literary Mind,* 24–25; Ticknor, *Prescott,* 7. I am indebted to Mr. Walter Whitehill for showing me the portrait of Gardiner in the Boston Athenaeum.

20. *Life,* I, 8–9, 12; Ticknor, *Prescott,* ch. i.

21. Morison, *Otis,* I, 218; Gardiner, *Recollections,* 94.

22. *Life,* I, 19; Quincy, "Social Life," 2–8, 17–19; Morison, *Otis,* I, 228.

23. Adams, *History of the United States,* I, 92; Hale, *Old Boston,* 12.

24. Griswold, *Republican Court,* 8; Ticknor, "Memoirs of Buckminsters," 3; Oscar and Mary Handlin, "Radicals and Conservatives," 353–355; East, *Business Enterprise,* ch. iii; and see Labaree, *Patriots and Partisans,* 96–97, for a comparison of merchants in Newburyport.

25. Anna Eliot Ticknor, *Samuel Eliot,* 6–10, 11, 16, 144, 153; Grund, *Aristocracy,* ch. x; Quincy, *Figures,* 42.

26. *Life,* I, 43–47; Gardiner, *Recollections,* 105–106.

27. Livermore, *Twilight of Federalism,* 267; Commager, "Leadership in Eighteenth Century America and Today," 652–671.

28. Ticknor to Jefferson, Aug. 10, 1818, LC; Simpson, *Federalist Literary Mind,* 56; Alexander Everett to Ticknor, Sept. 5, 1815, DCL.

29. *Life,* I, 21; Quincy, "Social Life," 13; Adams, *History of the United States,* I, 83–84.

30. Sullivan, *Familiar Letters,* 366–367; Miller, *Federalist Era,* 108–121; Smelser, "The Federalist Period," 391–408; Ames, *Works,* I, 263.

31. Hillard, *Mason,* 172–173; Sullivan, *Familiar Letters,* 367.

32. Miller, *Federalist Era,* 99; Simpson, *Federalist Literary Mind,* 56, 217–218.

33. Simpson, *Federalist Literary Mind,* 97; Ticknor, "Memoirs of Buckminsters," 192. It should be noted that Buckminster was not advocating total withdrawal from politics. Instead, he espoused the Ciceronian union of letters and statesmanship, not the epicurean position of Atticus. Ticknor seemed to agree more with Buckminster's attack on political life than with his Ciceronian model; in fact, one of Ticknor's friends accused him of being an Atticus.

34. Ticknor, "Memoirs of Buckminsters," 188; *Life,* I, 12–14.

35. Sullivan, *Familiar Letters,* 366; Livermore, *Twilight of Federalism,* ch. i.

36. Livermore, *Twilight of Federalism,* 45–46, 52–53; Hillard, *Mason,* 197.

37. Ticknor to Jared Sparks, n.d., HL; *Life,* II, 186–187.

38. Ticknor, "Memoirs of Buckminsters," 8–9; *Life,* I, 17–18; Quincy, "Social Life," 2.

39. Hale, *Old Boston,* 32; Lee, *Memoirs of Buckminsters, passim; Life,* I, 9–10.

40. Ticknor, "Memoirs of Buckminsters," 176–179, 182; Gannett, *Gannett,* 50–52; Ticknor, *Prescott,* 86–87; Norton, "Letter to Ticknor," 196–203.

41. Gannett, *Gannett,* 51, 52–55; Norton, "Letter to Ticknor," 197–201; Simpson, *Federalist Literary Mind,* 27. For an excellent study of the origins of "liberal Christianity" during the period of Ticknor's youth see Wright, *Beginnings of Unitarianism,* chs. x–xii.

42. *Life,* II, 195; Wright, *Beginnings of Unitarianism,* 259–264. Ticknor became a friend of William Ellery Channing, Ezra Stiles Gannett, and Andrews Norton, defenders of the faith, and wrote a fund-raising pamphlet for the Harvard Theological School called *Report of the Committee of the Association of the Federal Street Society for Benevolent Purposes on the Application of the Directors of the Theological School in Cambridge;* for later developments in Unitarianism see Miller, *Transcendentalists,* 3–15, and the perceptive account of Ezra Stiles Gannett's life by his son, William C. Gannett.

43. Lee, *Memoirs of Buckminsters,* 228–229. I am much indebted to Lewis P. Simpson's studies of the Anthology Society and its milieu cited in general bibliography. Also useful are the following: Howe, *Journal,* and Dole, "The Anthology Club." Ticknor was secretary of the Anthology Society in its last years and left its MS Journal to the Massachusetts Historical Society.

44. Howe, *Journal,* 6–8; Simpson, *Federalist Literary Mind,* 83–102; letters from Buckminster in Ticknor's Autograph Collection, DCL.

45. Lee, *Memoirs of Buckminsters,* 240; Ames, *Works,* I, 440; Ford, "Ticknor's History," 1.

46. Everett to Ticknor, Jan. 18, 1815, DCL; Simpson, *Federalist Literary Mind,* 84–85, 96, 57.

47. Simpson, *Federalist Literary Mind,* 146–147, 176–177; Simpson, "Crisis," 261–262.

48. Ticknor, "Ridiculous Literary Blunders," and "Criticks." On a trip abroad Buckminster also became uncomfortably aware of the defects of the *Anthology:* "I am in great doubt about the propriety of applying to any societies here for an exchange of publications, for alas what have me to exchange with them . . . I cannot say that I am entirely pleased with some of the last numbers of the Anthol . . . I feel too on this side of the water, those defects which are almost inherent in the work and which will keep it a bar from being interesting in Europe." Buckminster accused the authors in the *Anthology* of being dull and derivative, of striving for "fine writing, and sentimental beauties" (Buckminster to William Shaw, n.d., DCL). For the vogue of judicial criticism see Charvat, *American Critical Thought.*

49. Simpson, *Federalist Literary Mind,* 25–27, 196–202, 204–207; Lee, *Memoirs of Buckminsters,* 229.

50. Howe, *Journal,* 19; Simpson, *Federalist Literary Mind,* 154.

51. Ticknor (as secretary of the Anthology Society), MS Records of the Anthology Society, June 13, 1811, MHS; Simpson, *Federalist Literary Mind,* 40–41.

52. *Life,* I, 9–11; Ticknor, "Study of the Law"; Davis, "Early American Lawyer," 191–205. The list of books Ticknor sold before going to Europe indicated his chiefly literary interests: *Catalogue of Books to Be Sold at Francis Amory's Store #41 Marlboro St. Boston on Wed. Dec. 21, 1814* (a copy of this printed catalogue is deposited in the Harvard College Library).

53. Sullivan, *Address to the Bar*; Ticknor, "Mr. Sullivan's Address," 227–229. It should be noted that Ticknor dwelt mostly on Sullivan's discouraging remarks on the legal profession and not on his more optimistic comments. Eliot also

decried the law as a career "that throws wide open the door of temptation to practices of the most nefarious kind" (Anna Ticknor, *Eliot,* 171).

54. Story, *Discourse,* 3; Anna Ticknor, *Cogswell,* 18; Thompson, *Young Longfellow,* ch. vii; Brooks, *New England,* 43–45; Ticknor, *Prescott,* 26; also see Davis, "American Lawyer and Profession of Letters."

55. *Life,* I, 11–12, 22–23; Simpson, *Federalist Literary Mind,* 100. Samuel Eliot wrote his son that "Mr. Buckminsters's Phi Beta Kappa oration gives my sentiments completely . . . If you attempt being a scholar, be a thorough one or quit the pursuit" (Ticknor, *Eliot,* 170).

56. Anna Ticknor, *Cogswell,* 26; Simpson, *Federalist Literary Mind,* 217.

57. *Life,* I, 23; Simpson, "Not Men, But Books," 167–184. William Taylor perceptively discusses Ticknor's motives for going to Europe and the problem of provincialism in *Cavalier and Yankee,* 38–51.

58. Everett, MS Autobiography, 10, MHS; *Life,* I, 11–12; Phelps, "The Idea of the Modern University," 183–187; Brown, "Discovery of the German University," is a thorough study of the motives of Ticknor and his friends for going to Göttingen and their experience at the university. Mrs. Brown discovered that when Ticknor matriculated at Göttingen he indicated jurisprudence as his field (81).

59. Ryder, *Ticknor's Werther,* Introduction, xi–xv; Professor Ryder summarizes the scholarly literature on early interest in German culture in New England.

60. Elisha Ticknor to Jefferson, Aug. 7, 1815, MHS; Ticknor, "Edward Everett," 137; *Life,* I, 12–14.

61. *Life,* I, 14–15, 26–27.

62. *Life,* I, 15–16.

63. *Life,* I, 27–33; Livermore, *Twilight of Federalism,* ch. i. Francis Calley Gray accompanied Ticknor on this journey; his account of the trip has been edited by Rowe and Coolidge in *Jefferson in 1814.*

64. Adams, *Education,* 47; *Life,* I, 34.

65. *Life,* I, 34–38; Long, *Jefferson and Ticknor,* 8–9.

66. *Life,* I, 38–41; Long, *Jefferson and Ticknor,* 8–9; Irving, *Sketch Book,* 11.

67. Thomas Jefferson to Elisha Ticknor, Feb. 9, 1816, BPL.

II. A Yankee Abroad

1. Ticknor, Typescript of MS Journals of first trip to Europe, 1815–1819, IV, 453 (translated from French). The first five and part of the sixth of Ticknor's nine MS Journals of his European experience have been copied, on the whole quite accurately, in a typescript on deposit in the Dartmouth Archives together with the MS Journals. Because of the irregular pagination of the MS Journals and for ease of reference I have cited the Typescript Journals of the 1815–1819 trip (checked for accuracy against the MS Journals). I will list these as TJ with volume and page numbers; the MS Journal of his first trip I will cite as MSJ with volume number and date and pages (where given in the Journal).

2. *Life,* II, 501. As literary executor for Buckminster, Ticknor had an opportunity to read letters Buckminster wrote to friends while traveling in Europe,

letters now deposited in Ticknor's Autograph Collection at Dartmouth. Emerson, *English Traits*, 299; TJ, VI, 681.

3. *Life*, II, 500–501; Higginson, *Carlyle's Laugh*, 332.

4. Anna Ticknor, *Cogswell*, 113; Ticknor to Francis Gilmer, April 2, 1815, in Davis, *Gilmer*, 82; Adams, "Ticknor's *Life, Letters and Journals*," 211.

5. *Life*, I, 49; Ticknor's friend Haven died at an early age, and Ticknor edited his papers.

6. *Life*, I, 49–50; TJ, I, 2–11.

7. Buckminster to William Shaw, June 9, 1806, DCL; MSJ, IX, April, 1819, 316; TJ, IV, 423.

8. Ticknor to Richard H. Dana, Sr., Oct. 28, 1837, MHS; TJ, I, 21, 25–28, 32–33.

9. TJ, I, 71, 36–82.

10. Whipple, "George Ticknor," 441–449; *Life*, I, 274.

11. MSJ, IX, April, 1819.

12. "Life of George Ticknor" (anon. rev.), *Quarterly Review*, 161; "Life of George Ticknor" (anon. rev.), *Saturday Review*, 479.

13. TJ, I, 61; TJ, III, 289; *Life*, I, 85, 264.

14. TJ, IV, 453; *Life*, I, 174.

15. Long, *Literary Pioneers, passim;* TJ, I, 64–65, 74–75, 82.

16. TJ, III, 340; Edward to Alexander Everett, Nov. 16, 1816, MHS; Ticknor, *Cogswell*, 56–57; Long, *Literary Pioneers*, 28.

17. TJ, IV, 416–418; TJ, I, 104; Ticknor, *Cogswell*, 77; TJ, V, 516; Long, *Literary Pioneers*, 175.

18. *Life*, II, 504; Webster, *Writings*, XVII, 533; Long, *Literary Pioneers*, 140–141.

19. TJ, I, 112; TJ, III, 398; *Life*, I, 82, 73. In Ticknor's alumni file at Dartmouth there is a photograph of the house in which he lived in Göttingen.

20. Davis, *Gilmer*, 82; TJ, II, 152–153; 157; TJ, I, 117; *Life*, I, 72n; Higginson, *Carlyle's Laugh*, 329.

21. Ticknor to Jefferson, March 15, 1816, LC; *Life*, I, 95; TJ, II, 146–147, 169, 193–195; Ticknor to Jefferson, April 23, 1816, LC; *Life*, II, 503; Howe, *Bancroft*, I, 31–32, 56; Ticknor to Longfellow, March 29, 1836, HL.

22. TJ, III, 178–180, 182–183, 202–205, 325–328, 329, 335–336; Cogswell, "University Education," 109–136.

23. *Life*, I, 99–102; Ticknor to Jefferson, March 15, 1816, LC.

24. Howe, *Bancroft*, I, 56; *Life*, I, 95, 103–105; Blumenbach to Elizabeth Ticknor, Oct. 20, 1817, DCL; *Life*, I, 85.

25. Edward to Alexander Everett, March 31, 1816, MHS; MSJ, April 8, 1816. See Ryder, *Ticknor's Werther*, xxvii–xxix, for a discussion of the attraction between Ticknor and Mrs. Perkins and the appeal of Werther to Ticknor. I surmise from the evidence that Mrs. Perkins' relationship with Ticknor (and Everett, for that matter) was at most a mild flirtation, in which Ticknor could indulge because of its very implausibility. But at the least her visit induced a severe case of homesickness.

26. TJ, III, 397–398, 390, 391–403; Ryder, "An American View of Germany—1817," and "George Ticknor on the German Scene."

27. TJ, I, 138, 126–127; Long, *Literary Pioneers*, 120–123, 128–129; Ticknor, *Cogswell*, 110; Brown, "Discovery of the German University," 180.

28. TJ, III, 399–400; Long, *Literary Pioneers,* 120; Hillard, *"Ticknor's History,"* 5; TJ, I, 136; Higginson, *Carlyle's Laugh,* 327.

29. Long, *Literary Pioneers,* 128–129; *Life,* I, 99.

30. TJ, I, 133–134; Everett to Bancroft, Aug. 18, 1818, MHS; TJ, III, 318. "Perhaps it may be a part of the original sin of my Education," Ticknor remarked, "but I verily believe this corruption to have been occasioned by the sort of theology taught there."

31. Higginson, *Carlyle's Laugh,* 12–13; *Life,* I, 85; TJ, III, 400.

32. The correspondence between Ticknor and Kirkland is in the Harvard College Corporation Papers, HUA. *Life,* I, 116–118, II, 504.

33. Buckminster to Arthur Walter, Dec. 20, 1806, to Jan. 10, 1807, DCL; TJ, IV, 436, 448; Howe, *Bancroft,* 117, 119.

34. TJ, IV, 436–486, V, 527; *Life,* II, 503; *Life,* I, 148–150.

35. TJ, IV, 453, 455, 456–457, 468, V, 535; Hawkins, *Madame de Staël,* 8.

36. TJ, IV, 440, 443, 455, 459–460, 468. Probably the persons Ticknor met in Paris were those most likely to confirm his prejudices.

37. TJ, IV, 473; *Life,* I, 311–312n. A friend wrote Ticknor from Paris that a French family was sending a wastrel son to Boston "to study the Banking business and to get him out of the dissipations of Paris, as it is supposed by his parents and their advisers that that town will correct him of a little taste for expense and folly" (Mary Clarke to Ticknor, June 4, 1848, DCL).

38. TJ, IV, 464–466, 469–470.

39. *Life,* I, 141–146; TJ, IV, 464–466, 469–470, 498.

40. *Life,* I, 156, 173; TJ, V, 528–529.

41. TJ, V, 558, 566, 555–676.

42. TJ, VI, 281, 667–668; Adams, *Education,* 89; Life, I, 169, 172.

43. TJ, V, 606–609, 619, 623, VI, 674.

44. MSJ, VI, Feb. 1818; Wolcott, ed., *Correspondence of Prescott,* 633; TJ, II, 233–245.

45. Ticknor's MS translation is in the Dartmouth College Library; the parts quoted are on pp. 4–5. TJ, II, 243, V, 701, 816.

46. Ticknor to Richard H. Dana, Sr., Feb. 22, 1837, MHS. Ticknor was one of those who gave Allston money in advance for painting "Belshazzar's Feast" — the indenture is in the Boston Athenaeum. Typescript Journals of 1836–1837 European trip, V, 795–796, DCL; Larkin, *Art and Life in America,* 182.

47. *Life,* I, 188, 251. Williams' *Spanish Background* is a thorough study of the cultural relations of America and Spain.

48. MSJ, VII, May 17–23, 1818, 48–49.

49. MSJ, VII, Summer 1818, 54–76, 109, 114–116.

50. MSJ, VII, Summer 1818, 92–94, 100–102.

51. MSJ, VII, Summer 1818, 56.

52. MSJ, VII, Summer 1818, 56–60.

53. MSJ, VII, Summer 1818, 95–96.

54. MSJ, VIII, Sept. 1818, 13–20, 133–150.

55. MSJ, VIII, Oct. 1818, 186–188; *Life,* I, 243.

56. MSJ, VIII, Nov. 21, 1817, 207–208.

57. *Life,* I, 251–252.

58. MSJ, VIII, Dec. 10, 1818, to Jan. 12, 1819.

59. MSJ, IX, Jan. 1819, 235–238; Smith, "Seybert's *Annals,*" 78–79.

60. MSJ, IX, Jan. 1819, 244–247.

61. MSJ, IX, Feb. 1819, 259–269.

62. MSJ, IX, March 16–18, 1819, 277–282, March 15, 1819, 275; Hart, *Ticknor,* 10.

63. MSJ, IX, March 19–22, 1819, 285–291.

64. MSJ, IX, June 6, 1819, 338.

65. Jefferson to Ticknor, Dec. 24, 1819, LC; Ticknor to Jefferson, Feb. 10, 1820, LC.

III. *The Cause of Sound Learning*

1. Kirkland (based on MS by Edward Everett), "Literary Institutions—University," 274.

2. Cogswell, "Means of Education," 550; Emerson, "Historic Notes," 330–331.

3. Cogswell, "Means of Education," 640, 546–547; Everett, "University of Virginia," 118. The missionaries took a somewhat strident tone in some of their writings; Sidney Willard, a Harvard professor, angrily reviewed Cogswell's anonymous *Edinburgh* article in the *North American Review,* 240–259 (Cogswell had attacked the superficiality and provincialism of American schools and colleges).

4. Cogswell, "Means of Education," 550; Kirkland to Everett, Oct. 25, 1816, College Papers, HUA.

5. Bancroft and Cogswell left Harvard to found the Round Hill School, and by May 4, 1825 (MHS), Bancroft was writing Everett to congratulate him on beginning his political career. Eliot, *Report for 1883–84,* 10.

6. Ticknor to Kirkland, Nov. 9, 1816, in Ticknor Letters, hereafter cited as TL. This collection of letters and another box of manuscripts, newspaper clippings, and other documents relating to Ticknor's work at Harvard (hereafter cited as TP — Ticknor Papers) were deposited in the Harvard University Archives in 1896. Kirkland to Ticknor, Oct. 26, 1816, College Papers, HUA; *Life,* I, 116–117, II, chs. xvi, xviii; Peabody, *Reminiscences,* 170; Morison, *Harvard,* chs. ix–x.

7. Long, *Jefferson and Ticknor,* 29, 30–31.

8. Howe, *Bancroft,* 155–156; the Sully portrait is in the Baker Library at Dartmouth College (a copy hangs in the Rare Books Room of the Boston Public Library); *Life,* I, ch. xvi. Ticknor's Autograph Collection, a multi-volume set of letters, indicates the range of his acquaintance with eminent Americans and Europeans.

9. *Life,* I, 390–392; Quincy, *Figures,* 99–100; Adams, "Ticknor," 212.

10. *Life,* I, 117, 334–335; Ticknor to Bancroft, May 11, 1826, MHS; Anna Ticknor to Bancroft, April 24, 1826, MHS.

11. Suffolk County Probate Records, vol. 120, 172–173; the same records show that Ticknor's property, real and personal, at his death was valued at $237,975.89, $82,000 of which was invested in his mansion at 9 Park Street, vol. 308, 52. *Life,* I, 335; Grund, *Aristocracy,* 156.

12. Emerson and Forbes, eds., *Journals of Emerson,* IV, 471, VI, 256; Emerson, "Historic Notes," 330–331; Quincy, *Figures,* 21–22; Blanshard, ed., *Letters of Storrow,* 210; Life, I, 312n.

13. Long, *Literary Pioneers*, 73; Emerson and Forbes, eds., *Journals of Emerson*, VI, 256.

14. *Life*, I, 274, 326; Ticknor, *Remarks on Harvard*, 44; Morison, *Harvard*, 236–237.

15. *Life*, I, 354; Long, *Jefferson and Ticknor*, 30–31; Hofstadter and Smith, *American Higher Education*, 254–273.

16. The annual Harvard *Catalogues of the Officers and Students* published for the years 1825–1835 contain useful information on the size and scope of the college. Ticknor, *Prescott*, 13n; *Course of Instruction in Harvard in 1820*, 1–3.

17. Clarke, *Autobiography*, 36, 40, 34–42.

18. Peabody, *Reminiscences*, 200; Canby, *Thoreau*, 40–41, ch. iv.

19. Peabody, *Reminiscences*, 197–198; Morison, *Harvard*, 204, 198–206.

20. Morison, *Harvard*, 211; *Course of Instruction in Harvard in 1820*, 4, 1–3; Ticknor, *Remarks on Harvard*, 7; Ticknor to Kirkland, Oct. 19, 1822, TL.

21. Ticknor, *Remarks on Harvard*, 8; Morison, *Harvard*, 262. In his correspondence with Kirkland in the first years of his career at Harvard Ticknor frequently commented irascibly on the futility of his lectures (TL).

22. Ticknor to William Prescott, July 31, 1831, TP; Dwight, *Travels*, 446.

23. Norton to Channing, Sept. 10, 1824, TP; Quincy, *Harvard*, II, ch. xxxv.

24. *Life*, I, 355; Ticknor to Prescott, July 31, 1821, TP.

25. Ticknor to Kirkland, April 6, 1822, TL; *Law of Harvard Regulating Dress*, April 29, 1822.

26. Donald, *Sumner*, 15.

27. Ticknor to Kirkland, Sept. 3, 1821, TL; Ticknor to William Prescott, July 31, 1821, TP.

28. A MS copy of the Corporation's questionnaire or "Circular," dated Sept. 12, 1821, is in TP; Ticknor's answer to the questionnaire, dated Oct. 23, 1821, is also in TP; the replies of the faculty are collected in a file entitled "Condition of College, 1821 and 1824," HUA; Ticknor to Kirkland, Sept. 17, 1821.

29. Morison, "Great Rebellion," 65–68; Norton to William Ellery Channing, Sept. 10, 1824, TP.

30. In his collection of papers dealing with reforms at Harvard — the Ticknor Papers — Ticknor separated the documents into categories, the most important of which were the following: "Reform attempted in 1821 to its failure 1823. — This was undertaken chiefly through the Corporation, — and the only purpose entertained was that of making the College a good High School, but no hope was entertained of soon making it a University" and "Reform attempted 1823 to its failure 1827 in all Depts. except the Modern Languages. This was undertaken chiefly through the Overseers, and with the purpose of Opening the College and making it an University". MS Remarks read by Ticknor at the meeting at his home on July 23, 1823, 9, TP; Ticknor to Kirkland, Oct. 9, 1822, TL.

31. Ticknor to Bancroft, March 16, 1824, MHS; *Life*, II, 410, I, 354. For this section I have found the following studies especially useful: Storr, *Graduate Education;* Crane, *Colleges and the Public;* Rudolph, *American College and University;* and Hofstadter and Smith, eds., *American Higher Education.*

32. Cogswell to Henry W. Longfellow, June 12, 1840, HL; Grund, *Aristocracy*, 154; Cogswell, "University Education," 111.

33. MS Remarks read by Ticknor at the meeting, July 23, 1823, TP; Ticknor, *Harvard*, 34–46.

34. Clipping in TP; *Life,* I, 372–376; Curtis, ed., *West Point in 1826.*

35. Howe, *Bancroft,* I, 167–168; Ticknor to Jared Sparks, Aug. 7, 1824, HL; Cogswell and Bancroft, *Prospectus of a School.*

36. Jefferson to Ticknor, Oct. 3, 1820, LC; Ticknor to Jefferson, April 4, 1825, MHS; *Life,* I, 348; Adams, *Jefferson and University of Virginia,* 123.

37. Ticknor to Jefferson, April 4, 1825, MHS; *Life,* I, 348; Adams, *Jefferson and University of Virginia,* 123–130.

38. Adams, *Jefferson and University of Virginia,* 126–127; Ticknor to Jefferson, Feb. 13, 1819, MHS; Cabell, ed., *Letters of Jefferson and Cabell,* 201.

39. Several of the responses of the Harvard faculty to the Corporation's questionnaire, in the file "Condition of College, 1821 and 1824," HUA, reveal views parallel to those of the Yale faculty. Hall, *Travels,* II, 200; Jefferson to Ticknor, Aug. 15, 1824, LC; Yale Faculty, "Report," 300.

40. For the structure and functions of academies at this time see Sizer, *Academies,* 1–46.

41. Cogswell, "Means of Education," 546; Yale Faculty, "Report," 313.

42. Yale Faculty, "Report," 315–317, 300.

43. Yale Faculty, "Report," 312, 316–317, 350–351.

44. Ticknor, *Remarks on Harvard,* 39; Williams, *Spanish Background,* I, 375n; Pickering to Ticknor, Sept. 7, 1826, TP. In a letter to C. S. Daveis (Ticknor, *Life of Cogswell,* 161) Ticknor's fellow-reformer Cogswell wrote, "Do not, I beg you, come round to the new doctrine of exploding classical studies. If not checked it will bring destruction to the cause of sound learning in our land. I am persuaded that nothing can be substituted for this kind of early discipline for the mind, be the destination in life what it may."

45. Ticknor to Jefferson, Dec. 25, 1823, LC; MS Remarks read by Ticknor at the meeting, July 23, 1823, TP.

46. Kirkland, "Literary Institutions — University," 270–272; Kirkland to Ticknor, Nov. 8, 1816, TP; Morison, *Harvard,* 196; Gardiner, *Recollections,* 94.

47. Long, *Literary Pioneers,* 74–75; Everett, "University of Virginia," 118; Frothingham, *Everett,* chs. ii–iv; Donald, *Sumner,* 257; Everett to Story, April 13, 1821, MHS; Emerson and Forbes, eds., *Journals of Emerson,* VI, 256.

48. For faculty attitudes see MS remarks of instructors in file "Condition of College, 1821 and 1824," and "Report of the Immediate Government," May 21, 1825, College Records, 1819–1827, HUA; *Life,* I, 353–360.

49. See Ticknor's annotated copy of his *Remarks on Harvard,* 33, in HUA; *Life,* I, 356–360.

50. MS Remarks read by Ticknor at the meeting, July 23, 1823, TP; Ticknor, *Remarks on Harvard, passim.* Compare Francis Wayland's views on free academic enterprise in Crane, "Wayland: Political Economist as Educator."

51. MS Remarks read by Ticknor at the meeting, July 23, 1823, TP; Ticknor, *Remarks on Harvard,* 3–10, 35–36, 38.

52. *Life,* I, 359–360.

53. *Life,* I, 359–362; Quincy, *Harvard,* II, 344–351; Ticknor, *Remarks on Harvard,* 11–35; Norton, *Speech,* 3–5.

54. Story, *Report,* 3–11.

55. Story, *Report,* 10; Pickering to Ticknor, Sept. 30, 1823, TP.

56. Norton, *Remarks,* 4–11; Harvard Overseers, Records, VII, 102–190, HUA; Quincy, *Harvard,* II, 340–344.

57. Everett to Story, Feb. 6, 1823, Corporation Papers, HUA; Morison, *Harvard*, 233–234.

58. Harvard Overseers, Records, VII, 102–161, HUA; Norton, *Speech;* Everett, *Letter to Lowell*; Everett to Norton, Feb. 6, 1823, March 3, 1823, Feb. 19, 1825, Aug. 23, 1825, Corporation Papers, HUA.

59. Norton, *Speech,* iii–iv, xvii, 12, 27.

60. Norton, *Speech,* 28; Harvard Overseers, Records, VII, 190, HUA; Quincy, *Harvard,* II, 341–342.

61. Ticknor to Webster, Feb. 19, 1825, DCL; Ticknor to Jefferson, March 28, 1825, LC; Ticknor to Thomas Hill, Feb. 4, 1863, College Papers, XXX, 38, HUA; *Boston Courier,* Oct. 27, 1825, TP.

62. Ticknor, *Remarks on Harvard,* 31.

63. Henry W. Longfellow, MS Journal, 1840–1841, Jan. 3, 1840, HL; apparently unaware of his own strategic myopia, Ticknor declared that he thought everyone "except the teachers, or rather a part of the teachers" believed the reforms essential (*Life*, I, 360).

64. Sparks to Ticknor, Jan. 22, 1825, DCL; Ticknor, *Remarks on Harvard,* 3–10, 31–48; Ware's reply is in file "Condition of College, 1821 and 1824," 102, 156, HUA.

65. Ticknor, *Remarks on Harvard,* 44; Edward Everett to Alexander Everett, Dec. 16, 1827, MHS.

66. Ticknor, *Remarks on Harvard,* 40; Sullivan to Ticknor, July 21, 1824, TP; Morison, "Great Rebellion," 99n; Bowditch, "College History," 71, HUA; copy of letter by Ticknor to Corporation of Harvard College remarking on President's Report for 1825–26, April 11, 1827, 16, 27, TP. Ticknor pointed out that the students who were not candidates for a degree (only four) were substantially members of some one of the old classes, down even to the ceremony of wearing its uniform."

67. Resolution of Corporation, Dec. 1824, and William Channing to Kirkland, Feb. 25, 1825, Corporation Papers, HUA; Ticknor to Story, Jan. 6, 1824, TP; Sparks to Ticknor, Jan. 22, 1825, DCL; Kirkland to Ticknor, Oct. 20, 1825, TP.

68. Bowditch, "College History," 73, HUA; Bowditch said that the members of the Corporation "passed over without notice" Kirkland's hint that he would like to be rid of Ticknor. Henry Ware, Sidney Willard, and Edward Everett, Letter to Harvard Corporation, May 8, 1824, College Papers, HUA.

69. Bowditch, "College History," 109, 13–14, HUA; Ticknor to Corporation, April 11, 1827, 2, TP.

70. Marsh to Ticknor, Feb. 3, 1826, DCL; Edward Everett to Norton, Aug. 23, 1825, Corporation Papers, HUA. Everett said that Sparks was stymied because he feared the loss of Ticknor's pen for the *Review* yet thought the article too one-sided; Alexander Everett to Ticknor, Jan. 7, 1828, DCL.

71. Ticknor to Corporation, April 11, 1827, 13–15, TP; Morison, *Harvard,* 234–236.

72. Ticknor to Corporation, April 11, 1827, 10, 29, TP; Morison, "Great Rebellion," 102–112; Bowditch, "College History," 22–32, 48–53, HUA.

73. Quincy, *Harvard,* II, 333–335; Morison, "Great Rebellion," 58–63; Bowditch, "College History," 6, 104–105, HUA.

74. Morison, "Great Rebellion," 110–112; Bowditch, "College History," 119–121, HUA; N. I. Bowditch, *Remarks,* 19; John L. Sibley, MS Private Journal, 1846–1865, I, 557–558, HUA — Sibley commented that Ticknor, too, spoke

harshly to Kirkland; Amos Lawrence to N. I. Bowditch, Jr., Dec. 11, 1840 (letter inserted in Bowditch, "College History," HUA). In a letter to Edward Everett, Peter C. Brooks gives a different account of the episode involving the room in Hollis Hall, claiming that a faculty committee had recommended to Kirkland that Ticknor not move (April 14, 1828, MHS).

75. Edward Everett to Sparks, Oct. 6, 1828, MHS; Blandshard, ed., *Storrow*, 233; Charlotte Everett to Edward Everett, April 14, 1828, MHS.

76. Ticknor to Bancroft, March 24, 1828, HUA; photocopy of letter from Ticknor to Biddle, July 9, 1828, HUA — he commented that he would be willing to serve under any of these candidates; Edward Everett to Alexander Everett, Sept. 15, 1828, MHS.

77. Peter C. Brooks to Edward Everett, April 14, 1828, MHS; Peabody, *Reminiscences*, 33; Emerson and Forbes, eds., *Journals of Emerson*, VII, 168; Story, *Story*, I, 565. Story wrote to Bowditch (Jan. 1, 1828, College Papers, HUA) that "if our friend Mr. Ticknor is to be passed by, I am ready to vote for Mr. Quincy."

78. Peabody, *Reminiscences*, 30; Dana, *Autobiographical Sketch*, 59–60.

79. *Life*, I, 365–369, 399–401; Storr, *Graduate Education*, 134, ch. xi; Crane, ed., *Colleges and the Public*, 1–8, 15–27.

80. Longfellow to Ticknor, Sept. 28, 1837, DCL.

81. Lowell, *Addresses*, VI, 157; Longfellow, MS Journal, 1838–1839, Sept. 10, 1838, HL.

82. *Life*, I, 116, 324.

83. Kirkland, "Literary Institutions — University," 276; Higginson, *Carlyle's Laugh*, 348.

IV. The True Uses of Literature

1. Channing, *Works*, I, 248.

2. Josiah Quincy, "The Elegant Literature of France and Great Britain," MS Commencement Part, 1821, HUA.

3. Ticknor, Varia (2 vols. of miscellaneous short pieces), I, 321, DCL; Levin, *History as Romantic Art;* Thackeray to Ticknor, Jan. 13, 1850, DCL.

4. Ticknor to Jefferson, Aug., 1818, LC; Ticknor, MS Lectures on French Literature, V, 8, HUA (hereafter cited as FL); Hart, "Ticknor's *History*."

5. *Life*, I, 283. For discussion of literary nationalism see Simpson, *Federalist Literary Mind*; Miller, *Raven and Whale*; Charvat, *American Critical Thought*; Spenser, *Quest*.

6. Ticknor, Varia, II, 27, DCL; Hart, "Bouterwek," and "Ticknor's *History*"; *Life*, I, ch. iv–v.

7. Everett, "Peculiar Motives," 7–8.

8. Ticknor, FL, V, 3–4; Quincy, "The Elegant Literature of France and Great Britain," MS Commencement Part, 1821, HUA.

9. Ticknor, FL, V, 8.

10. Ticknor, FL, V, 9, I, 4–7.

11. Ticknor, FL, I, 7–8, V, 4, 6; the poem is a translation of the "Cancion" of Juan II of Castile (MS in DCL).

12. Ticknor, FL, V, 2–3.

13. Ticknor, FL, V, 16, 12–17, 10; *Life,* II, 140; Gilman, ed., *Journals of Emerson,* I, 54.

14. Amory, *Proper Bostonians,* 14.

15. Hillard, "Ticknor's *History,*" 4; Miller, *Errand into the Wilderness,* 213; Taylor, *Cavalier and Puritan,* 98–99; Dahl, "American School of Catastrophe."

16. Ticknor, MS Lectures on Spanish Literature, III, last sentence, HUA; Ticknor, FL, I, 10.

17. Hart, "Ticknor's *History,*" 78–79. There is a curious discrepancy in the comments which Ticknor and his wife and daughter made about the relation between his Harvard lectures on Spanish literature and his published *History.* In the preface (x) to the *History* Ticknor wrote that the tone of discussion in his Harvard lectures seemed unsuited for "a regular history. Destroying, therefore, what I had written, I . . . prepared the present work, as little connected with all I had previously done as it, perhaps, can be, and yet cover so much of the same ground." In his *Life of Prescott* (67) Ticknor wrote that his Harvard lectures "became . . . the basis of a work on that subject." The *Life* (II, 243) asserted that Ticknor "threw aside" his Harvard lectures in composing the *History.* I agree with Hart that Ticknor had foreshadowed the central concepts and organization of his *History* in his Harvard lectures. See "Labor Ipse Voluptas" in part V for an interpretation of this discrepancy.

18. Whitney, *Catalogue,* preface; Williams, *Spanish Background,* II, 46–77.

19. *Life,* I, 387–390.

20. *Life,* II, 252–254.

21. *Life,* I, 320–321.

22. *Life,* I, 232n; Hart, "Ticknor's *History,*" 80; Ticknor, *History,* I, 115, 119; Ticknor, Varia, 27, DCL; Ticknor, *History,* I, 182.

23. Ticknor, *History,* I, 474, 475–501.

24. Ticknor, *History,* II, 307–308, 290, 293, 473, I, 258.

25. Ticknor, *History,* I, 280, II, 484, 384, 162–164, 178; Hart, "Ticknor's *History,*" 84–85.

26. Ticknor, *History,* III, 437.

27. Ticknor, *History,* III, 437–438; Georg, ed., *Briefwechsel,* 157.

28. Obituary of Ticknor, *Boston Journal,* Jan. 26, 1871; Hillard, "Ticknor's *History,*" 8; Bancroft, *History of U.S.,* I, 6.

29. Grund, *Aristocracy,* 156.

30. *Life,* II, 252–254, 256–257, 260; Ray, ed., *Letters of Thackeray,* III, 530.

31. Ford, "Ticknor's *History,*" 24; Lawrence to Ticknor, Feb. 14, 1850, DCL; Prescott to Charles Sumner, Oct. 16, 1840, HL; Ticknor, *Prescott,* 212n.

32. Ames, *Works,* I, 429; Sydney Smith, "Seybert's *Annals,*" 78–80; Spiller, "Verdict of Smith," 3–13.

33. Ford, "Ticknor's *History,*" 6; Cogswell, "Means of Education," 647; *Life,* II, 189.

34. Parsons, "Merits," 30; Ticknor to Hillhouse, April 2, 1825, Yale University Library.

35. Channing, "Models," 207.

36. Streeter, "Nationalism," 244–246; Charvat, *American Critical Thought,* ch. iii; Clive, *Scotch Reviewers,* 159–160; Alison, *Essays on Taste.*

37. Orians, "Romance Ferment," 408–431; *Life,* I, 477; Clark, ed., *Transitions,* 107, 202–204.

38. *Life,* I, 328.

39. Cogswell, "Means of Education," 647; Streeter, "Nationalism," 251.

40. Longfellow to Alexander Smith, July 24, 1844, HL; by 1844 Longfellow had changed his earlier view that American literature should be unique — see Higginson, *Longfellow,* 33.

41. Hillhouse, *Works,* II, 92–93; Gilman, ed., *Journals of Emerson,* I, 298.

42. Shapiro, *Dana,* 14–16 (Dana, of course, changed his mind about Webster as a politician when he opposed the Free-Soilers); Mrs. Anna Ticknor, MS Journals of second European trip, Nov. 17, 1835, DCL; Ticknor, "Criticks," 22.

43. There are numerous letters from these authors to Ticknor in his Autograph Collection, DCL; on these authors see Ward, *Percival*; Warfel, *Percival*; Adams, *Dana*; Clark, ed., *Transitions,* 144.

44. Brooks, *New England,* 161; Lowell, "Nationality in Literature," 197.

45. Lord Holland to Ticknor, July 16, 1839, DCL; Rogers to Ticknor, 1840, DCL.

46. Hillhouse, *Works,* II, 96–97.

47. Whipple, "Ticknor," 457–458; Kohn, *American Nationalism,* 69.

48. Ticknor to Bancroft, June 21, 1832, MHS.

49. Channing to Ticknor, 1833, DCL; Hillhouse, *Works,* II, 65.

50. Norton, *Mrs. Hermans' Forest Sanctuary,* 6; *Discourse,* 29–30; Norton, ed., *Letters of Lowell,* I, 377.

51. Brooks, *New England,* 129; Hillard, *Poet,* 5, 16, 18–19.

52. Story, *Discourse,* 29–30; Ticknor, *Prescott,* 173. Compare Francis Jeffrey, who had admired Wordsworth's poetry in private but who excoriated him in the *Edinburgh Review* with the famous words, "This will never do" (Clive, *Scotch Reviewers,* 157, 160).

53. Longfellow, MS Journal, Sept. 24, 1838, HL; *Life,* II, 194.

54. Ticknor, *Prescott,* 339; Dana to Ticknor, March 5, 1838, DCL; Everett, MS Diary, August 28 and 30, 1838, MHS.

55. Everett, MS Diary, Sept. 6 and 9, 1838, MHS; Longfellow, MS Journals, March 8, 1838, HL.

56. *Life,* II, 287; Ticknor, "Memoirs of Buckminsters," 28–29; Norton, "Letter to Ticknor," 196–203; Whipple, "Ticknor," 457.

57. Webster, *Works,* I, 48; Everett, *Peculiar Motives,* 61; Ticknor, *Webster,* 3–6.

V. Gentlemen of Letters

1. Hillhouse, *Works,* II, 129–130.

2. Morse, *Letters of Holmes,* II, 222.

3. Boyd, ed., *Papers of Jefferson,* VIII, 636; Norton and Howe, eds., *Letters of Norton,* II, 62–63.

4. Hillhouse, *Works,* II, 129–130.

5. Ticknor, *Prescott,* 68.

6. James, *Eliot,* I, 31.

7. Quincy, *Figures,* 99–100; Massachusetts Historical Society, *Proceedings,* V, 97.

8. Morse, *Letters of Holmes,* II, 157; Morison, *Maritime History,* 225–240; Shlakman, *Factory Town,* 37–45; Stromberg, "Boston," 591–598.

9. Grund, *Aristocracy,* 169; Pierson, *Tocqueville,* 391; Pierce, *Sumner,* III, 2; Gardiner, *Recollections,* 11.

10. Stromberg, "Boston," 591–598; Grund, *Aristocracy,* 162.

11. Whitehill, *Topographical History,* 60–67, 142–144; Winsor, *Boston,* III, 232–233; Lawrence, *Old Park Street,* 81–82; Anna Ticknor to Bancroft, March 15, 1825, MHS. The Boston Athenaeum and the Dartmouth Archives have pictures of the interior and exterior of 9 Park St.; in Ticknor's will the mansion was valued at $82,000 (Suffolk County Probate Records, vol. 308, 52).

12. Stewart, ed., Hawthorne's *American Notebooks,* 246–247.

13. Hart, *Ticknor,* 2; Godwin, *Bryant,* II, 372; Gannett, "Christian Scholar," 520; Prescott to Mary La Bouchère, June 13, 1856, MHS; Rusk, ed., *Letters of Emerson,* I, 136; Brooks, *Allston,* 66.

14. Perry, "Ticknor," 631; *Life,* II, 495.

15. Thompson, *Young Longfellow,* 82; Longfellow, MS Journal, Jan. 3, 1840, HL; *Life,* II, 496.

16. The Sully and Healy portraits are in the Baker Library at Dartmouth; the Milmore bust is in the Boston Public Library.

17. *Life,* I, 387–395; Houghton, *Victorian Mind,* 342; Grund, *Aristocracy,* 213. Even in informal letters to close friends Ticknor normally referred to his wife as "Mrs. Ticknor" and it is hard to realize that Anna Ticknor and her daughter wrote the reticent and impersonal narrative sections of the *Life.*

18. Houghton, *Victorian Mind,* 343. In 1897 a group of Miss Ticknor's colleagues in the Society to Encourage Studies at Home edited a volume describing the work of the Society and including Anna's correspondence with students and eulogies by Samuel Eliot and Elizabeth Cary Agassiz — *Society to Encourage Studies at Home, Founded in 1873 by Anna Eliot Ticknor.*

19. Anna Ticknor, *American Family,* 167.

20. Anna Ticknor, *American Family,* 275.

21. *Life, I,* 398–399, 401.

22. Channing to Ticknor, May 29, 1835, and April 22, 1837, DCL; *Life,* I, 402.

23. Ward, *Ward Papers,* 137.

24. Grund, *Aristocracy,* 48.

25. Wolcott, ed., *Correspondence of Prescott,* 498.

26. *Life,* I, 403–404.

27. Mrs. Anna Ticknor, MS Journals, I, July 25, 1835, DCL; *Life,* I, 402–450, II, 144–183; Ticknor to Thomas W. Ward, Sept. 22, 1835, MHS; Mrs. Ticknor to Willard Phillips, May 17, 1838, MHS. For a discussion of the landed aristocracy, see Thompson, *English Society.*

28. MSJ, III, Nov. 20, 1835, to May 4, 1836; Ticknor to Thomas W. Ward, Jan. 28, 1836, MHS.

29. MSJ, IV, June 24 and July 1, 1836.

30. MSJ, III, July 1, 1836.

31. MSJ, III, July 1, 1836; *Life,* II, 20 (translated from the French); MSJ, III, June 26, 1836.

32. *Life,* I, 480–481; Ticknor to Dana, Feb. 22, 1837, MHS.

33. Ticknor to Dana, Oct. 28, 1837, MHS.

34. MSJ, VI, Jan. 27, Feb. 7, and March 4, 1837.

35. MSJ, VI, Jan. 24, 1837; Dec. 10, 1836.

36. Mrs. Ticknor, MS Journals, VII, April 9 and Jan. 2, 1837.

37. MSJ, VI, Jan. 19, 1937; Dec. 21, 1836.

38. *Life*, II, 140; MSJ, VIII, Dec. 22 and Oct. 6, 1837.

39. Gannett, "Christian Scholar," 520; Ticknor to Sumner, April 12, 1839, HL; Donald, *Sumner*, 48; Ticknor to Sumner, April 10, 1838, HL; Ticknor to Sumner, Dec. 3, 1839, HL.

40. Ticknor to Sumner, April 22, 1839, HL; *Life*, II, 184.

41. *Life*, II, 269n; Ticknor, *Prescott*, 339, 305, 312.

42. Otis, *Barclays*, 210; Wecter, *Society*, 321–322.

43. Pierson, *Tocqueville*, 364; Adams, "Ticknor," 213.

44. Adams, *Education*, 32; Tocqueville, *Democracy*, I, 288; Hillard, *Dangers and Duties*; Calhoun, *Professional Lives*, 178, 194–195.

45. Holmes, *Venner*, 1–2; Otis, *Barclays*, 128; Amory, *Proper Bostonians*, 171.

46. Hillard, *Dangers and Duties*, 41–42.

47. Channing to Ticknor, April 22, 1837, DCL; Prescott to Bancroft, June 19, 1849, MHS.

48. Holmes, *Venner*, 3–4; Pierson, *Tocqueville*, 364–365.

49. Holmes, *Autocrat*, 20, 260.

50. Ticknor to Charles Daveis, April 13, 1843, MHS; Howe, ed., *Letters of Lowell*, I, 71; Higginson, *Contemporaries*, 271–272.

51. *Life*, II, 420; Ticknor, *Prescott*, 449.

52. Crawford, *Famous Families*, and Winsor, *Boston*, contain a wealth of biographical information on Boston families; Saveth, "Patrician Class," indicates the rich mine of information available to historians interested in the American elite. Prescott, *Papers*, 248; Amory, *Proper Bostonians*, 38; Grund commented that Yankees "in the absence of a law of primogeniture, preserve their wealth by marrying cousins" (*Aristocracy*, 169).

53. Pierson, *Tocqueville*, 378, 364, 365; Welter, "Cult of True Womanhood," 154–158.

54. Adams, *Education*, 30; Marryat, *Diary*, II, 170–175, 185; Martineau, *Society*, III, 36–37.

55. Wolcott, ed., *Correspondence of Prescott*, 627; Longfellow, MS Journal, June 2, 1840, HL; Quincy, *Figures*, 138–139.

56. Adams, *Education*, 56–59.

57. *Life*, II, 410; Holmes, *Venner*, 5; *Life*, II, 417–418.

58. Lyell, *Travels*, I, 106–109; Winsor, *Boston*, IV, 293; Adams, *Education*, 30.

59. Lyell, *Travels*, I, 109; Ticknor, *Prescott*, 335; Grund, *Aristocracy*, 140–143; Tocqueville, *Democracy*, I, 187. For the "decline of the gentleman" in politics during this period see Hofstadter, *Anti-intellectualism*, 154–171.

60. Adams, *Education*, 32; Hillhouse, *Works*, II, 123, 129–130; see part VI below and Saveth, "Patrician Class" (249–252), for further discussions of the patrician's role in politics. Donald (*Lincoln Reconsidered*, 19–36) points out that displaced members of the gentry, "educated for conservative leadership," also entered the abolitionist crusade in large numbers.

61. Whipple, "Ticknor," 456; Hart, *Ticknor*, 2; obituary in the *Boston Post*, Jan. 26, 1871; Oliver Wendell Holmes, Sr., to Ticknor, Dec. 19, 186?, DCL.

62. Crawford, *Romantic Days*, 317; Otis, *Barclays*, 62; Morse, *Lee*, 346.

63. Pope-Hennessy, ed., *Aristocratic Journey*, 88; Ampère, *Promenade*, I, 29.

64. Adams, *Education*, 33; Lord Morpeth, copy of MS Diary, Oct. 22, 1841, HL; Ray, ed., *Letters of Thackeray*, III, 318–530.

65. Grund, *Aristocracy*, 156, 160–161; Pierce, II, 366.

66. Pierce, *Sumner*, III, 10, 7–8, 50–51, 90, 96, 119; Sumner to Longfellow, May 14, 1842, HL; *Life*, II, 235.

67. Sibley, MS Private Journal, I, 669, HUA.

68. Donald, *Sumner*, 94; on the splintering of Boston society see Shaler, *Autobiography*, 198–199, and Whipple, "Ticknor," 456.

69. *"Our First Men"* (anon.), 3–6.

70. Longfellow, MS Journal, Jan. 11, 1840, HL; *Boston Morning Post*, Jan. 11, 1840. Another variant of the story was that Thackeray had made the same remark about Theodore Parker, whose theological opinions Ticknor abhorred.

71. Emerson and Forbes, eds., *Journals of Emerson*, V, 469.

72. Grund, *Aristocracy*, 153, 155–156.

73. Tocqueville, *Democracy*, II, 250.

74. Ticknor, *Prescott*, preface, 119–120, 137–138, 146, 133.

75. *Life*, I, 324; Wolcott, ed., *Correspondence of Prescott*, 451. Prescott declared, perhaps with ironic intent, that Ticknor's judgment of King John of Castille was too severe, when Ticknor wrote of the king that "he turned to letters to avoid the importunity of business, and to gratify a constitutional indolence" (Prescott, *Miscellanies*, 685).

76. See the list of Ticknor's manuscripts and printed essays in the bibliography — most of his translations were written before or during his stay at Göttingen. *Life*, I, 475n; Ticknor taught Dante to a special class of juniors at Harvard and gave lectures on Shakespeare in Boston during the winter of 1833–34.

77. Irving to Ticknor, Feb. 15, 1850, DCL; Ticknor, *Prescott*, 441; *Life*, II, 467, 478.

78. *Life*, I, 318n; Adams, *Dana*, I, 15; Lowell, *Works*, IX, 57; Ticknor to Dana, Oct. 28, 1837, MHS.

79. Ticknor to Dana, Feb. 22 and March 2, 1837, MHS; Otis, *Barclays*, 37.

80. Higginson, *Carlyle's Laugh*, 12; Trent, *English Culture*, 134; Dickens, *American Notes*, 26.

VI. Clouded Destiny

1. Emerson and Forbes, eds., *Journals of Emerson*, VI, 88.

2. *Life*, II, 485.

3. Ticknor to Charles Daveis, April 26, 1848, MHS; *Life*, II, 402–404.

4. Ticknor commented that "Tocqueville's acute book . . . contains so much truth as well as error about us" (*Life*, I, 480); *Life*, II, 361–362, 364–367; Pierson, *Tocqueville*, 362, 768. I am indebted to Marvin Meyers' analysis of Tocqueville in *Jacksonian Persuasion*, ch. iii.

5. Meyers, *Jacksonian Persuasion*, 37.

6. For analyses of conservative social thought in this period see Hartz, *Liberal Tradition*, ch. iv; Schlesinger, *Age of Jackson*, ch. xxii; Bilderback, "Cotton Whigs," ch. ii.

7. Rufus Choate uses the encampment metaphor in *Addresses,* 147. I am indebted to Professor Richard Storr for suggesting the concept of *paideia* in this connection.

8. Ticknor to Jefferson, Oct. 14, 1815, LC; Jefferson to Ticknor, Jan. 14, 1817, LC.

9. Everett to Ticknor, Sept. 5, 1815, DCL; Howe, *Journal,* 8; Bowditch to Ticknor, Aug. 5, 1836, DCL; *Life,* II, 464.

10. Du Pan, *Considerations,* preface; *Life,* II, 274.

11. *Life, II,* 234–235; Everett, "European Politics," 153.

12. Obituary by "Warrington" in *Springfield Republican,* ca. Jan. 26, 1871, clipping in Rare Books Room, BPL; Georg, ed., *Briefwechsel,* 28.

13. Georg, ed., *Briefwechsel,* 158; *Life,* II, 404. For discussions of the concept of national character see Potter's *People of Plenty,* chs. i–ii, and the unpublished syllabus and bibliographies for the 1955–56 conference on "The American Character," Princeton University.

14. Choate, *Addresses,* 144; Bowditch, too, believed that "nations advance and thrive, and die, like men; and can no more have a second youth than their inhabitants can" (*Life,* II, 464).

15. Everett, *Orations,* II, 622–624.

16. Ticknor, "Hon. William Prescott," *Boston Daily Advertiser,* Dec. 14, 1844; Choate, *Addresses,* 138.

17. Hillhouse, *Works,* II, 113–114; Curtis, *True Uses,* 3, 22, 12, 14–16; Pierson, *Tocqueville,* 381.

18. Curtis, *True Uses,* 10–11, 28–30; Curtis took a dim view of the contemporary rebellion in Rhode Island (Curtis, *Merits of Dorr*).

19. Ticknor, *Remarks on Webster,* 38–39; Webster, *Writings,* VI, 230–231; Ticknor, "Lafayette," 179, 151.

20. Choate, *Romance,* 22–23; *Life,* II, 268; Everett, *Orations,* III, 28; cf. Gentz, *French and American Revolutions,* 3–4, 60–61, 76, and the introduction by Russell Kirk.

21. Taylor, *Cavalier,* 114–115.

22. Choate, *Addresses,* 160, 143.

23. Tocqueville, *Democracy,* I, 288; see bibliography for works by or about these lawyers.

24. Choate, *Addresses,* 137–138, 140.

25. *Life,* II, 287; MS copy of letter from Parker to Sumner, Feb. 1855, MHS.

26. *Life,* II, 194–195.

27. Curtis, *History of Constitution,* x–xi.

28. Quincy, *Figures,* 158; Tocqueville, *Democracy,* I, 289.

29. Schlesinger, *Age of Jackson,* 330; Tocqueville, *Democracy,* I, 282–297; Story, *Story,* II, 134–136, 139.

30. Cogswell, "National Education," 194; Daveis, *Address,* 42, 49–50.

31. Story, *Lecture,* 26; Story, *Exposition,* 267–268; Elson, *Guardians,* chs. vi, x; McGuffey's *Readers* also played an important part in inculcating the conservative persuasion.

32. Massachusetts Historical Society, *Proceedings, 1871–73,* 24–25; Anna Ticknor, *American Family,* 250; *Life,* II, 148, 188.

33. *Life,* I, 379; Ticknor, "Free Schools," 456.

34. Ticknor, *Remarks on Webster,* 4; for Webster's pleased response to Ticknor's biography see Webster, *Writings,* XVI, 209, 216.

35. Webster, *Works*, I, 42; Welter, *Popular Education*, ch. v.

36. Emerson and Forbes, eds., *Journals of Emerson*, V, 250.

37. Everett, *Orations*, II, 229, 316–320.

38. Everett, *Orations*, III, 606; *Life*, II, 300; Whitehill, *Boston Public Library*, 29. For a general study of the public library movement see Shera, *Foundations*.

39. *Life*, I, 336; Ticknor to the Rev. D. Nichols, Feb. 15, 1827, DCL.

40. See Simpson, "Not Men, But Books," 167–184; Trent, *English Culture*, 138; *Life*, I, 23, 371; Ticknor, *Union of Athenaeum;* Whitehill, *Boston Public Library*, 40.

41. *Life*, II, 300; Whitehill, *Boston Public Library*, 15–16; *Life*, II, 301–303.

42. *Life*, II, 303; Anna Ticknor, *Cogswell*, 264–265.

43. *Life*, II, 304–308; Ticknor, *Union of Athenaeum*, 6–9; Quincy, *Appeal;* Whitehill, *Boston Public Library*, 40.

44. The report was *City Document No. 67: Report of the Trustees of the Public Library to the City of Boston, July 1852;* Ticknor wrote pages 9 to 21; *Life*, II, 304.

45. Whitehill, *Boston Public Library*, 34–36; Everett, *Orations*, VI, 603–614; Ticknor to Thomas Willard, Nov. 3, 1852, MHS.

46. *Life*, II, 307, 318; Ticknor to A. A. Lawrence, June 25, 1860, DCL. Whitehill, *Boston Public Library*, 64, points out that the experiment in purchasing multiple copies of improving books like Smiles's did not prove very successful.

47. Whitney, *Catalogue; Life*, II, 319; Whitehill, *Boston Public Library*, ch. iv.

48. *Life*, II, 309–310, ch. xvi.

49. Ticknor to Jared Sparks, n.d., HL; *Life*, II, 185–187; Richardson, ed., *Messages of Presidents*, I, 216–218; Wolcott, ed., *Correspondence of Prescott*, 501.

50. Ticknor to Bancroft, March 19, 1838, MHS; Ticknor, *Prescott*, 358. In his biography of Webster, Curtis commented that Webster had an opportunity to exercise true statesmanship at the Massachusetts constitutional convention of 1820 because he could work "without the bias and the trammels arising from that minor organization in the republic that is constituted by a party" (I, 180).

51. Story, "Statesmen," 89–96; *Life*, I, 393; Curtis, *Webster*, I, 161; Ticknor, *Remarks on Webster*, 33, 3.

52. Suffolk County Probate Records, vol. 120, 172–173, vol. 308, 52; *Life*, II, 198–200, 208, 210–211; Richard Leach, "George Ticknor Curtis and Daniel Webster's 'Villainies,' " 391–395.

53. Ticknor, *Remarks on Webster*, 3; cf. the "hero worship" described by Houghton, *Victorian Mind*, ch. xii.

54. Ticknor, *Remarks on Webster*, 3; *Life*, I, 330.

55. Gilman, ed., *Journals of Emerson*, I, 9–10; Emerson and Forbes, eds., *Journals of Emerson*, VI, 341–346; Gunderson, *Log Cabin*, 174; Adams, "Ticknor," 213; *Life*, I, 378–379; Longfellow, MS Journal, Jan. 9, 1840, HL; Lord Morpeth, MS Copy of Diary, Dec. 14, 1841, HL; Choate, *Addresses*, 521; Everett, *Orations*, III, 398–400; Ticknor to S. G. Ward, Sept. 2, 1840, HL.

56. Pierce, *Sumner*, II, 179, 186.

57. Lord Morpeth, MS copy of Diary, Dec. 11, 1841, HL.

58. Anna Ticknor, *Cogswell*, 212.

59. Howe, *Bancroft*, I, 193.

60. Sullivan, *Familiar Letters*, 401, 405.

61. Sullivan, *Familiar Letters*, 401.
62. Hillard, *Mason*, 359–360; Story, *Story*, II, 49, 154, 273.
63. Channing to Ticknor, 1836, DCL.
64. *Life*, II, 199; Benjamin Curtis to Ticknor, Feb. 16, 1855, DCL; Grund, *Aristocracy*, 200; Hofstadter, *Anti-intellectualism*, 164–166.
65. Curtis, *Webster*, II, 22; Gunderson, *Log Cabin*, 174–181. According to a newspaper, even the scholarly Hugh Legare, Ticknor's friend, gave up "expatiating upon Sparta and Lycurgus" and orated "right sturdily about 'gammon' and 'scarecrow' and 'scape goat' " (Rhea, *Legaré*, 191–193).
66. Pierce, *Sumner*, II, 186; Webster, *Works*, II, 42; Curtis, *Webster*, II, 128, 672; Georg, ed., *Briefwechsel*, 165.
67. *Life, II*, 197, 188, 220–221.
68. *Life*, II, 215; Ticknor to Longfellow, Aug. 28, 1842, HL; *Life*, II, 214, 223; see Webster's plea for the payment of state debts in Curtis, *Webster*, II, 224.
69. Miller, *Federalist Era*, 230.
70. Georg, ed., *Briefwechsel*, 69, 74–75.
71. Ticknor to Thomas W. Ward, Sept. 22, 1835, MHS; Handlin, *Boston's Immigrants*, ch. iii; *Life*, II, 240–241; Winsor, *Boston*, III, 231.
72. Georg, ed., *Briefwechsel*, 95–96.
73. *Life*, I, 26–40; *Life*, II, 216–218; Choate, *Addresses*, 400–401, 423–424; Everett, *Orations*, IV, 652.
74. Georg, ed., *Briefwechsel*, 56–57; Prescott to Charles Sumner, June 19, 1845, HL.
75. Curtis, *Webster*, II, 401, 506; Current, *Webster*, ch. viii.
76. Van Tassel, "Compromise Sentiment," 307–319; Curtis, *Webster*, II, 474; Webster, *Works*, V, 325–326.
77. Webster, *Works*, V, 332, 365.
78. Webster, *Works*, V, 363–365.
79. Webster, *Works*, V, 437; Winthrop to John Clifford, March 10, 1850, MHS; Webster, *Writings*, XVI, 543–546.
80. Donald, *Sumner*, 184; Adams, MS Diary, April 2, 1850, in no. 71 of microfilm copies of Adams Papers made by the MHS.
81. Curtis, *Webster*, II, 410.
82. Ticknor, "Mr. Webster as a Senator," clipping from the *Boston Transcript*, 1850, DCL; Curtis, *Webster*, II, 438; *Life*, II, 265, 263–264. Ticknor visited Washington during the spring of 1850 and frequently saw Webster, Clay, and Winthrop; he conferred with Webster about strategy and wrote articles (practically dictated by Webster) for the Boston press. Later Webster thanked Ticknor for upholding "my name and fame, through recent events" (Webster, *Writings*, XVI, 562, 546, 543).
83. Gannett, *Gannett*, 286–287, 289. Cf. statement of Nathan Appleton that "sin is a matter that rests between the individual and his Maker" (*Letter to Rives*, 5).
84. Choate, *Addresses*, 397–399, 411, 407.
85. Shaler, *Autobiography*, 198–199.
86. Adams, *Education*, 30; Bowditch, *Bowditch*, I, 101.
87. Georg, ed., *Briefwechsel*, 59, 60–64; Ticknor had discussed the slavery issue while in Washington in 1850 with Clay and Henry Foote (*Life*, II, 264).
88. Georg, ed., *Briefwechsel*, 59.

89. Georg, ed., *Briefwechsel*, 64, 61.

90. Woodward, *Burden*, 90, 81; Lord Morpeth, MS copy of Diary, Dec. 14, 1841, HL.

91. Shaler, *Autobiography*, 197; *Life*, II, 212–213.

92. Curtis, *Webster*, II, 663–664; Nevins, *Ordeal*, II, 40; Curtis, *Webster*, II, 698.

93. *Life*, II, 283–284; Whipple, "Webster," 263–268; Emerson and Forbes, eds., *Journals of Emerson*, VIII, 335–336; *Life*, II, 284; Choate, *Addresses*, 240.

94. Choate, *Addresses*, 241, 355–357; Georg, ed., *Briefwechsel*, 165.

95. Frothingham, *Everett*, 362; *Life*, II, 287; Georg, ed., *Briefwechsel*, 89.

96. Georg, ed., *Briefwechsel*, 96, 105.

97. Brown, *Choate*, 326.

98. Everett, *Orations*, IV, 50–51.

99. Frothingham, *Everett*, 411; Georg, ed., *Briefwechsel*, 126.

100. Pierce, *Sumner*, IV, 18–20; Ticknor to Nathan Appleton, March 21, 1860, MHS; Winthrop to John Clifford, Dec. 20, 1860, MHS.

101. Curtis, *Constitutional History*, II, 328, 338.

102. Winthrop to John Clifford, Aug. 24, 1861, MHS; Winthrop to Clifford, April 23, 1861, MHS; Shaler, *Autobiography*, 194–195; Frothingham, *Everett*, 450, 463.

103. Georg, ed., *Briefwechsel*, 119; Ticknor to Laura Cranworth, July 14, 1864, BPL; Georg, ed., *Briefwechsel*, 129; *Life*, II, 433–434.

104. *Life*, II, 440; *Life*, II, 459; Curtis, *Constitutional History*, II, 558.

105. Curtis, *Constitutional History*, II, 558; Curtis, *Buchanan*, II, 282; Georg, ed., *Briefwechsel*, 158.

106. *Life*, II, 442; Winthrop to John Clifford, Nov. 16, 1864, MHS; Ticknor to Winthrop, Nov. 13, 1864, MHS; Howe, *Boston*, 289.

107. Georg, ed., *Briefwechsel*, 136; *Life*, II, 470; Howells, *Literary Friends*, 130.

108. Ticknor to Benjamin Curtis, July 29, 1865, DCL; Anna Ticknor, *Cogswell*, 320, 293–294.

109. *Life*, II, 448; Ticknor to Charles Eliot Norton, May 1, 1870, HL; Georg, ed., *Briefwechsel*, 148, 151.

110. Georg, ed., *Briefwechsel*, 147, 154–155; *Life*, II, 485; Adams, *Education*, 45, 261.

111. Shapiro, *Dana*, 146–150; Hofstadter, *Anti-intellectualism*, 173n.

112. Ticknor to Longfellow, Feb. 19, 1835, HL; *Life*, II, 419; Anna Ticknor, *Cogswell*, 310; "Life of George Ticknor" (anon. rev.), *Quarterly Review*, 196.

113. Georg, ed., *Briefwechsel*, 138; *Life*, II, 493–494.

114. Norton and Howe, eds., *Norton Letters*, II, 63; Adams, "Ticknor," 215; Norton, "Ticknor," 149; Curtis, *Webster*, II, vii; Saveth, "Henry Adams," 302–309.

115. Ticknor's last major project, the biography of Prescott, distracted him from the horrors of the war, and gave him an opportunity to illuminate all that he felt was worthwhile in his Brahmin world. Ticknor's *History* is still widely used as a reference work, the latest edition being by the Gordian Press in 1965. For the information on this recent edition I am indebted to Mr. Phillip Newbauer of Chicago.

Index